Lucy Bethia Colquhoun, at the age of seventeen / The Kylin Archive

Recollections of a Scottish Novelist

Lucy Bethia Walford

Dedication

*For Majorie McInroy
who would love to have seen this revival
of her mother's work*

*Designed by Peter Tucker, typeset in Plantin
and printed at The Alden Press, Oxford
All rights reserved*

*The Kylin Press Ltd, Darbonne House, Waddesdon, Buckinghamshire
© The Kylin Press Ltd 1984*

ISBN 0 907128 16 5

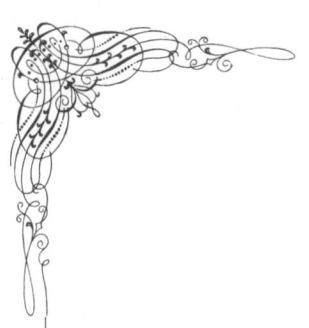

Contents

The Course of True Love	3
My Birthplace	14
The Crimean Winter	25
An Early Victorian Household	40
Strange Sights in the Hebrides	52
Edinburgh Society in the 'Fifties	68
A Youthful Author	79
The Colquhoun Country	90
Personages and Personalities	105
The Gay Isle of Bute	122
My Marriage	135
Wanted: a Hero	146
Publication of 'Mr Smith'	158
Last Days at Arrochar	173
Literary Memories	183
Chapter Notes	196

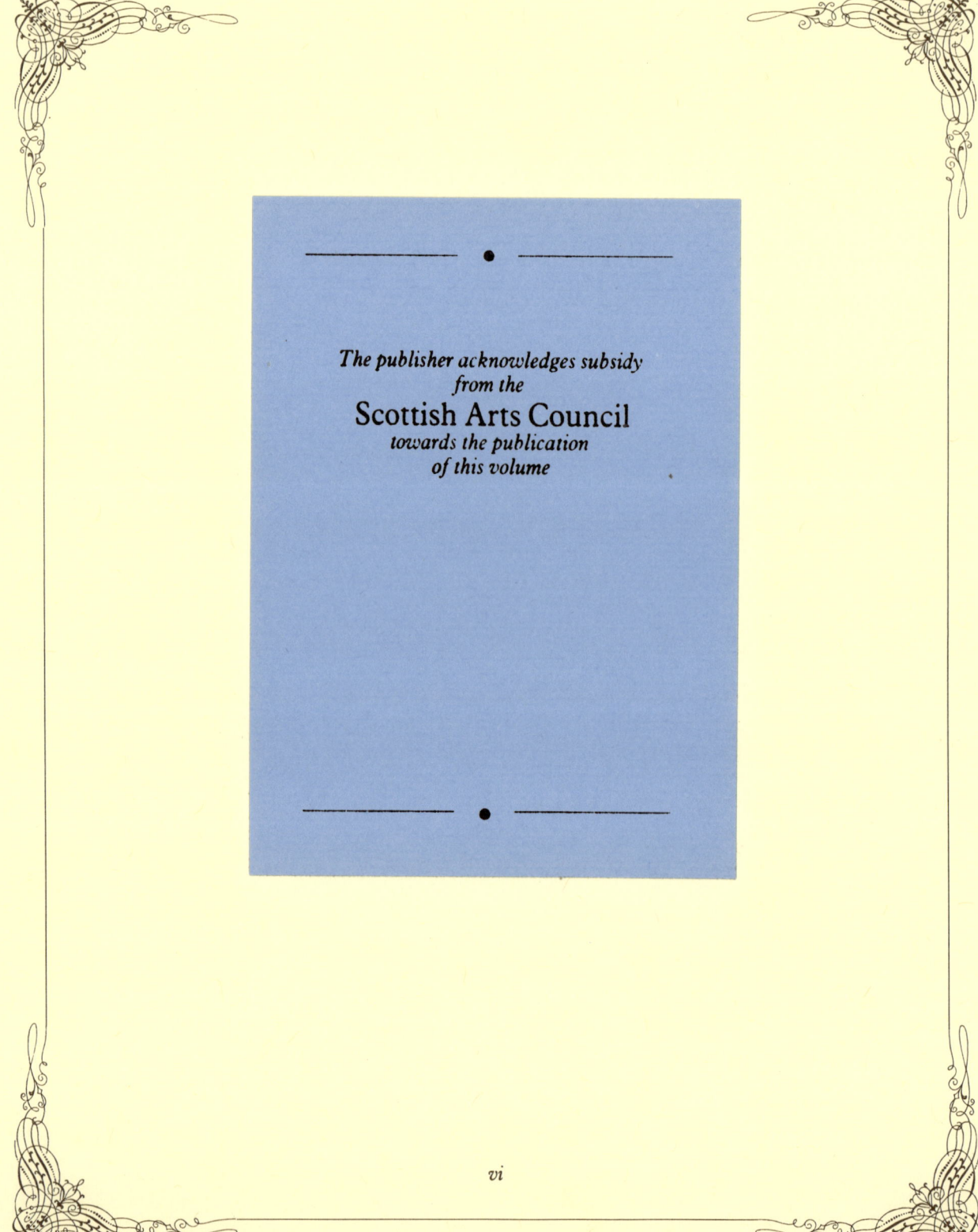

The publisher acknowledges subsidy
from the
Scottish Arts Council
*towards the publication
of this volume*

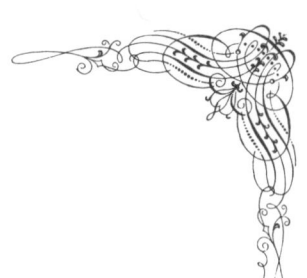

Introduction

When these 'Recollections' were written in 1910, Mrs Lucy Walford was looking back over a lifetime of 65 years, in which she had published over 45 novels and children's stories, to her girlhood in the Scotland of the 1850s – a time when Queen Victoria was still a young woman in her early 30s. She gives us a fresh and vivid picture of life in the country, watching the rafts being steered down the river to Aberdeen, or waving as the Queen and her family drive past on one of their first visits to Balmoral – the Queen distracted from her clumsy efforts to tighten the bonnet strings of the Princess Royal – or seeing Harriet Beecher Stowe, the author of 'Uncle Tom's Cabin', arrive at Oban pier.

Lucy also gives us a delightfully humorous picture of old Edinburgh, the independent-minded capital of the 1850s and 60s, with a gallery of highly individual characters, who spoke their minds and did as they pleased. It is a picture seen from the point of view of a young girl just entering 'Society', and she was fortunate in being born into the large, happy family of the second son of the Chief of the Clan Colquhoun. Her early days were spent among her numerous Scottish relations, the Sinclairs, the Campbells, the Colquhouns, or at the various country houses her father, a passionate sportsman and author of a classic book on field sports, rented for a few years at a time. There were also annual trips to her wealthy, but less forceful, maternal relations, the Fuller-Maitlands of Park Place, near Henley, providing a fascinating look at an early Victorian English household, and the difficulties of travel during the early years of the railway.

In 'Recollections' she records the mid-nineteenth century upper class world not only with the freshness and vivid observation of an old lady remembering her experiences and adventures as a child, but as a practised writer. Most of this book is set in the period before her marriage, in 1869, but the final chapter deals with the beginnings of her literary career, when she was living in England and in poor health after the loss of her first child. Her first novel 'Mr Smith' was a runaway

1

best seller and even came to the notice of Queen Victoria, as Lady Errol reported to Mrs Walford 'I have been reading "Mr Smith" to the Queen ever since it arrived, and I can say with what interest the Queen listens to the readings". After that, the Queen requested copies of all Lucy's books as they were published, and Mr Walford bound them himself. At first 'Leddy Margret' was not a great success and the Queen listened coldly to this tale of a gay-spirited old widow. But then she had a change of heart. Lady Errol was asked to read the book to her a second time, and looked up to behold the tears running down the face of her Royal Mistress. *"Afterwards I saw her Majesty rereading it quietly to herself"* continued Lady Errol *"and as for my opinion, if it is worth having, I do not think I have ever read a more beautiful book . . ."*

Further praise came from the famous critic, Coventry Patmore, writing in the 'St James's Gazette':

'Among living writers are two – one well, and at present comparatively little known – whose work ... can scarcely be surpassed: namely, Thomas Hardy and L B Walford.' While she herself heard Gladstone call out of his railway carriage window to a friend on Chester Station 'If you want the third volume of "Troublesome Daughters" you will find it on the little table beside my bed'.

For almost a quarter of a century Mrs Walford's literary output and popularity was enormous, but when she died on the 11th May 1915 her fame had to some extent predeceased her. The last chapter of 'Recollections' gives some clue to the reasons for this, and provides a fascinating account of a working author's methods at this period. Her great strength was the ability to tell a story, and her novels are carried forward by the irresistible movement of the plot. Her technique was especially suited to the three-volume novels of that period and when, towards the close of the century, the shorter novel became fashionable she was, as she says, *"one of the writers of fiction hit hardest"*. Her book 'The Matchmaker' was the last 'three-decker' ever ordered by Mudie's, the powerful library chain which, in its own interests, had done so much to keep the longer, more expensive, novel alive.

Another factor was that her style was going out of date, her good-hearted love stories were no longer in tune with the spirit of the age as the confident 'Victorian high noon' shaded into the 'decadent' naughty 90s.

Her novels became the symbol of a bygone era – but her 'Recollections' live on, as fresh and amusing as ever, to give us a picture of a fascinating vanished world.

Park Place, Berkshire, her mother's home / The Kylin Archive

The Course of True Love

A group of very little children, all dressed up and starched out, were being shepherded along the corridor of an English country house, to be ushered into the dining-room with dessert, according to the fashion of a bygone period – when one of them, the youngest, called a halt outside the door, and lifting up her face to the solemn butler in charge, demanded of him to blow her nose for her.

    This is my earliest recollection; for the suppliant was myself, and I was but three years of age. The country house was Park Place, near Henley-on-Thames, the residence of my grandparents, Mr and Mrs Fuller-Maitland, where my mother was born, and from which she was married in 1834.

My mother was one of a large family, twelve in all, of whom there are at the present time many descendants in various parts of England; but she alone crossed the Border for a husband, and the story of her wedding the son of a Highland chief is rather dramatic, and, as all concerned are long since dead, may fearlessly be told.

The Fuller-Maitlands led a very secluded life, in accordance with the taste of my grandmother, who was of Puritan descent, possessed of ultra-strict ideas and an innate and piously cultivated abhorrence of society. Her health was not good; perhaps it was that, – but at any rate the fact remains that she hardly ever went anywhere, and left my grandfather to enjoy by himself and in his own way the pleasures of fashionable life.

Her mother, Miss Fanny Fuller-Maitland / The Kylin Archive

When, however, he desired to return hospitality by invitations, it was another matter. Occasionally indeed he was permitted, grudgingly permitted, to do so; but if there were no very good report of the people in question – and this was not infrequently the case – the 'No' was adamant.

No: such worldlings could not and should not be made welcome within the guarded precincts of Park Place; and upon a certain occasion it was conjectured by the family that a battle-royal had taken place, for a terrific ringing of bells and hurrying of servants ensued, and orders were sent to the stables for the master's own travelling carriage to be prepared to start on a journey next day. My eldest unmarried aunt (who afterwards became Mrs Herschell, stepmother of the late Lord Herschell) her sister Fanny, some years her junior, and their brother William were ordered to have their trunks packed in readiness to attend their father. My mother, the said Fanny, thought that they did not even know where they were going, but dutifully accepted whatever was in store, and set out for Scotland – she, all unwittingly, to meet her fate.

And what a place to meet it was Rossdhu, on the 'bonnie, bonnie banks of Loch Lomond'! Thither our little party of travellers wended their way, since a distant connection with the Colquhouns of Luss warranted an offer of a visit while exploring the beauties of the neighbourhood; and the Sir James and Lady Colquhoun of that day were friendly, sociable people, always ready to open their doors. Perhaps they were even more glad to do so than usual on the present occasion, since all their three sons were at home, and here were two pretty and well-endowed young ladies – *et voilà tout*.

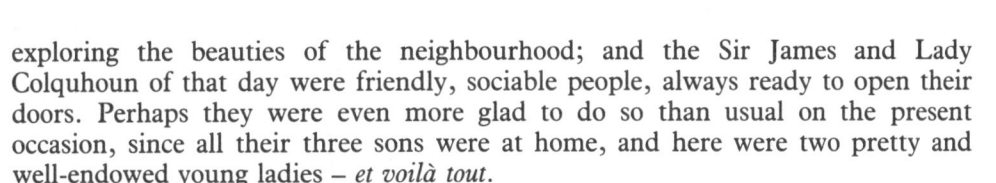

Of the eldest son (who was to end his life so tragically by being drowned in his own beloved loch many years afterwards) I shall say no more here, for obviously there was nothing between him and either of the Misses Maitland; but there was John, a dashing young cavalry officer, with blue eyes and curling hair, and he and Fanny – oh! it was the old, old story over again.

They climbed the purple heights of the mighty Ben; they sailed over the blue loch, and landed at the various wooded islets; they whispered to each other the romantic legends of the countryside – (how romantic, how enchanting it must all have seemed to the young girl from the south, especially to one brought up as Fanny had been!) In this case the course of true love certainly did run smooth, for the engagement which speedily followed was hailed with acclamation by both families, and the following January – why not sooner, I cannot tell – but on the 28th of January 1834 the gallant young Scotsman arrived at the Red Lion, Henley – an inn known far and wide now, by reason of the famed Regatta – where he put up for the night, and the next day was married to Miss Frances Sara Fuller-Maitland at the little church of Remenham, a mile or two away.

I do not know to what was due the fact that on his marriage my father, whose regiment was the 4th Dragoon Guards, retired from service. It seems strange that he should have done so, in the fullness of health and strength, and when only twenty-seven years of age; but one may be permitted to fancy that the influence of his future mother-in-law was thrown into the scale. She certainly made *some* terms with the bridegroom, one of which had a considerable – and delightful – bearing upon my own early life, and that of my brothers and sisters; for it was to the effect that every year as long as we were alive, this dear daughter and her husband should pay her a visit at Park Place; and I may add that the promise then given was loyally kept, though if often entailed some effort to keep it, and the old lady lived for thirty years to exact it.

Railways were rare in those days; and if steamboats were in use, they were of such a nature that only on one occasion did my parents venture on the experiment of going by sea from Leith to London. Their experience was such that they never went again.

I will not, however, anticipate. Before starting on their long posting-journey north, the newly wedded couple went for their honeymoon tour – think of it, brides and bridegrooms of to-day who fly to the uttermost parts of the earth – this very young and very well-off pair contented themselves with a wedding trip round the Isle of Wight! To be honest, neither of them ever cared, then or thereafter, for foreign travel; and it is quite likely that they enjoyed the sunny Under-cliff, the rushing waters in Black Gang Chine, and sunsets reflected by the coloured rocks

Honeymooning at Alum Bay, Isle of Wight / The Kylin Archive

of Alum Bay, as much as future generations have enjoyed Alpine heights, Venetian gondolas, or starry nights on the Nile, – while as their after-life was full of variety and interest as regarded the picturesque scenes of Nature, they had nothing to regret in the way of having lost an opportunity. A little set of sand pictures – we all know the kind, we who can now look back across the lapse of half a century – I possess as relics of this little, happy, humble wedding-tour.

I have also been told that the bride travelled in a large, wide bonnet, with a drooping feather laid across, and a short, round silk dress. She was very pretty, and no doubt looked it in the first flush of youth and happiness, despite the early Victorian quaintness, not to say ugliness, of her attire. Of my father's appearance I have also heard it said that he looked well in everything, and that his sisters-in-law vied with each other in embroidering waistcoats for him. He was married in one of white satin, embroidered by my mother in dark and pale-coloured heather – and a very lovely piece of work it was – or, I might say, 'is,' for it is now in the possession of his eldest grandson.

Off set the young pair at last for the 'North Countree,' travelling in their own carriage, with post horses; and their first home was Arrochar House, at the head of Loch Long, which my grandfather, Sir James Colquhoun, handed over to them, expecting that they would settle down and live always there.

Little he knew. My father was a sportsman and a naturalist – *his* father was neither. They had not, I fancy, an idea in common, though there was always perfect good-will between them; but, as for being tethered to one spot, when there was all the length and breadth of Caledonia stern and wild to choose from, when eagles were to be found in Glencoe, and seals in the Sound of Mull, and ptarmigan here, and capercailzie there? – John Colquhoun shook his head and cocked his eye. He was going to fish as well as to shoot, and he was going to write *The Moor and The Loch*; he very soon knew the rugged outline of The Cobbler from Arrochar doorstep too well, and commenced what was termed later by a friend his 'Residential tour of Scotland.'

In the course of a long life, for he lived to be eighty-one, very few people could have covered a greater variety of sporting-ground, shot over more moors, or fished more rivers, in his native land, than did my very fortunate father, who was able to begin so early, and to devote himself so exclusively, to his favourite pastime.

Not that it engrossed him to the neglect of duties and responsibilities. Let this be distinctly understood. My mother was profoundly religious, my father was not 'profoundly' anything – it was not in his simple nature to be so; but he was conscientious and highly-principled, even before being united to one who fostered and developed all that had been early inculcated in a Christian home. In after years he took up more than one good work, and with one in particular his name will ever be associated by those who recall the Grassmarket in the Old Town of Edinburgh as it was in the last century. Of that more anon.

We will return to our young couple in their heyday. A son was born, and by the desire – perhaps we might hint 'command' – of the Colquhoun grandparents, was given the name of 'James,' and none other. They had an eye to the future. Who could say if this were not a 'Sir James' in embryo? – and at any rate it was well to be provided against such a contingency. A venerable relation, the Countess of Caithness, gave a christening robe of Honiton lace and held the infant on the solemn occasion; but, as it was received into the Church of Scotland, there were no godfathers. In rapid succession more children followed; in fact, for some years it was a case of the 'hardy annual,' and as a move had to be made to Edinburgh for each occasion, a desire arose on the part of the young parents to have either there or in the neighbourhood a house of their own to winter in, even though the 'Residential tour' of Highland homes had begun with the renting of Leny House near Callander, and farewell for the present had been paid to Arrochar.

This move, and the suspicion of a slight to their own lands conveyed by it, had already given rise to soreness on the parts of Sir James and Lady Colquhoun; and my mother, in telling us once about it, added that when a further extravagance had to be confessed, in the purchase of a house at Portobello, although it was made with her own money (and turned out to be an excellent investment), her heart was in her mouth. The deed was done, however, and Lady Colquhoun was the last person to make herself unpleasant to no purpose. She was the first visitor to the new abode, and took a keen interest in all its arrangements.

Portobello, a small seaside resort about three miles out of Edinburgh, was, at the time I write of, a very different spot from the Portobello of to-day. It may have been a suburb, but it was a suburb innocent of omnibuses and tramways; it had no sea-wall, no band, no trippers; the cavalry regiment quartered for the time being at Piershill Barracks, midway between it and the ancient city under whose wing it nestled, did indeed use the long stretch of sand for manoeuvres, and delighted the natives thereby – but this was almost the only excitement of the place.

It was old-fashioned, peaceful, absolutely quiet. It suited my father from one point of view, my mother from another. Both desired to be let alone, after a summer of visitors and entertaining on her part, of hardy exercise and varied sport on his, – and they saw the very house they fancied in a small crescent in which it held the proud position of 'The big hoose.'

All the others were semi-detached, with nice little gardens before and behind; but 'The big hoose' stood on its own feet, with a carriage sweep in front, and two large iron gates, one at each end. NB – Later, my father let the house for a year to the future Duke of Beaufort, then Marquis of Worcester, whose regiment was quartered at Piershill; and an aged crone who was in the habit of coming up to receive a dole every now and then, thus described what she saw: 'There was a poothered[1] heid at tae gate, an' a poothered heid at the tither gate, an' savin' your presence, a poothered heid at the door! Me? I jist gaed awa'; and she did not return till the 'poothered heids' had vanished, when the poor, bent, old figure of Henny Rose reappeared as if by magic, and came as regularly as before.

To return. I may perhaps be forgiven for lingering over a description of my birthplace, as No 11 Brighton Crescent proved to be, though not for some four or five years after it came into my parents' possession.

It was a delightful house of its kind; plain and solid, with two wings. The windows ran in a straight line from end to end; the door was precisely in the middle; there was nothing of the *villa* about it.

It was indeed unfortunate that the front rooms faced the north, and that the blue Firth, for whose sake this might have been forgiven, although so near, was hidden from view; but there were other rooms, spacious, sunny rooms at the back, which caught the first beams of the morning sun, and overlooked a pleasant, shady garden, to which a flight of steps, running down from a small balcony, gave access.

Anyone who knew my mother might be sure that among these choice apartments were the nurseries, and later, the school-room. She thought much of such matters. I recollect her saying once with emphasis 'How *can* one expect children to be happy in a dark room?' Perhaps other youthful matrons may take the hint.

The walls of the house were very thick: of grey stone, as were most of the Portobello houses; and however small and squat they might be – and some were very small and squat – they always looked as if they had endless powers of endurance, and might also be snug and comfortable within. A childish fancy of mine was to pick out a tiny building and think it would be just the place to hide in, if all the world were in pursuit. No one would ever think of looking into such a little, small house!

My parents were singularly lucky in their purchase, rash though they were thought, and thought themselves; for they had 'rushed in where angels fear to tread,' and bought a domain which had somehow got *blocked* for no conceivable reason, – and had furthermore bought it as it stood, furnished, and stocked with glass and china. The furniture turned out to be of the best – in the drawing-room it was of rosewood; and the massive sofas, tables, chairs, even the unconsidered trifles, of which there were many, were upholstered in pale green satin-damask, which formed an exquisite contrast to the polished shine of the dark wood. Formal the room might be, but it was stately; it was wonderful for a place like little Portobello.

And then the china, the china was a still greater 'find.' It proved to be Crown Derby of the best period; Worcester with a glaze that made collectors stare; and Lowestoft. And these were the ordinary breakfast, tea, and dinner sets, put down in the house-agent's list as 'Table China'!

Their value apparently was unsuspected by seller and buyer alike; for, though strangers often noticed and admired, my mother, who liked to see pretty things about her, never dreamed of their being too good for daily use; and in later years we were all so well accustomed to see our dinner-table gleaming in crimson and gold like the cohorts of the Assyrian, that it was only after I had left the paternal roof, and when I was much in contact with people who pursued the supremely fascinating study of the moment, that I discovered and finally established the real status of the cups and platters so lightly esteemed, so familiarly treated.

They were nevertheless still used, and continued to be so while my parents lived. Now they are in glass cases. I like the old way best.

A wild triangle of marsh land fringed with willows was the centre round which Brighton Crescent circled, and was frequently the resort of birds of passage, as well as others. This was what happened one morning not long after my parents had taken up their abode in their 'own house.' Enter Duncan, a youthful manservant, with an air of excitement – not having yet attained the correct impassivity of the thoroughly trained butler.

'Oh, sir, if you please, sir, will you look out of the window?'

Look out of the window? His master, who was eating his breakfast, looked at him instead. What on earth did the creature mean?

But the creature stood its ground. 'Would you please to look out of the window, sir?' Then despairingly, as his words seemed to produce no effect, 'Mistress Aitken told me to say it, sir.' (Aitken was the children's nurse, of whom more, much more, anon.)

'Humph!' My father still hesitated, reluctant to leave his porridge and scones – but Duncan was almost weeping by this time. 'They'll be gone, they'll be gone; –

Tempestuous seas around the Bass Rock / The Kylin Archive

and Mistress Aitken *said* I was to tell you, – and they'll not stay, though they're there still,' taking a glance out himself.

'Well, I saw I had got to give in,' related my father, who often told the tale with zest, 'and there, what d'ye think? On a branch of the green daphne at our right-hand gate, there was a perfect cluster of exquisite little Bohemian Waxings, birds I had never seen before! I was off to the gun-room like a streak of lightning, and by a lucky right-and-left secured three specimens for my museum – where I identified them for what they were. That woman, she had had the wit to notice them' – he would himself grow excited over the recollection; 'not one in a hundred would have seen anything different from our own goldfinches, at any rate; and but for her and Duncan, I should have lost my chance.' More than once, in the future, he was indebted to this humble observer of Nature for information of a similar kind, and always acknowledged it with gratitude.

The museum alluded to, was in its infancy at the time the little waxings were included in it. I do not know, but I think they were the only foreigners ever given the *entrée*, for it was, with that possible exception, composed entirely of British creatures – either bird, beast, or fish, contributed by my father himself or by one of his four sons. The whole interesting little collection is now at Rossdhu.

From Portobello my father had many a wild, delightful day's sport round the Bass Rock, going thither from North Berwick; but I expect I am anticipating, for he certainly made the short journey to the latter point by train, and when that line was opened I either have forgotten or never knew. But I was very, very small when he first began to come back from North Berwick, smelling of the sea, and dangling for our admiration nice, soft, fluffy things, some of whose plumage we were allowed to keep for ourselves, if, on second thoughts, they were not considered worthy of being sent to Sanderson, the bird-stuffer.

Does anyone who reads this remember still Sanderson's little downstairs shop in George Street? My father rarely let a week pass without visiting it.

Among the denizens of the Bass Rock were solan geese, puffins – yclept 'Tommynories' in the dialect of the countryside – and other kinds of sea-fowl too numerous to mention. Naturalist as well as sportsman, my father would dilate on them to my mother, who all her life took a keen delight in his prowess (though but for the museum she might have deprecated slaughter of the innocents); and had her health at the time permitted, I feel sure she would herself have braved the jumbling waters round the storm-beat Bass, for her eyes used to kindle at descriptions of it. Her poetic imagination cast a halo over exploits by sea and land, and well fitted her to be the right hand and literary helper of the author of *The Moor and The Loch*.

How far this book had progressed before I was born, I cannot tell; it could be easily ascertained, but I prefer to give here only my own impressions, either acquired from the lips of others, or from personal observation,[2] – so that all I can say is that one of my very earliest memories, following hard upon the blowing of the nose incident, is of passing an open door in the Portobello house, and seeing within, a sunny room, a blazing fire, my father seated on a table littered with papers, and my mother reclining on a sofa, but sufficiently propped up to enable her to write upon the sheet of foolscap in her hand. 'Come awa'; your papaw and mamaw's busy,' exhorted the nurse, hustling us past; but I hung back a minute. My mother had paused to mend her pen (she always used a quill, and pointed it with a pen-knife), and something slipped off her lap, and, oh joy! she hailed me in to pick it up. I lingered, hoping something else would fall, but it did not, and I had to go – to go out in a cold, March wind, along a bleak, sandy shore, and drink the water of a certain yellow little stream, whose mineral properties were supposed to be beneficial! It seemed to me then – it seemed even after I had got over the horrid taste of the horrid water, and was all in a glow from running with my hoop – that grown-up people had the best of it on mornings like those.

Nor was that peep of warmth and comfort and pleasant occupation a solitary one. The room was on the ground floor, with windows accessible from the garden balcony. We could all take a look as we passed in or out; and as we older grew, it came to us, let fall casually no doubt, that our parents were writing a book.

Advisedly, I say 'our parents' – for no one would have been more ready to allow how much he owed to the critical and cultivated perceptions of his pen-woman than her husband.

Their plan of work was this. He, having previously collected his material – and I take this opportunity of asserting that every statement, every incident jotted

11

down in the diary he kept for over forty years, may be relied on for absolute truth – read aloud from a pencil draft, noting and correcting as he went. If there were no fault to find, she, in her elegant, clear handwriting, which was as easy to read as print, wrote down from this dictation, and then it was her turn to read aloud. 'We went over each page many times,' this patient secretary told me in after years.

For herself, her solitary literary achievement was a remarkable one – remarkable in that it was not followed by others. She was asked, in common with others, if she would try her hand at finishing the hymn begun by Henry Kirke White, 'Oft in danger, oft in woe' – or, as it originally stood, 'Much in sorrow, oft in woe.' My grandmother, Mrs Fuller-Maitland, an ardent hymnologist, wished to include this in a small volume she was preparing for private circulation.[3]

At that time her daughter Fanny was only sixteen; but her three and a-half verses, which she produced, I believe, very quickly, are now in every English hymn-book, sometimes with their source acknowledged, sometimes not. The first six lines only are by Kirke White.

It seems strange that so promising a beginning should have had no sequel to speak of. A few pretty verses were indeed gathered up and published by Macmillan towards the close of my mother's life,[4] but I cannot honestly ascribe to them any merit; nor did two quaint little tracts written for the fish-wives of Newhaven, penned during her residence at Portobello, and inspired by the constant appearance of those stalwart vendors of their husbands' catches, contain anything particularly striking or original. The best part of them was the woodcut on the title-page of each, in which the picturesque costume then universally worn, is done full justice to.

Scottish fisher-wives, a calotype by Hill and Adamson / Scottish National Portrait Gallery

Our fish was regularly brought to the door of the house in Brighton Crescent, by one of those Newhaven dames. She would dump her creel outside the kitchen door, which opened into the garden, (hence our view of the lovely vision), wipe her brow with a red cotton handkerchief, and thunder a knock.

'Aweel, Maggie, what hae ye for us the day?' would then be heard from inside; and Maggie's hand would go slipping about among fine flapping soles, whitings, and haddocks, till a selection was made.

A good dish of fish, often of mixed fish, fresh out of the water, could be had for a shilling in those days. Oysters were a shilling the 'half-thunder.' Think of it, gourmand! Half-a-hundred fine, delicately-flavoured Firth of Forth oysters, for a paltry shilling – and the bell-like tones of 'Caller oo!' filling the outer air with melody, thrown into the bargain!

If my two Colquhoun uncles were coming to breakfast any day, fish was always provided, as sea-fish was an agreeable change from the trout, perch and 'powan'[5] of Loch Lomond. Why they should have cared to walk down from Edinburgh, where they would be located at the time, to *breakfast*, instead of to some more reasonable meal, one wonders; but it may have been that the fashion set in London by Rogers, and his contemporary wits and poets, had permeated other kinds of society.[6]

Anyhow, they came; when I was old enough to remember, they had long got into the habit of coming every now and again; and though my parents kept very early hours – from choice, for they were among those who, having nothing to do, had all day to do it in – there was no change made for the guests.

Who that knows a Scottish breakfast will not confess that it is hard to beat? I can see my parents' breakfast-table yet: the many and varied dishes, hot and cold; the dark and light jellies – (black currant and white currant – what has become of white currant jelly? – one never sees it now); then such potato scones, barley scones, and scones that were just 'scones' and nothing else, each kind nicely wrapped up in its snowy napkin, with the little peak that lifted and fell back, falling lower and lower as the pile within diminished; the brown eggs that everyone prefers to white – and why? – the butter, the sweet, old, yellow butter, framed in watercress. It does not seem strange, all things considered, that the two bachelors who appeared at half-past eight o'clock on the door-steps of their brother's house found it worth their while to bring to the long, leisurely meal before them sharpened appetites and pleasantly tired limbs.

My birthplace

My parents had resided at various Highland places during the summer and autumn months, returning punctually to their winter quarters at Portobello as the days shortened, for a period of ten years, before I, their youngest daughter and seventh child, was born.

So far, I have put down only what came to me from highways and byways of their early married life; but only a short time elapsed between my being ushered into the world, on the 17th of April 1845, and my beginning to 'take notice,' as nurses say, for myself – the art of putting two and two together being speedily acquired. Looking backward, moreover, it is not difficult to fit in the pieces that may have then been missing, and a tolerably clear map of the past unfolds itself before my eyes.

It was maintained by my mother, and the saying was backed up by my nurse, the 'Mistress Aitken' afore mentioned, that at four years old I could read with ease. They also alleged that on urging this as a reproach and incentive to a younger brother not so far advanced, they were silenced by the sturdy retort, 'Girls read; boys doesn't'; which, we will hope, settled the matter. I have no recollection of it.

That at seven I read with avidity is certain, for some of the books given me at that age created impressions never effaced in after years, and even now I can quote passages from them and behold in my mind's eye the scenes depicted in their pages. *Ministering Children*[7] affected me greatly, and is a volume I should like to see in every child's hand. *The Little Duke*,[8] to my view incomparably the best of Miss Charlotte Yonge's many and popular tales, was a still greater favourite. I possess still the old worn copy, and would fain see it reproduced in that, the original edition, with its large print, broad margins, and excellent paragraphing: I fancy the story of young Richard the Fearless, with his thrilling adventures at the unfriendly Court of France, and his escape therefrom concealed in a bundle of straw, would still find delighted readers, if such were the case.

Of Miss Yonge's other writings – dare I confess it? – even as a little girl, I was no great admirer, – though I have since learned to appreciate *Heartsease*,[8] a tale full of human interest on a quiet level; but *The Little Duke* is perfect: there is not a false touch in it.

Next followed a gem of another kind, the evergreen *Struwelpeter*[9] – so green and so fresh after all these years have come and gone, that one still meets it in the same guise in which it first rejoiced the hearts of countless small denizens of the schoolroom.

Is it not a sign that whatever is good of its kind *endures*, that elderly men and women of to-day, finding themselves in sympathy over *Shock-headed Peter* and *Augustus was a Chubby Lad*, will wax excited to the point of shouting line after line; while if one stumbles or hesitates for an instant, the other dashes triumphantly in, and stops only with the dire catastrophe at the close?

There was another book, a German book; but, alas! it had no particular name, and I have never been able to procure a copy since I lost my own. If anyone who reads these pages and remembers *Dame Mitchell and her Cat*, Prince Hempseed and his animals, Rol, the cruel footman whose punishment was to drink tumblers of water till he burst – and, above all, dear, delightful Godpapa Drosselmeyer, and Princess Perlipita, and the army of rats, and the land of sweet cakes – if anyone, I say, could and would tell me if that never-to-be-forgotten book is anywhere to be had, I should be grateful indeed.

How young was I when *Holiday House*[10] was first put into my hands, I do not know; but *Holiday House* and its author deserve more than a passing recognition, since the latter, Miss Catherine Sinclair, was my father's aunt, and figured largely on our childish canvas, as did the whole of her well-known and gifted family.

They did everything, went everywhere, and knew everybody – or so we believed. Their father – my great-grandfather – was that Sir John Sinclair[11] of Ulbster whose portrait is one of Raeburn's masterpieces; and some at least of his sons and daughters inherited his singular beauty of person, though he did his best to rob them of it, if report be true. It was said at the time, and I have heard it repeated since, that having had several of his daughters inoculated for smallpox, and being dismayed at the result – for some were marked for life – he urged upon the doctor to *skin their faces*, and was furious at a refusal.

My own father would chuckle over this. 'He wanted to flay them alive,' he would say.

Among the unfortunates whose looks were thus ruined was my aunt Catherine, the authoress – and I believe she felt it keenly, though her talents afterwards gained for her considerable reputation, and her charm of manner and witty conversation made her a universal favourite.

She principally wrote novels. Her half-sister, Lady Colquhoun, gave to the world a series of feeble, religious booklets,[12] which went down, as books of that sort did then, fairly well; but Catherine boldly struck out into the realms of fiction, and conveyed a moral – always a moral – so subtly, beneath vivid descriptions of fashionable life and pages of racy dialogue, that they had a real and far-reaching success.

To what extent *Modern Accomplishments* and *Modern Flirtations* would appeal to the present generation, it is perhaps as well not to inquire; but we, of another, loved them and pored over them; while *Beatrice*,[13] the most ambitious and ingenious, had a special hold on our imaginations because of its being, as we learnt with awe, 'founded on fact.'

Holiday House was indeed also founded on fact – or facts – but that was a different thing. 'Harry and Laura' might be Archie and Catherine Sinclair (the author and her brother), and the deer-park at Rossdhu the scene of the suppositious Lord Rossville's flight from the bull – while Laura's starched frock? – we drew from my great aunt's own lips the history of that thrilling misadventure which happened to herself; but the realism of these simple episodes was one thing, and that of the mysterious depths of *Beatrice* another. On the latter, however, I need not enter.

Sir John Sinclair was said to have jocularly asserted that he had 'six-and-thirty feet of daughters' – which, being interpreted, meant that he had six, all six feet high.

The remark is legendary, and much more likely to have been said for a parent given to *bon mots*, than by him; but certainly the Sinclair ladies, as well as their brothers, were, as Pet Marjorie might have had it, 'more than usual' tall. We could always detect the corkscrewy figures of the two old gentlemen as they grew into old gentlemen, among any number of people; and our aunt's bonnets towered high above the crowds in Princes Street, or George Street.

Sir John Sinclair of Ulbster, a portrait by Raeburn / National Gallery of Scotland

Moreover, there was a piece of pavement in front of their Edinburgh house, which Sir John had caused to be paved with immense slabs brought from his own lands in Caithness, and did not some wag christen that piece 'The Giants' Causeway'? And did not the name stick?

Yes, they were very tall – very large altogether, but at the same time handsome – nay, some of them were beautiful. Julia, Countess of Glasgow, was the belle of the family; and how lovely we children thought her when she came to dine at the Portobello house, robed in pale blue velvet, which showed off to perfection the milky fairness or her neck and shoulders, and with plenty of diamonds in her hair and bosom! After her widowhood, Lady Glasgow was irresistibly drawn back to the lively house in George Street, which was doubtless a contrast to a dull dowager residence in the country, and she regularly took up her abode there every winter, going on to London in the spring, accompanied by her sister Catherine. My father used to laugh a little at the coalition; hinting that the handsome Julia, for all her looks and her diamonds, would never have collected such fine company as she did in Chesham Place, but for the wit and wisdom of poor, plain, pockmarked Catherine. 'She can *talk* – and that's the thing,' he would aver. 'Catherine keeps a whole table going.'

N.B. He said 'Catherine,' because the second family of the Sinclairs were his own contemporaries, and it was reserved for his children to call them uncles and aunts.

Sir John Sinclair was dead, and his bones laid beneath a grey tombstone in Holyrood Chapel, before I can remember; but his unmarried sons and daughters continued for long to reside at '133 George Street,' and to make it a centre of Edinburgh society.

They loved entertaining, and carried to a high pitch the art of entertaining *well*. Also they adored impromptus, and loved especially to show impromptu hospitality. Albeit an affectionate family, they rarely sat down to dinner by themselves; they wanted someone from without – someone to warm up their powers of conversation – notably someone on whom a *pun* would not be wasted. I am ashamed to say that these really clever talkers were sadly given to puns; and the story went that, in place of having the tendency checked in childhood, it had been fostered by the promise of half-a-crown for every good pun proved to be original. Now, a good pun is the worst kind of pun. Any other pun might be borne, but our Uncle Alexander Sinclair's puns made his audience wince.

Besides his partiality for this cheap form of wit – if wit it can be called – Sir John had other naïve fancies, one being for framing aphorisms which his children were expected to appreciate, but which they were not always in a position to profit by. I suspect that there are not a few young people to whom the following will come home, even as it did to my brothers and sisters and me when it was handed down to us.

It chanced that our great-grandfather was in need of a shilling to complete a cab-fare, and applied to his eldest son, a schoolboy, who had to confess his inability to produce the coin. However, it came from somewhere, and Sir John, with portentous solemnity, proceeded to improve the occasion. He leaned on his stick, and thus addressed the delinquent in slow, emphatic, measured accents:

'Archie – in future, Archie – recollect that – *a gentleman – should always – have change in his pocket.*'

'But where the change was to come from was quite another pair of boots,' my father added, when telling the tale; 'not out of *his* pocket, you may be very well assured. He was a regular screw to them all.'

I once heard another old gentleman deliver himself of a rebuke and an aphorism which brought this old memory up before me.

It chanced that I was at a country railway-station when the late Earl of Mansfield, a very high and mighty grandee, appeared, accompanied by a youthful grandson, who was all attention to his venerable relative, whom he had been deputed to see off by train.

Servants and luggage had gone on by a preceding train, and so it came to pass that when the old lord had seated himself in his corner seat, and suddenly discovered that he had no morning paper, there was no one to scold for omitting to bring it, and no one – yes, there was: the long-limbed lad was off like a shot to the bookstall.

In half a minute he was flying back at the top of his speed, breathless but triumphant. What was his reward? Pleasure, gratitude? Lord Mansfield scowled as he took the paper. Note, he took it; but all he said to the donor was: 'Edward – recollect, Edward – that *a gentleman should never hurry himself in public.*'

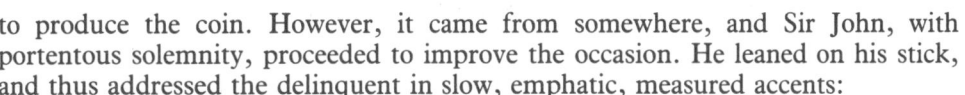

The talk round the dinner-table of the Old George Street house must often have been stimulating, even brilliant. Edinburgh was in its intellectual zenith at the time, and attracted savants and wits of all nationalities. The Sinclairs were not content with having an enviable circle of friends and acquaintances, they were for ever on the lookout to add to it; and it was expected of each brother and sister by the rest, that he or she should do his or her part. Next to Catherine, whose literary reputation opened for her every door, the brothers Archie and Alexander had the most opportunities; and my father used to say that it was their first business every morning on entering the New Club, to ascertain if any person of note, and distinguished stranger or foreigner, had appeared on the scene – then obtain an introduction, and ask him to dinner on the spot!

And very well pleased that distinguished personage would be to go, no doubt. He would find hosts, accomplished and cultivated in themselves, and surrounded by agreeable people – occasionally by scions of royal houses – or again of scientific or intellectual eminence.

'Every second person at table was a celebrity!' exclaimed a young American, on one occasion – 'and I was only invited a few hours before!' But such a *tour-de-force* was easy for a Sinclair, with resources at command and energy to grasp the situation.

Those who have experienced the cordial and courteous hospitality of the Chapter House, St Paul's Cathedral, at the present time, will easily perceive whence the Archdeacon of London inherits his delightful gift. Well pleased indeed would his venerable uncles and aunts have been, had they lived to see the traditions of their house so ably carried out.

The family of Sinclair was, however, under a shadow about the date of my birth, owing to the demise of the eldest sister, my grandmother. Lady Colquhoun had been a widow for some years, during which she had headed her eldest son's household; but as he married in 1843 Miss Jane Abercromby, daughter of Sir Robert Abercromby of Forglen, she retired from the scene – to return only too quickly, however, for the young wife died at the birth of her first-born child, a son and heir. The little boy, delicate, and difficult to rear, was the supreme object of his grandmother's care, and must have cost her many anxious hours – as I gather from her letters written to various members of the family, and now in my possession; doubtless she would have been surprised could she have known he would live to be over sixty. He succeeded his father in 1874, and died in 1907.

To return. 'The good Lady Colquhoun' being taken to her rest, it behoved her two daughters, who were her literary executors, to have her Memoirs written; and will it be believed that the person they pitched upon for the task had never seen its subject?

But he was a clergyman – or rather a minister – and a Free Kirk minister to boot; and her ladyship, with all her family then resident at home (save and except her eldest son), had 'seceded' in the 'Disruption.' In addition, Dr Hamilton was a writer of religious literature, and bore a high reputation among 'devout and honourable women.' The ladies were confident that he would do every justice to their mother's memory.

Nor were they disappointed. There was a certain poetic vein in all Dr Hamilton's writings which took greatly with the public; and probably his present task appealed to his imagination, for he gave it full rein in passages which, though too flowery and sentimental for the present taste, are not without merit. The book was also well illustrated, and excellently printed.

In consequence, it flew over Scotland like wildfire; soon there was not a house with any pretensions to piety or culture which did not boast a copy; the daughters were enchanted – and only my father raised a discordant note.

Whether he did so at the time or not, of course, I cannot say, though I believe there was some coolness between him and his sisters, for a whisper of it reached my ears later; but it was reserved for his own fireside to hear his real opinion, as I have often heard it, after arriving at years of discretion.

'*That* my mother! Why, he makes her out a perfect saint! You would think she was a sort of angel! And she was nothing of the kind; she was only a cheerful, sensible creature, with a kind heart and a very good temper. Of course she was a religious woman, no one could doubt that; and did her duty, and made a wonderful wife to a rather tiresome husband.' (If this candour shocks anybody, I beg them to understand that it was simply due to my father's extreme and innate truthfulness, which made him revolt against the extravagant and, as he conceived it, artificial attitude enforced on children towards their parents in the days of his own youth). 'I always used to admire the way in which she listened to and laughed at all his old stories, told over and over again,' my father would continue; 'he would address himself to her; and as soon as she saw he was nearing the point, her laugh rang out and led the rest. She never failed him. But Hamilton's idea of her? I wonder now what he would have thought of this? I have known my mother rise up and leave her seat in church, a great Edinburgh church, right in the middle of one of Chalmer's finest perorations, – and away she would go, sailing down the aisle to the door, with a whisper to a friend as she passed, 'It's getting near Sir James's dinner-hour."

⇒|⇐

Sir James's dinner-hour, everyone's dinner-hour, at that time was five o'clock; and though we had passed the period when only a tray with cakes and fruit and wine was brought in as a stop-gap, luncheons were light and were often dispensed with by the hardy and strong. My father never touched a morsel between breakfast and dinner until he was well past middle age, when he so far yielded to entreaties as to partake of a 'hunk' of cake and a bunch of grapes, and these in their turn yielded in old age to a bowl of soup.

By then, I must add, the dinner-hour had also advanced, as well all know – but our home was always one of the last to move with the times.

My mother had, however, a fancy of her own; she did not like the friends and relations who had driven down to Portobello from Edinburgh, or in from some place in the surrounding country, perhaps many miles away, should come and go without experiencing any kind of hospitality, and accordingly instituted – I had almost said 'invented' – offering them coffee – coffee, not tea – and the coffee was of a quality to satisfy the most epicurean taste. This I have often been told since, and also that it was accompanied by cake and biscuits, so that it must really have been a precursor of the afternoon-tea of to-day.

When that popular institution could no longer be warded off, the men – yes, the men – began it in Edinburgh. It was the judges in the law-courts who first succumbed to 'Kettledrum'; and a certain Lord Benholme,[14] a dear and intimate friend of my parents, was, if I mistake not, the first to fall. He described once in my hearing the pleasures of that cup of tea secretly partaken of in the robing-room, after a long and arduous sitting; and one can fancy how the witty Lord Neaves[15] shone on such an occasion. A cup of good tea is one of the most inspiring of stimulants.

Dinner being then so early, and luncheon so quickly disposed of – while it did not exist for my father, – he was free to be off betimes on his afternoon walk, which, during the months he resided at Portobello, was the substitute for tramps 'o'er crag and corrie, flood and fell' at other seasons of the year. As soon as a child was old enough, he or she was permitted, nay, desired to join in long, leisurely rounds by Duddingston Loch, Craigmillar Castle, or the quaint little seaports of Joppa and Musselburgh; and as quite little creatures we trotted happily along, for it is amazing what staying power a healthy child possesses, provided the pace is adapted to its requirements.

Then our father entertained us. He was never dull; never morosely sunk in his own thoughts. On the contrary, he would talk, talk, talk, the whole time, and that without ever boring or wearying his audience.

Nor did he talk *down* to us – a practice abhorred of children; whatever his theme was, he discoursed on it as naturally and unguardedly as though among his own familiars; and often, I know, we would giggle to each other in the supreme delight of hearing stories of his youth, of his tutors, of his brothers, sisters, and even parents, which a more cautious, possibly a more prudent spokesman would have kept to himself.

After years of experience we got to know tolerably well the subjects which would afford us the best amusement, and would turn on one of these as easily as a tap. He would perhaps offer a feeble protest: 'Hoots, you've heard that often enough;' but a few adroit leading questions soon set him off, and the only interruption would be from his attention being arrested by some sight or sound in Nature, for which he always kept eyes and ears on the alert.

'See, what's that?' He would stop dead, and point with his stick. It would be the first swallow of the spring skimming over the water of some lakelet.

Or he would suddenly break off short, head on one side, as a warble descended from the Salisbury Crags, and immediately we were instructed how to distinguish the note of a lark from that of a thrush, a blackbird, or a wheatear.

Then there was the hedge in a sunny lane between Duddingston and Craigmillar – the hedge that was so extraordinarily in advance of its kind that it put forth tiny shoots of green in February or even earlier, for during one very mild winter I have distinct recollection of seeing it in full leaf during the last week of January! We always called it 'The Hedge'; and I believe that on the occasion I refer to, my father wrote to some paper an account of 'The Hedge's' prowess.

Even if sometimes not over well disposed to start on these walks – and girls and boys do have their own fancies – we were sure to come home in good spirits. On the homeward way, moreover, a small voice might occasionally be heard in petition. A few pennies would buy us a goodly packet of brown sugar to make toffee, and we had the first authority in Europe for asserting that toffee was good for us. How was this? Sir James Simpson,[16] the famous physician, though not yet 'Sir' James, was beginning to make the name which was afterwards to ring so far and wide, – and my parents were among the first to divine his greatness. He attended my mother in all her serious illnesses; and one day on leaving her room at Portobello his nostrils were assailed by a powerful and delicious odour. He snuffed it up, and pronounced without hesitation, 'I smell toffee. Toffee's very wholesome.' Do I need to add that the enchanted toffee-makers surrounded their enlightened friend and protector like a swarm of bees; that he had more of the hot savoury condiment pressed upon him than he knew what to with; and that his dictum was our joy and bulwark forever after?

Dear little fat 'Simmy'; we owed him so much – apart from toffee. He was never too grand nor too busy to attend us in our childish ailments, confident that he would not have been sent for if another would have done; and when I was eleven years old one of these summonses was despatched on my behalf. I had an abscess in both ears, contracted from bathing in the sea too late in the season, and had been hurried into Edinburgh from Oban by my anxious parents. These abscesses were frightfully painful, and also rendered me stone deaf. Part of the journey was made by steamboat, and I lay in my berth still as a stone, when a hoarse, tremulous whisper in my ear, 'Dearie – dearie, *are ye deid*, dearie?' made me laugh even then. It was only the well-beloved Aiky, our nurse; but a few hours later when I again woke to consciousness there was a sense of something warm, soft, heavy and suffocatingly close, hanging over me. It was 'Simmy' putting on leeches!

It was the middle of the night, but he had come, as I learned afterwards, on the instant; and as the little patient was sleeping, he proceeded to apply his leeches without waking her; finally forgetting his proportions in the ardour of his task, he well-nigh smothered the poor little unresisting body. But he brought her through.

I remained deaf for a month or more, but subsequently quite recovered my hearing, and mention this as it may encourage others suffering for a time in like manner from a like cause.

※

In later years I went occasionally with my mother to Dr Simpson's well-known breakfasts, this being the only meal at which he ever received, or, as some said, 'sat down.' And it was not always he was there! On the contrary, an assemblage would have gathered, ushered straight into the breakfast-room as they came – and there would be no host to receive them! They would be people of many kinds and nationalities; occasionally one could not but surmise that they bore names not unknown to fame, but as no member of the Simpson family was present to act as intermediary, nothing could pass but polite interchanges of civility between strangers, or snatches of subdued conversation among such as belonged to the same party.

All would be eating and drinking with a sense of disappointment: the busy man, whose moments were precious, would be frowning; the nervous lady, whose fears had sent her flying from her bed at this unearthly hour, would be trembling, – when on a sudden carriage would dash to the door, there would be a general cry of 'There he is!' and all would be on their feet.

Then some to the window, among them myself; well, and what do we see? The very short, very broad, very great little figure, enveloped in its familiar sealskin coat, waddling across the pavement. We turn to fix our eyes on the door of our room. It opens, and there he stands, he of whom it has been said that some beholding his noble, his sublime countenance have thought it was the face of an angel!

He has been travelling all night: he has come from London – from Paris – from St Petersburg; it matters not from where, – he makes nothing of it, has no intention of secluding himself, is delighted to see so many kind friends, and goes round the table with warm and cordial greetings.

He pours out his own coffee – says the servants never give him enough milk; and chats of this and that in an easy, natural, unaffected manner, while never for a moment usurping the general attention.

With consummate tact he contrives to make known to each other people who he considers will be congenial. He is as leisurely over this delayed meal and as free to enjoy it socially, as though he had all the day before him; but at length there is a pause, and those who out of consideration are willing to postpone their coveted interview, withdraw. They will look in another day.

The rest are seen immediately, each in turn; and often it is a long, close, searching cross-examination the patient has to go through; and when the last is gone, the real labours of the day are only supposed to be beginning in the plain, undistinguished, world-known house in Queen Street, in which *chloroform* was first given and taken.

The Crimean Winter

Blackhall Castle, on the banks of the river Dee, in Aberdeenshire, was the first of our many moorland homes of which I retain a clear and distinct recollection. My father took a three years' lease of it in 1852, when I was just seven years old.

'Castle' is a somewhat grandiloquent term for a white-washed tower with two wings – just as 'Park' is hardly that for a piece of grass land with wooded islets by which Blackhall was surrounded; but it was certainly a good, comfortable house, beautifully secluded, and approached by an avenue of considerable length, whose gates were close to the bridge of Banchory Ternan, then little more than a village – now, I understand, a town.

The avenue ran along the banks of the river, of which my father had the fishing for some miles, and many a fond and longing glance he must have cast at it, as he steadily marched to church on a Sunday morning when it was 'in trim;' but of this I am certain, never once did he yield to the temptation of casting a fly over either the 'Rosepot' or the 'Sandy Havens' – the two pools which lay in our path. No, he held stoutly on his way, heading his band – a goodly band too, as I shall presently show – till we filed into our front seat of the gallery, yclept, 'loft' in those days, which we filled from end to end.

At that time there were nine of us, the whole family, in short; and all were at home the first year, though soon after my eldest brother went to Cambridge. And why to Cambridge, I cannot say, since it was always his intention to enter the army; and at the close of his University career at Trinity College, Cambridge, he went into the 4th Dragoon Guards (our father's former regiment) in which he remained fifteen years.

To return. All the other front seats in the gallery of the parish church of Banchory belonged to neighbours, and it was an exciting time for us youngsters when these

The fourth Dragoon Guards / National Army Museum

began to fill. Exactly opposite were the Davidsons of Inchmarlo, who were also our exactly opposite neighbours on the other side of the Dee. There was a very little boy – he is now a grey-haired laird, and I wonder if he will read this? – whose pranks were a continued source of delight to us, his contemporaries. One of these remains in my memory by reason of its tragic ending. For our entertainment our friend stuck in his eye the penny provided for putting in the collecting-plate; and being caught, and hastily endeavouring to conceal what was going on, his fingers somehow missed fire, and out flew the penny, struck the edge of the seat in front, and bounced to the pavement below. Not even then did it stop: it rolled and rolled away down the aisle, till a foot protruded from a side seat, and stamped it down

– by which time every pair of eyes that had seen the beginning of that penny's career were straining delightedly from above to note its end. I don't think Master Duncan Davidson ever attempted that little feat again.

When we came out of Banchory church, a fine row of carriages would be in waiting outside, notable among them my mother's, by reason of her fancy to have a postillion instead of a coachman. This was not uncommon in those days; still no one else in the neighbourhood did it, and I fancy my parents adopted the plan chiefly because they liked to occupy the box seat themselves, as they always did when travelling and often at other times, in fine summer weather.

Our horses were denominated by my somewhat imaginative mother, Sheik and Bedouin, from some strain, real or supposed, of Arab blood in their veins – and I doubt if she ever knew that they were only Tom and Dandy, (Scotch for Andrew) in the stables. Robert Macdougal, our dapper little postillion, rode on Bedouin *née* Dandy, and such of us as were too small to walk both ways – it was two miles each way – were bundled into the large landau, though we much preferred as we grew older to walk. Shall I say why? There were small green lizards basking in the sun on a certain paling just inside our own gates, and we were not allowed to catch them on our walk to church; but coming home – well, my father looked the other way.

There were adders also – poisonous, ill-conditioned adders – in the woods round Blackhall, and these even invaded the immediate precincts of the house. On one occasion we rushed in from the garden to report that a great snake was lying coiled up upon the bank on which we were about to play, outside the kitchen-garden. Eagerly we guided my father to the spot. He had a big stick in his hand, and with a single tap on the head, he stunned the creature, and next moment dexterously caught it up by the tail.

An adder thus stunned soon recovers consciousness, but what is it to do? It can only twist and writhe; it cannot extend its head high enough to bite the hand of its captor. How the one in question was got into the high, wide-mouthed, glass bottle filled with whisky, in which I saw it thereafter – and where it is still – I do not know. My father had ere long a row of these bottles filled with specimens; and we looked at one with special interest, as a protruding stomach betokened, we were told, a mouse inside.

None of us were ever bitten, and this is rather wonderful, as within our own precincts we were allowed to rove at will during holiday hours; but a little son of one of the gardeners fell a victim one day, and was cured by a remedy thought highly of by natives of the place. The child had flown screaming to his mother; she instantly caught and killed a chicken, severing it in two, and applied the reeking sides to the wound, with the effect that the poison was, as it were, sucked out. At any rate the patient recovered, and everyone lauded the deceased chicken, save and except Nurse Aiky, who sniffed – perhaps because she had no hand in the affair. More than once, however, she detected an adder; once, lying along a grass path in the flower-garden under the box-edging, and she had the honour of seeing her quarry in a bottle afterwards. It proved to be the largest of the set.

Our Sundays in those days *were* very strict – the Presbyterian Sunday of the early Victorian era is well known, but I will affirm it had its alleviations in our home. Arrived back from church at Blackhall, we all, down to the youngest, accompanied by our tutors and governess, dined in the dining-room – a thing we never did on any other day of the week. As there was usually guests besides, we were often a very large party, and the Sunday dinner, albeit in the middle of the day, was a merry meal. A fine salmon, or lusty grilse, would be uncovered, smoking hot, and needing no sauce but the water in which it had been boiled. It would have been caught the afternoon before. My father, as he tore the rough skin off its back, disclosing the bright pink flesh beneath, would be sure to have something to tell about the catch – whether it were in the rush of the 'Grey Mare's Tail', or the depths of shadowy 'Cairnton,' or the bubbling bends of 'Ferroch.' 'Ferroch' was our favourite pool, because of its smooth shore of glittering pebbles on which the brambles sprawled, whose fruit, large and sweet and warm from the sun, shone like jet. The rest of the dinner might be unexciting – of the usual kind; but we all took an interest in the salmon.

And the meal was over, we were free to do as we chose throughout the long afternoon – than which children can have no greater boon. We were indeed expected to read 'good' books, but the supply was varied, and how much or how little we perused was not inquired into; we were not looked after; we were not herded; we walked or sat at our own sweet will, and I can truly say that unless the day were wet, necessitating our being kept indoors, we were never bored.

Even on rainy Sunday afternoons we had a resource; for, being handed over to our brother's tutor, (a reliable and safe person), to be kept out of harm's way, we prevailed on him to tell us ghost stories.

Mr M'Ewan was an adept in the art. His stories were glorious, cumulative, shuddery – so much so that when he was careful, as he always was, most conscientiously careful, to 'explain' the ghost, I was thankful in the depths of my heart, however bolder spirits among the audience might protest.

I have said that afternoon-tea was not born or thought of in the days whereof I write – but what about a certain sunny little room in the back regions, where Nurse Aiky sat with a tray before her, and a brown teapot with a broken nose? Aiky's tea was sure to be going on about four o'clock, and towards that time there was a strange desire for Aiky's company in more breasts than one.

She never said us nay. She had little ornamental cups and mugs at disposal, to say nothing of saucers – and her tea! Years afterwards she met an eulogium on tea fresh from China or India or Ceylon with 'I ken naethin' aboot your furrin teas.

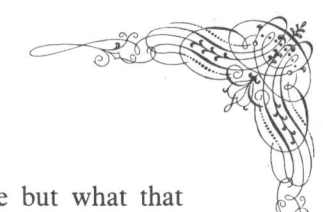

Gie me Melrose,' – and to the end of her life would drink none but what that fine old Edinburgh firm supplied, though it probably did not occur to her that even tea at four shillings a pound might have come from 'furrin' parts.

The chief event of the Sunday took place a six o'clock. At that hour we all assembled in the dining-room for an evening service, and rows of chairs and benches had been placed at the far end. Then streamed in, with much etiquette and nicety of precedence, a congregation often amounting to over forty people, which is the limit set by the 'Conventicle Act' for a religious meeting in Scotland held by a layman. The Act has, of course, fallen into abeyance; but it was frequently a mild jest on the lips of those who knew, that my father might be 'had up' for breaking it! How and when he had begun thus to assemble outdoor retainers and their families for Sunday evening prayers, I do not know, but it was in full swing when we went to Blackhall. Many not merely among our gardeners and keepers were glad to come; for there was no evening service at Banchory, and, without being uncharitable, one may suspect they did not know very well what to do with themselves. The men had talked and smoked and slept long enough; the women had the sense of doing their duty, and the sight of all the ladies at the castle in full evening dress at the same time.

It is possible that this last was not lost upon the other sex also. At any rate, Nurse Aiky did not altogether like it, especially as her own bairns grew into young ladies; but my mother was adamant on the point. She could not see that we should be worse dressed on Sunday evenings than on other nights of the week, when we were always attired in white or pale-tinted muslin, with low necks and short sleeves; and her indignation was roused by a hint that the young keepers and gardeners were not accustomed to sights of the kind. They had come, she fully believed, actuated by very different motives – and we will hope that at any rate in some cases she was right; but certainly we did present a somewhat dazzling tableau, especially when the family party was reinforced by guests equally elegantly turned out – and certainly our Sunday evening services were appreciated at Blackhall, and elsewhere. Throughout his life my father never failed to hold them wherever he might be.

If a clergyman were present, he would indeed be called upon to take the place of the master of the house, and conduct an extempore service, including an extempore sermon. This we young ones did not altogether approve of. We preferred my father's well-known voice, and a discourse by Blunt, or Melvill, or Jay, long though it might be, to the never-knowing-when-it-would-end feeling evoked by a preacher left to his own devices. He might indeed politely inquire to the usual order of ceremonial, and make believe to adhere to it; but though it was simple enough – a sermon, a hymn, and a prayer – he always, or so it seemed to us, contrived to spin out all three.

Prayers over, a short interval would elapse during which we flew out-of-doors if possible, at any rate out of sight; but the sound of the gong soon summoned all together again for a gigantic repast – the precursor of the 'Sunday evening supper' of to-day. By this time youthful spirits were, it must be confessed, getting sadly out of hand; and I think there must have been some sneaking sympathy with them even among our elders, who, after all, were young themselves, though I thought them old then. I recall being apologised for to a godly divine who had just delivered a homily on strictest Calvinistic lines, and the gentle indulgence of his response and the benevolence of his smile won my affection ever after. His heart was soft and loving, whatever were his tenets.

If we relaxed a little at supper, however, there was no chance of doing so throughout the evening which followed. It was of the nature of a Sunday School, and none were exempt from attending and contributing to it. We had to repeat hymns or sing them – but with no piano, nor musical instrument of any kind; we had divers Biblical exercises, such as repeating texts in turn, all beginning with the same letter of the alphabet, or turning on the same Scriptural subject; and, with the whole party under her eye, my poor mother exerted herself to the very best of her ability to keep us 'good and happy,' according to her ideas; but when it is added that even after we broke up at night, she re-assembled all her children, sons as well as daughters, yet again for further exhortation and prayer within her own chamber, I think it will hardly be wondered at if she found us, as she would tearfully lament, wild and unmanageable.

We had been 'kept at it' the whole day long – (for I have not mentioned that before descending to breakfast, we were expected to sing several hymns outside her bedroom door, and that in the interval between breakfast and preparing for church she read to us from some missionary or other religious work) – so that the few afternoon hours were our sole relaxation, – and though I speak of this prolonged effort on the part of the best of parents with reverence and gratitude, I cannot but think such Sundays were an almost unbearable strain for all concerned.

Moreover, the above was Sunday at its best in the old Scottish home. It was Sunday amid beautiful surroundings, and under summer skies. When we went into Edinburgh, as soon after we began to do, for the winter and spring months, the same domestic routine was observed, but with additions and subtractions. We were taken twice to church – the one service following hard upon the other – and we had no afternoon outlet. The days, short and dark, did not admit of our going out after dinner, whose hour was altered to four o'clock; also we had not guests beneath our own roof, neither did we ever see a single fresh face from without. The door-bell never rang. No one would have been admitted, if it had.

Those were terrible Sundays indeed; yes, I fear I must say it, they were. I do not believe anyone of us young ones ever went to bed at night without a sense of relief that the day was over. Yet let me not be misunderstood. We were so far from being uninfluenced by our parents' example, or incapable of being advantaged by their teaching, that the impress of both was indelible; but it was the mistaken idea of 'winding ourselves too high' on one day of the week which bore so hardly on our tender years, and I rejoice to think no Presbyterian child of to-day is likely ever to suffer from it.

One word more. I have said nothing about the church services, because it is well known how thoroughly these have been reformed since the period I write of; but let me give one glimpse of what the musical portion must have been like at St Cuthbert's Edinburgh, where it is now so beautiful, when it could draw forth the following comment from my outspoken father. Our pew was close beneath the precentor's desk, and the raucous nasal twang which burst out over our heads as the latter led each psalm or paraphrase invariably brought a frown to his brow; but we had never heard his feelings put into words till one day, when, as he issued from the porch, out it came: 'Well, I suppose that horrid din that horrid creature, Gibson, makes, is the correct thing for church? I suppose you like it,' (to my mother), 'and other people like it; but for my part I'd sooner hear a dog howl or a donkey bray.'

Governesses were naturally important personages with us in the Blackhall days. We were five sisters, and my parents were great educationalists: accordingly one preceptress was not considered sufficient, and we had two – both Germans, and related to each other.

The German craze in the educational world was at its height, taking its cue no doubt from the Royal schoolroom, then in full swing; furthermore, I believe that my mother, when debating the question of having a Parisian for our No 2 was daunted by the fear of internecine warfare, or at any rate of jealousy between Fräulein and Mademoiselle. Accordingly there they were. Fräulein Lindemann, fair, soft, pretty, with heavenly blue eyes, and a pure soprano voice; and Fräulein Muller, ugly, dark, eager, strenuous, with spectacles, and a fierce contralto.

Both were singers, and musical evenings soon became *de rigueur* in the house. The two voices not only blended charmingly, but had been trained to sing together. An invitation having been sent in due time to the schoolroom, the pair would enter arm-in-arm, carefully and becomingly dressed, with rolls of music in their hands. By-and-by, when the sweet songs of the Vaterland thrilled a delighted audience, some of the latter would be proud to join in; the group round the piano would swell, and my mother – an excellent musician – would readily act as accompanist, adding her own sweet low tones from time to time, timidly, but with keen enjoyment.

It needed but a very little pressure on the part of us younger ones to gain her permission to sit up an extra half-hour on these occasions; hence I remember them now. Let it be remembered how early were the hours we kept.

At other times the Fräuleins spent their evenings together in the schoolroom, happily enough, no doubt, reading, working, and writing letters. It would have been a tax on them to have had to dress and go into company every night, and it was not as though one poor exiled girl had been left to solitude and her own devices. They were both clever, efficient, and thoroughly trained, with diplomas from various colleges. They taught us well; and we acquired from them many things besides the knowledge they were engaged to impart.

Our schoolroom was a kingdom in itself, and there we might do as we chose, and as the Fräuleins chose. If, under their auspices, we elected to cook nice little puddings and pastries such as were compounded in their native land, no one had anything to say. We sent to the kitchen for what we wanted; we brought in fruit from the garden, berries from the hillsides; and the kind creatures, especially if we had been diligent at our lessons, would hasten to bring out the little stewpans. Then what a delicious odour arose, and how ravishing tasted the small, steaming mess cooked by our own hands! I doubt that if any English preceptress, either of that date or any other date, would have so condescended with her pupils.

We strove to emulate their needlework; the blonde was an exquisite embroidress – her patterns grew by magic; the other, I think, rather despised the art – or would in any hands but those of 'Emma.' She adored Emma. Her pride in Emma's beauty was intensified by having none of her own, and it was a joy to her to gather up the long, thick, flaxen tresses, and coil the plait round Emma's head. When Emma, fully dressed, with a pale pink, gauze scarf floating from her plump, milk-white shoulders, would come to be looked over before an evening of music and company, Helen's unalloyed admiration of her younger, fairer colleague had in it not a tinge of envy.

We children used to mimic, but not ill-naturedly, the two contrasting voices, – Emma's soft piping treble, and her 'Ach so, Helene,' then Helene's deep-toned response, her '*So*, Emma,' which resembled the bass note of a drum.

Helene was, I think, the more intellectual; and she had also a talent for drawing, which, if not very profound, gave much pleasure to the household, for she took likenesses of everybody from my father downwards, and I know that the sitters were pleased. Of course, *we* thought them works of genius. And again, each lady excelled in an accomplishment which if not particularly useful, was quaint and uncommon: they could weave the most wonderful little bouquets of hair, arranging the different colours so as to form the light and shade of flowers. In a large party of children, some very small, there were plenty of golden heads to cull from, and I possess one of these little relics of the past to this day.

What the governess thought of our Scottish Sunday as represented at Blackhall, can only be surmised, for they were at once too cautious and too loyal ever to let it out.

They were completely happy with us – that I know. Their warmly affectionate natures made them soon look on our house as a home, and they learned to climb the hills and rove over the surrounding country as to the manner born. Only once do I remember Emma's courage and endurance giving way, after hours and hours of steady tramp, during which we had insisted on following unknown 'short cuts' home, patiently attended by our faithful pair, (who, directly school-hours were over, became the most mild and docile of guardians); she offered not a syllable of remonstrance, but when desired to mount a high, stone dyke, and leap a deep ditch on the far side, Emma could no longer restrain herself, and wept aloud. She really was at her last gasp, poor thing; and we were all so contrite we would cheerfully have carried her home. Luckily a farmer's cart came by, and she was popped in and borne to safety.

The governesses were never tired of one sight – namely, that of the rafts on the river. It is probable that those rafts are no longer to be seen swinging down from the wooded heights of the Upper Dee to the dockyards at Aberdeen; but they were the only means of conveying there timber to be used for shipbuilding and railway sleepers, fifty or sixty years ago.

The rafts were built of pine trees, roped together roughly but very strongly – for the river was rapid and beset by rocks, seen and unseen, and guiding this rude craft among them was dangerous in the extreme. The two men – always two – who stood at either end, steering, had need of all their watchfulness and all their strength as they wended their perilous way; and how they ever had a footing

Rafts of pine trees on the Dee near Aberdeen / The Kylin Archive

at all on the slippery pine stems stripped of bark, was a marvel.

They often shouted and laughed as they went by. We little ones, paddling in the shallows, thought they did it from sheer lightness of heart – but I have wondered since. Could such joviality have proceeded from the same sort of feeling as that which prompts the Italian or French boy to sing, and shout, and caper when conscription time comes round? The other day I witnessed a scene of the kind in Italy. You would have sworn the olive-skinned lads were all mad with joy, such hilariousness – such tomfoolery – the air resounded with their merriment and laughter. 'Ah, no; they are all very sad *really*,' quoth a gentle matron, gazing at the revellers out of dark, pitiful eyes. 'But this is it, they *have* to sing to make their spirits, you see?' Did the bold raftsmen of the Dee use the same device to 'make their spirits' as they plunged into the swirling and foaming waters?

One day we were setting forth on our daily walk when our attention was called to people running across the park from different points, and as one of them passed us, he shouted, 'There's a man droonin;' The Kelpie's i' the river.'

The Kelpie (water-sprite), so nicknamed from that element being presumably his own, as he was the most reckless and fearless of raftsmen, was known to us all, and not very favourably so, being an arrant poacher when not otherwise employed. He had his good points, however; and my father had a sneaking fondness for him as a deadshot, and something of a naturalist besides.

Horrified at his danger, but wild to see what there was to be seen, we broke from the poor little Emma, who chanced to be alone in charge, and raced to the spot.

As usual, rumour had outstripped reality. The Kelpie was not yet drowned, but he and his fellow-raftsmen were in momentary danger of being so. The river was in flood, and their raft had been hurled upon a rock and broken up. All that remained were a few cross logs, on which the apparently doomed men balanced themselves with difficulty, and which swayed to and fro, as though at any moment fated to be overpowered by the raging torrent.

It seemed hours before a rescue came, in the shape of a rope, which was flung by the strong arm of a wader venturing in as far as he dared, with a rope round his waist, whose other end was held fast by those behind.

The Kelpie caught the rope. We all drew a breath, and our eyes started from our heads. Could he, dared he, leave his pole, with which he alone battled for his life – could he trust to the single strength of his mate at that awful crisis? He did, and a low groan burst from the spectators; but it was a groan of admiration and sympathy, for the brave fellow calmly tied the rope first round his friend, and them himself, when both were drawn to shore. The same instant the wreck, released, tilted forward, crashed into the boiling current, and was instantly out of sight.

And what did The Kelpie say? Did he emit any sentiment of satisfaction or

Giulia Grisi the opera singer / The Kylin Archive

gratitude or piety? He did not. He stood and dripped for a moment, then shook himself, and walked away.

Another day we had an excitement of a different nature. Some neighbours had brought word of a forthcoming event which to them and to others whose tastes were musical, was of much importance; Grisi,[17] famous soprano, and Mario, the equally famous tenor, were to sing at a concert for one night only at Aberdeen; and though Aberdeen was eighteen miles off and no Deeside railway was then in existence, my mother and elder sisters were on fire to go, and my father was submissive. The carriage stood at the door; the parents mounted the box, the daughters, the dickey behind; the maids were inside with the small luggage, and a huge 'Imperial,' containing the gala dresses, was strapped on behind.

How gay and grand it all looked! We children hopped about, and wondered what it would be like to be grown up – or nearly so – and be going to a concert, and sleep the night in a hotel? But when, on the following day, the party returned, we did not hear so much of Grisi and Mario as of something else which eclipsed their glories utterly – with us at any rate. *The Queen* was coming to Balmoral,[18] and would pass our gates on her way thither!

I believe, though, I am not absolutely sure, that this was Her Majesty's first visit to her Highland home. I think it must have been so: the excitement was so great, and the loyal enthusiasm so widespread. Far and wide the lairds left their houses and the cotters their huts, to line the roadside and bid their sovereign welcome.

The gates of Blackhall abutted on to the main road, and were high and imposing. A flag was affixed to the topmast point, and a daring Highlander, spurred on by his fellows, stood on the narrow ledge by its side, prepared to yell a notification when the cortège came within his view.

Below, the family and household were assembled in the circle of ground just without the gates; and my younger brother and I were on our little Shetland ponies in front. We had, I think, to wait some time, for my little animal, a hot-tempered

Queen Victoria on her visit to Stonehaven, Scotland / The Kylin Archive

chestnut, grew restive, and I was terribly afraid I should be ordered off him; but after a while he quieted down, and that happily before a cry broke out from above: 'She's comin'! – she's comin'! – she's comin'! Ay, it's *Her!*' shrieked Sandy Macgregor, and almost instantly outriders appeared round the corner of the road.

What a moment that was when the *real* moment came! Prince Albert – he was always called 'Prince Albert' then – ever courteous and kindly, and on the lookout to acknowledge loyal greetings, laid his hand on the Queen's arm – for we could see him do it – to draw her attention to our little assemblage; but at the moment Her Majesty was taken up with tying the Princess Royal's bonnet-strings, which she was tugging at in the fashion peculiar to arbitrary mothers. The little princess was holding back, pouting: and as the carriage slowed down (no doubt by previous orders) to enable a considerable crowd which had collected round us, the nucleus, to give vent to their feelings, and have also a good look into the open barouche, we had the satisfaction of seeing our gracious Sovereign Lady obliged to postpone her maternal inclinations, and bestow the light of her countenance elsewhere.

Her face, we then saw, was radiant with sweetness and happiness. She wore a dark blue 'Ugly'[19] a concoction of silk and wire, supposed to be a protection from the sun, when attached to the small bonnet then in vogue, – and it did not misbecome her. She also wore a tartan cloak, and the little princess opposite wore the same, and also the hideous thing rightly named an 'Ugly.' That is all I remember. Whether Prince Albert, and his son, our late King, were in the kilt or not, I cannot tell.

We heard afterwards that the Royal party did not know at the time that they were passing the author of *The Moor and The Loch*, or would have called a halt, as that book did much to lead their steps northward. Her Majesty's Librarian, Mr, now Sir Richard Holmes, showed it to me, thumbed and worn, years and years afterwards, in a selected group of the Prince's favourite works at Windsor Castle.

At the end of our third summer at Blackhall, my parents decided to stay on there for the winter – the Portobello house being let to Lord Worcester, – (and it was on this occasion that the 'poothered heids' of his footmen scared poor old Henny Rose from the door). Blackhall was a good, comfortable house, and its situation was ideal, but – the winter proved to be the historic Crimean winter! For weeks we should have been snowed up but for the snow-plough which plied incessantly up and down the long avenue, and by-and-by the river, the rushing Dee itself, was frozen over.

My father was in his element, however, enjoying a novelty in sport, namely, the chase of the roe-deer, which, driven from the heights, abounded in the woody banks of the river. We were allowed to join occasionally in the hunt, as the youngest of us could keep a pass as well as a full-grown person; and though we little girls only wore – will it be believed? – short socks, and our poor little knees were sadly chapped by the cold, we would have endured anything rather than be ordered home before the day's sport was over. Wood cock and other northern birds were also plentiful that winter, and my father's enormously heavy 'duck gun' was scarcely ever off his shoulder.

The governesses were also quite content amidst snow and frost, which

Lucy's father, John Colquhoun

reminded them of their beloved Vaterland, and there were no grumbles from them when every road was impassable but that kept open by the snow-plough. They were the most cheerful of inmates. They devised all sorts of indoor games; and, best of all, told us in their own tongue such enthralling tales of the weird and mysterious Hartz Mountains, such legends of the Rhine, as made us fancy we were perpetually dwelling in fairyland.

Hans Andersen we read for ourselves; and it was a noble idea to make the translation of *The Snow Queen* and other tales form a part of our German lesson – and then came an idea still more noble, in fact rapturous. We were to have a real German Christmas tree – not the poor imitation to be found in this country.

My mother, who was very well and strong at the time, entered into the notion with spirit, and gave the Fräuleins permission to order what materials they needed from Stewart and Chevis, the Aberdeen grocers.

Then what designing and cutting, what pasting and stitching, what cabbage-nets and streamers of silver and gold and blue and crimson paper – what gilding of walnuts and oranges, what strings of raisins and figs – above all, what quaint little figures perched everywhere upon the boughs, with a mighty Father Christmas on the topmost!

Fastening him and his attendant tapers on, was only accomplished by putting one table on top of another, and a step-ladder on top of both. One of the menservants then mounted aloft, and his head appeared to touch the ceiling. Yet the room was a lofty one, and the tree stood in a tub on the floor. You may guess what a tree it was.

I think my parents themselves were proud of it. Certainly they permitted it to be seen by high and low, for it was lit up several nights in succession, and many of our own small contemporaries, as well as the children of our gardeners and foresters, gazed with envious eyes. It is borne in on my mind that one of the ladies who came on the 'gentry' night, appeared with small flat side-curls on either cheek, just in front of the ear, and that they were extremely becoming to her. She also wore a single curl depending from one side of her head; and we learned that this fashion, side-curls and all, had just been introduced by the Empress Eugénie. Soon there was hardly a pretty face in England which did not follow it, and my two elder sisters were among the first to begin.

The roll of drums and roar of battle in the East sent, I fear, but dim echoes into our quiet home. No very near relation was at the front, and my parents, albeit no doubt patriotically interested, were not personally so. They were, it must be owned, always much wrapped up in their own little world; and even when we grew to be more of companions and could have appreciated discussions on the affairs of nations, we did not hear them.

This was a pity. It was more; it was a serious loss. If children are to take an intelligent interest in the history of their own times, their elders must themselves show – not preach – love of the subject and a sense of its importance.

My mother seldom, if ever, opened a newspaper. It is true that in her day newspapers were usually left to 'the gentlemen;' but still it was inexplicable to me as I older grew that, with her powers of mind, she should have been content to take such knowledge of home and foreign politics as she possessed through the medium of my father. Even these communications were not usually made in our presence, since we led, as I have shown, a separate life all the days of childhood and early youth.

The names of Alma, Balaclava, and Inkermann were therefore, I have to own, but names and nothing more, at any rate to us younger ones. We had snow soldiers indeed, and had field-days on the mimic battle-field, and we demanded a holiday when news of a victory arrived, or sang 'The Red, White and Blue,' emphasising 'This Russian bear we must conquer now or never,' – but we were in reality infinitely more interested in seeing country carts cross the frozen bed of the Dee, and in all the other strange surroundings of our frost-bound fortress.

Then came the break-up of the ice – the awful, thunderous groaning and creaking, crashing and roaring which went on all one night, keeping everyone awake – and the sight next day as the huge blocks which still adhered to the banks, detached themselves and swung and circled down the foaming rapids.

Once begun, the thaw set in rapidly; and ere we left Blackhall, which we did in April (never, so far as I am concerned, to see it again), we had had plenty of warm and fragrant spring days to blot out the background of grey sky above and snowy hills beneath, throughout the earlier part of that historic winter.

Battle of Balaclava – news was left to 'the gentlemen' / The Kylin Archive

Twyford station, the nearest to Park Place / The Kylin Archive

An Early Victorian Household

My parents had now been married for twenty years, and had faithfully kept the promise made upon their wedding-day. No year was ever suffered to elapse without seeing them at Park Place, accompanied by a contingent of sons and daughters.

At first they travelled, as was then the fashion, in their own carriage, with relays of posthorses, taking something under a week over the journey; but by degrees this cumbersome and expensive mode of procedure was abandoned, for the age of steam had set in, and with fear and trembling, but resolved at least to try what it was like, they essayed to go by sea from Leith to London.

They never went again. One experience was enough.

But swiftly the railroad followed in the wake of the steamboat, and with marvellous expedition (only sleeping once by the way, think of that!) the hardy Northerners were transported to the metropolis, and thence to Twyford, the nearest station for Park Place at that period.

To be sure, it was five miles off; but my father was well pleased that it should be so, for reasons of his own. It exactly suited him to despatch all who chose in carriages awaiting us at Twyford, and to invite the rest to cover the distance, as he himself elected to do, on 'Shanks' nags.'

After we left Blackhall we went south in May, and this journey made a special impression upon me, both because for the first time I was allowed to attend afternoon service at York Minster, and sit up to late dinner afterwards, and because, after much pleading, I also obtained permission to accompany the walking party from Twyford to Park Place.

This last feat was looked upon somewhat dubiously by our kith and kin, and I caught asides on the subject: 'Such a little girl! Such a long walk!' – with more of the kind, which added of course to the 'little girl's' triumph. For, be it remembered, walking was the last thing in the world expected of the Early Victorian lady, and my English aunts were Early Victorian ladies or nothing. A stroll in their own grounds, their long dresses trailing behind, or only half caught up by ineffective fingers (how a French-woman would have despised them!), their fragile steps supported by a manly arm, if such were available – and my poor uncles were sadly victimised in this way – this was all they ever ventured upon in the way of walking exercise; and had it not been that my father was a favourite son-in-law and brother-in-law, and that they were fond of visiting his own wild Highland homes, where they saw for themselves the effect of rearing children in hardihood, they would have done more than merely murmur a remonstrance, which indeed only extended to me, the youngest. And they were very kind to us, and we enjoyed ourselves much in our own way beneath our grandfather's roof.

Not that we saw much of either him or my grandmother. Mr Fuller-Maitland[20] in Parliament, representing, I fear, somewhat rotten boroughs; but as he sat continuously from 1807 to 1830 – with the exception of six years from 1820 to 1826 – and was offered a peerage by Mr Spencer Percival,[21] which promise only fell through on the assassination of that Minister, he must have been of some use to his party, if not to the public. I may under-value his services; but I must honestly confess that I never heard of his doing, or being, or saying anything remarkable, and when he was at home we fled from his path. Ergo, he must have had a bad temper, whatever else he had or had not.

My grandmother[22] was more approachable, and the only thing we dreaded about her was her ear-trumpet. She was very deaf, and spoke in the peculiar voice of a deaf person; but she would occasionally carry on a conversation even with us very young ones, and this the shy and timid shrank from. Being neither myself, I was often thrust forward to bawl response down the trumpet, and partly on this account and partly because my second name of 'Bethia' was her own, the old lady took kindly to me after a grandiose fashion. She would send for me to her room, to repeat poetry, mainly sacred poetry (down the trumpet), and desire that I should accompany her in her daily airing – a compliment I would fain have dispensed with, as the carriage was a close one, with only a chink of window open, and it swung in a manner to make children very uncomfortable, even if they did not actually succumb.

But to get out of going was impossible, we all thought; – it was only once achieved, and the record of that achievement remains, thanks to the impression it made upon the old lady herself: 'I asked Willy if he would like to drive with

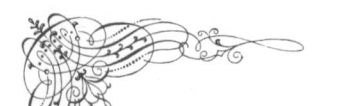

The Druid Temple at Park Place / The Kylin Archive

me,' she narrated; 'and what do you think he said? That he would like to drive with me in an *open* carriage; that was truth and politeness combined'; and at this she would whisk up her trumpet to hear what her auditor had to say to it, for she told the story many times over, as a person will who has few stories to tell – though it never seemed to occur to her that other grandchildren besides Willy might prefer an *open* carriage, though they had not the wit to say it.

My grandmother had a chaplain, Mr Young, at the time I write of, and Mr Young's reading prayers – no, I should say reading of the Bible at prayers – and finally praying into the ear-trumpet, was a sight. He had to kneel in the middle of the floor facing the extended line of servants – but mercifully their backs were turned – and, holding in his hand the tube, the other end of which was in my grandmother's ear as she lay upon her sofa, he raised the cup to his lips, and the effect was exactly as though he was about to quaff 'a full stirrup-cup.' His meek, unconscious face during the ordeal was its final touch.

Park Place[23] in the fifties was not the elaborate structure it has since become. It was a plain, pillared house in the Italian style of architecture, but if the building itself was not so large, the grounds were larger then than now. A considerable portion of these has been curtailed to form another domain, 'Temple Court,' so named from a Druids' temple – (a circle of stones which had been brought from somewhere or other and placed in this chosen spot) – and the acres where my grandmother grew lavender for her own specially distilled lavender-water are now used for other purposes. There were also grottos, summer-houses, and a subterranean passage in the beautifully wooded slopes overhanging the river, which may or may not be still extant.

One of our favourite resorts was an ornamental cottage, yclept the 'Chinese Cottage,' nestling in a hollow below the Henley avenue, where dwelt a certain Mrs Irvine, much petted and pampered as a kind of 'show' woman by the ladies of the house. This wily cottager, it afterwards came out, had taken the measure of their feet to half an inch; but at the time she was all pious professions and honeyed words for the dear little masters and misses who honoured her by a visit; she allowed us to hold in our own hands the curly, china lambs and horned cows on her mantelpiece; she accepted our little offerings of fruit or flowers with humble gratitude; and she flattered – well, no matter. There was one person who had neither sweet looks nor dulcet tones from Dame Irvine. She had a brother whom she led so sorry a life (this also transpired later, *via* a tell-tale who overheard the scene) that one day in desperation, albeit a patient man, he threatened to throw himself down the well. The well, it must be explained, was built over a little bubbling fountain by the side of the cot, and was indeed the *raison d'être* of the latter's being there.

'Down the well!' shrieked the dame, now turned to a virago; 'you throw yourself down the well! And my young ladies comin' here to me for a drink of nice spring water, and *you* lyin' stinkin' there at the bottom!'

And apparently the enormity of his presumption did so strike the poor wretch that he continued to live and be miserable.

In our days, however, Mrs Irvine throve, and was specially favoured by my grandmother a little later on, because of her abstaining from *crinoline* at that lady's desire. In vain did the autocratic old lady try to impose like abstinence under her own roof. Not a maid would stay with her, if the command were enforced.

Then she tried bribery. A handsome donation was proffered to any woman-servant who would do as her mistress did.

The mistress did not take into consideration the fact that whereas she was herself comfortably puffed out by quilted eider-down petticoats, poor Molly must needs be as flat as a pancake. Moreover, Molly went into society, while her mistress abode at home; and Molly had sweethearts to consider, or, at any rate, her reputation among her cronies. Molly's 'No' was prompt and decided. With a solitary exception the bribe was spurned.

With one exception, I repeat, and that one was a certain aged and delightful creature, the head of the housemaids, who thankfully accepted her lady's reward for doing what she would have done at any rate. No shame to her; 'Great Jane,' as she was called among us, was a simple soul who disliked innovations as much as her mistress did, and not being troubled by too much thinking, pocketed her *douceur* with untroubled mind.

One other word about 'Great Jane.' There came to her a day some years after, when she was called upon to show the house to strangers, (this was after the death of both my grandparents, when Park Place was to be sold), and the old woman chanced to be in charge, in the absence of a higher authority. Upstairs and downstairs she stumped, opening doors and displaying cupboards – till the party had seen all they wished, and prepared to depart.

'Great Jane' was standing at the door seeing them off, when an elderly gentleman, after a moment's confab with an elderly lady now seated within the carriage, re-ascended the steps. 'Here is a sovereign for you, my good woman,' said he; then added with a chuckle, 'and *Her Majesty* desires me to tell you that *you have walked before the Queen to-day*!' 'And,' added the narrator, telling the tale afterwards, 'it was the Queen herself, God bless her, that looked up, and laughed, and nodded to me, as he said it!'

It was, I have heard, with a view to a possible purchase of Park Place as a residence for the Princess Helena[24] on her marriage that this visit took place; but if so, nothing ever came of it, and the property passed into the hands of Mr and Mrs Noble, whose family still reside there, and have done much to deserve the esteem and goodwill of their neighbours, rich and poor.

At Park Place, then, we younger children were deposited for some length of time in the summer of 1855, while our elders disported themselves in London, where the season was in full swing. For three whole months we were free of tutor and governesses, and this absence of supervision and education no doubt greatly enhanced the charms of our surroundings, and caused us ever after to regard that summer as memorable. For if our cousins – and we had a large party of delightful cousins within hail – hearkened eagerly to our description of a life in every way different from theirs, and regarded us (as we have since learned they did) as beings to be envied, dwelling in a sort of romantic Paradise, we on our part had many new and exquisite sensations.

A long spell of settled fine weather accustomed us to the glorious singing of the nightingales beneath our open windows as we lay awake at nights; we tracked the glow-worms on the chalky banks where the wild thyme grew, scenting the air; we wondered at the big bats flitting across our path in the twilight, – and even the tinkle of the sheep-bells coming up the slope, and the smock frock of the shepherd-boy husbanding his little flock, was something new, something poetic after a different fashion from the poetry of our native Caledonia.

There was the river too. The Thames is very beautiful at Henley; and just below Park Place there were the willowy 'eyots,' where the kingfishers rustle blue amidst the green, and the shy, brown rats creep in and out, carefully avoided by the mother dabchick piloting her brood among the waterlilies further out stream.

We were allowed free use of our grandmother's boats, and, having been taught to handle oars on Highland lochs, we soon grew accustomed to the different style of rowing, and covered with ease the three miles to Wargrave, where my uncle, Mr Thomas Fuller-Maitland, resided with his family, the aforementioned cousins. With them we would further explore the teeming islets and blossoming back-waters, where grew lovely snowflakes, irises, forget-me-nots, and other delights.

The river to-day is, alas! *the* river to countless thousands; every nook and crannie has its boat-load on a summer afternoon, and no vista of green but shows a red or white parasol at the other end. One ought not perchance to grudge the fretted Londoner this quiet outlet; and yet for those who can remember the exquisite peace of the gently flowing water in the old days, the hushed atmosphere, through which came only the rumble of a distant cart, or an occasional shout from haymakers resting in the shade for their noonday meal – for them the contrast is a sad one.

Everywhere there is, of course, something of the same transformation: villages grown into towns, towns into cities, cities into centres of gigantic suburbs; but nowhere to the view of a lover of 'quiet resting-places' is this spoilation by the influx of humanity more apparent –I would almost say more pitiable – than in the crowded surface of the Thames between Cookham and Maidenhead (though indeed one might instance a dozen other favourite reaches), when one looks back to what were the same beauteous landscapes some fifty years ago.

Henley Regatta[25] was indeed in existence, but there were no house-boats, no

An early view of the Henley regatta / The Kylin Archive

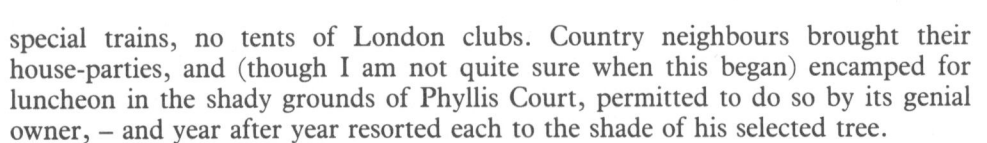

special trains, no tents of London clubs. Country neighbours brought their house-parties, and (though I am not quite sure when this began) encamped for luncheon in the shady grounds of Phyllis Court, permitted to do so by its genial owner, – and year after year resorted each to the shade of his selected tree.

Then there was the walk along the front – very different from the jostling promenade of to-day. Boats easily drew in to the bank at any point, to embark or discharge their several freights; the water itself, though presenting a gay and brilliant spectacle, was not one vast pack of human beings, playing the fool under the guise of merry-making – the whole scene, in short, was not a close imitation of the worst features of a race-course; and as night fell, there was not the frantically crammed lock to be got through at the peril of one's life!

And Henley itself, as yet unspoilt, was as pleasantly rural a little town as one could wish to see.

The shopkeepers came out to attend their customers, whose carriages stood before their doors. The market-day was a great day, when farmers dined at the Red Lion, and we from Park Place were desired to avoid the roads along which

High Street, Henley 'a pleasantly rural little town'/ Geo. Bushell & Son

cattle and sheep were being driven in. The school-children, sauntering leisurely homewards as the afternoon waned, thought no shame to drop their curtseys, or pull their forelocks to any gentry they recognised; whilst their parents bobbed at the cottage doors.

The church? – well, the church services may be much as they were; but to us youthful Presbyterians they seemed well-nigh perfect then; and indeed they were so beautiful and so unlike anything we had ever conceived in the way of church-going, that they excited mingled terror and indignation in the breast of one of our Scotch handmaidens: 'There was the twa o' them,' cried she, relapsing into the broadest vernacular, 'thae twa men, dressed oot like folk at a fair, booin' to each ither, an' answerin' each ither across the table, and the rest cryin' ower an' ower, "The Lord hae maircy upon us!" and a' the time there was the organ bummin' awa' owerheid! Me! I thocht it was the theatre!'

I am bound to own that we flew with this recital to our Puritan grandmother, whom we were shrewd enough to guess it would amuse; and it did – thoroughly. She did not, however, discountenance our attending Henley Church, being conscientiously desirous of fulfilling our parents' wishes while in *loco parentis*, and we never heard a word against the Church of England, dissenter though she was, at which I have since marvelled, religious feeling running strong at the time.

And that Mrs Fuller-Maitland held fast to her tenets the following will show. Among other visitors to Park Place, came from time to time the silver-tongued Samuel Wilberforce,[26] then Bishop of Oxford. He had a purpose in coming. It seemed to him an incongruity that my grandmother, a Nonconformist, should be the patron of several livings in the Church of England, and he much desired to have these in his own gift.

Bishop of Oxford – Samuel Wilberforce

I have heard that he used every argument in vain, and retired from the field worsted by an old woman upon whom his silvery tongue made no impression. It was even added that he professed himself afraid of her! We in the upper regions of the house, hearkened to the rumour with pride; we mentally backed our winner, and thought it fine and gallant of her to stick to her guns; but somehow, somehow in after years we were not quite so sure – however, all of that is an old, old story now.

Although the wild young things from the North must have been a somewhat disturbing element in the dull and prim household, which was so entirely a world within itself in my grandmother's latter days, the only days of which I am able to speak, – we had that vague sensation of being *in favour* which goes for much and compensates for much in a child's life. We did with impunity what many of our cousins never dared risk doing. We abducted books from the library, fearlessly bearing them off to devour within our own stronghold – a far-away room on the ground floor, where none of our elders ever intruded; we pillaged the garden, and romped among the curious old carriages in the stable, (of which we counted forty odd, their collection being a whim of my grandfather's), and we harried the beneficent and long-suffering housekeeper for jams and jellies from her storeroom.

She was a kind soul, and freely gave them – of a second-rate quality. But when, encouraged by her indulgence, we pointed to certain well-stocked shelves from which we noticed she never abstracted anything, she shook her head. 'No, my dears; no. Those,' she continued impressively, and swept her hand round the rows of jars and gallipots, 'those are not for *you*. They are all *for your Grandma's own eatin*'' – and so solemn was her air, and so convincing her tones, that it never occurred to us to reflect upon what must be our grandmother's own appetite!

In truth, the appetites of that generation were extraordinary when it is considered how little was done to deserve them – at any rate at Park Place.

Middle-aged women, even old women, career all over the world nowadays; climb mountains, play golf, toboggan down Swiss slopes, penetrate the desert on camel-back – in short, as we all know, there is nothing the hardy dame of sixty and seventy does not throw herself into with the zest of a school-girl; but half a century ago they were few and far between who indulged in any kind of vigorous exercise even when young, and even when full of animal spirits.

It was not 'the thing.' 'The thing' was to be musical, poetic, delicate, ethereal. Now and then, it is true, horsewoman might be found among families of position, who, clad in the flowing habits depicted by Leech, penetrated country lanes and put in an appearance at fashionable meets – and one of my Fuller-Maitland aunts did so far break loose from the traditions of her house as to keep her own horse for this purpose; but when not riding, she was as fond of the sofa and the carriage as her sisters.

Yet they ate – yes, I must say it, they ate enormously. Dinner, albeit at the unearthly hour of five, was a prolonged and stately function. We children, often perched upon the stairs above (to whom a friendly John Footman would surreptitiously pass a tempting remnant), found it amusing enough, even whilst feeling as though it would never end; but when we arrived at an age to join the party inside the dining-room, we soon grew bored with the multiplicity of courses, and secretly marvelled at our elders who partook of them all.

They also drank varieties of wine to suit. I once read the warning of a medical authority of that period. He implored lady patients to be on their guard against taking more wine than was wholesome and beneficial – 'taking wine in excess,' he termed it, adding that anything over four or five glasses at a meal *was* in excess.

What my grandmother and aunts took I am not prepared to say, but I expect they only just kept within the above limits, and always topped up with port at desert.

At last the doctor intervened. A word about Dr Cowan, beloved of all the family, who attended my grandmother throughout the latter years of her life. He came from Reading, driving over in the quaintest little vehicle, resembling a slice off an omnibus – it was indeed termed a 'Minibus.' There was only one seat on each side, and whether the inventor found his design did not answer, or had any other reason for not promulgating more, I cannot tell; but I have never seen another like it.

Once a week the worthy doctor appeared, and, after a confab in my grandmother's apartments, joined the dinner-party where he was hailed with effusion. He had a bald, peaked head, high forehead, mild, blue eyes, and an oracular manner which must have been pounds in his pocket to him. When he has prescribed gin, in place of wine, for his aged patient – she always called it 'Hollands' – it was universally felt that such a revolution in the habits of decorous Park Place could only have been effected by the master mind of Dr Cowan.

He played the flute. I can see him now putting it together; twisting and turning the component parts; essaying little trills and warbles – finally tooting away in excellent style, the while one fair lady accompanied him on the harp and another on the piano.

My aunts were all harpists. It was then considered a most elegant instrument, and, in addition to its musical value, it showed off a feminine figure, and the 'large, round, white arm,' beloved of Thomas Day.

This worthy, let me mention for the benefit of the ignorant, was the author of *Sandford and Merton*;[27] and in his memoirs we read that when desirous of marrying, he besought a friend to look out for him a lady of piety and culture, adding that, though he had no need to seek a fortune and would forego beauty, he must own he should like his proposed bride to have large, round, white arms.

To return to the evening concern in the Park Place drawing-room. Somehow I always think of it as happening on a summer evening, and see the figures of the musicians silhouetted against a sunset sky. No doubt it also took place at other seasons of the year, and the good Dr Cowan had many a dark and dreary drive over the nine miles between Reading and Henley; but with all drawbacks, there must have been a glow of satisfaction when the day came for a weekly visit, and he could look forward to an excellent dinner, an agreeable evening, and a fresh – and valuable – entry in his notebook ...

Before leaving the south in 1855, we younger children were permitted to stay at the pleasant Berkshire house of our uncle and aunt, Mr and Mrs Valpy, of which visit, delightful as it was, I have only one trifling incident to record, and only record it because it is characteristic.

We young Colquhouns never forgot that we were *Scotch* – that 'Scots wha hae' was in our blood, as it were; and that however fond we might be of our English relations, they were not to suppose we did not look down upon them as belonging to an inferior race.

Had they never heard of *Bannockburn*? Had not the very bows of the archers been cut from the yew trees on our own Loch Lomond islet, Inch Lonaig? Had we not actually given them *our* King Jamie? This was a great point, much and often enlarged upon; and as it met with its due retort, and as we were all equally warlike and ignorant, battles-royal on the subject were the result.

These culminated one day in our assembling the entire Enborne household within doors and without, and marshalling them upon the lawn. Our uncle and aunt were away from home, and the good-natured creatures from coachman to kitchen-maid, were highly diverted by the proceeding, wondering what the little misses would be at?

We soon enlightened them: my sister and I, the generals in command, went solemnly down the lines, demanding of each in turn, whether he or she were 'for' England, or 'for' Scotland? What was to be the outcome of their declaration of faith I am at a loss to conjecture; but am positive that in every case the answer very naturally came, 'For England,' till we reached a certain young groom who, possibly scenting a snug berth if he played his cards well, stoutly asserted that for his part he had no objection to go to Scotland, not he; and, still further courting our favour, added that he had *''eard there was uncommon good grub there.'*

As this material view of things did not, however, by any means please us – indeed, in our enthusiasm, we were repelled and disgusted – the base deserter got nothing for his pains but the black looks of his fellows, and if he ever had a chance of eventually judging of the Scotch 'good grub,' it was not through our instrumentality.

⁂

I cannot but think it strange that the Fuller-Maitlands, who as a family had considerable intellectual ability, and possessed appreciative and critical faculties in a marked degree, should have left so little trace on the world's tablets of bygone generations. Of that which flourished in the middle of last century, there would seem to be no trace whatever.

They were readers; they were thinkers; they were charming and often witty conversationalists; and there were many of them, for the most part highly cultivated, and having leisure and opportunities at command; yet something clogged the footsteps that surely ought to have made some 'footprints on the sands of time,' and I am inclined to think the creative power was absent. There was a lack of physical and mental energy; there were quick apprehension and receptiveness; but there was no inner force which must needs have vent. They were content to receive, and had no desire to give back any contributions[28] to intellectual, scientific, or artistic life.

That they left to their descendants, of whom I will only say here that while many are gifted in various directions, one at least is well and widely known. I allude, as may be divined, to my cousin, Mr J A Fuller-Maitland, who holds so high a place in the world of music.[29]

Those who take great pleasure in the graceful and original work of a certain writer, may wonder that I omit to add a further testimony to it; but to this I would reply that Mrs 'Ella' Fuller-Maitland[30] only bears the name by virtue of her marriage, and accordingly cannot count.

To return. The month of August saw us, the Northern contingent, once more homeward bound, and this time a fresh departure was made by our travelling the whole distance from London to Edinburgh without a break. Such a formidable achievement was considered feasible only by the acquisition of a private saloon-car with three compartments – one for the elder members of the family, one for the children and servants, and one for the luggage, – and we took sixteen hours over the journey, starting at eight one evening, and arriving at twelve the next day.

This was considered something to talk about and boast of, and I may add that we never afterwards travelled in any other way.

It was not always successful, however. On one occasion we had a disaster which might have been a very serious one. Our saloon was shunted in Preston Station to wait for the London Express (we having come from the South-west coast), and there was a fog, and the Express missed some signals and ran into us.

Perhaps I ought not to say 'ran,' for had it run, I had not been here to tell the tale – but its gentle touch was like the pat of a lion's paw. It was sufficient to pitch us all from our seats, while the man and maid in the next compartment were badly cut and bruised, and some windows were broken. The sensation was, as far as I was concerned, as though a dark blue wall suddenly rushed at me, and hit me a violent blow on the side of the head; then I found myself lying full length on the floor, without any idea of how I got there. We had been eating our luncheon at the moment the accident took place, and there was now a fine *debris* of broken plates and victuals; but when voices from without shouted anxiously to know if anyone were hurt, we could cheerfully answer, 'No,' till our poor maid popped her bleeding face round the door and we learned that she and her companion had suffered more than we had – probably because their compartment was not so well stuffed and cushioned.

As we approached the Border on these returns from southern raids, my father would be on the watch for the first glimmer of the Tweed.

Then, 'Now, children, cheer; cheer for your native land' he would cry; 'and you,' turning to my mother, 'groan for yours.'

To humour him she would laughingly comply, only bargaining that as *we* were to cheer when our faces were set to the North, *she* should do the same when they were set to the South. Nevertheless, in her heart of hearts, I believe that after a while she really loved the land of her adoption more than that of her birth.

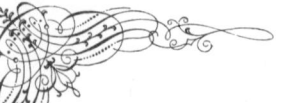

Oban pier, where we saw Harriet Beecher-Stowe / The Oban Times

Strange Sights in the Hebrides

The following year brought a visitor to our shores whose name was soon in every mouth.

Mrs Harriet Beecher-Stowe had just scored a second success with her novel *Dred*; and though it never attained the celebrity of its world-known precessor, it is, I venture to think, superior to *Uncle Tom's Cabin* in point of construction and concentration. Like the other, it has unsurpassably beautiful episodes, and the reader's attention is never called away from them by being forced to follow the fortunes of insignificant personages who have nothing to do with the main story.[31]

We were at Oban when the little party of Americans, whose movements were

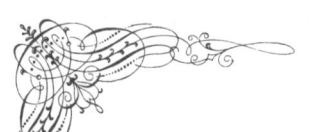

Harriet Beecher-Stowe, authoress of 'Uncle Tom's Cabin' / The Kylin Archive

being eagerly followed by thousands of eyes, took their way up the West Highland coast. My father had taken a shooting in the Isle of Mull; but as there was no good house attached, we were obliged to content ourselves with 'Rosebank Villa,' on a little height above Oban Bay.

The gay little harbour put on its flags one August day, and we were told that the next steamer from Crinan would have the noted authoress and her friends on board. Of course we were on the *qui vive* to see them – or rather her; but our enthusiasm was not shared by one person at least in the place. Mr Anthony Cumstie, the grocer, was weighing out to our esteemed order some of his brown sugar-candy – which was of the best – when, seeing through the doorway the passers-by beginning to run towards the pier as the red funnel of the *Mountaineer* rounded the last point, he thus delivered himself: 'All this fuss aboot a wumman just because she's written a *bouk*! A *bouk*! – What's a *bouk*? – Whae couldna write a *bouk*?' Words fail to convey the sour sarcasm of his accents as he kept on repeating the obnoxious word: and his long narrow chin, quivering with Scotch self-conceit, jerked itself higher and higher into the air: 'A *bouk*!' he muttered, 'juist a *bouk*!'

'You think we could all write a book if we tried, don't you, Mr Cumstie?' affably suggested one of our party. 'I didna say *you* could,' snapped Mr Cumstie. He saw he was being laughed at.

Then we all rushed off to the pier; but alack! the pier was so crowded that try as we might we could not wriggle our small selves to the front, and all that I ever saw of Mrs Stowe was a blue veil! It floated up for a moment, caught in a passing gust of air, and just sufficed to give me a throb of pleasure when a voice near by exclaimed, 'Thon's her, wi' the blue veil.'

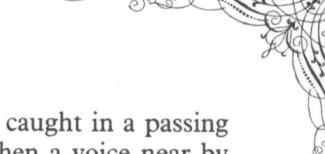

Oban has perhaps altered less than most other places of its kind during the past half-century. It has grown, of course; but it has not grown out of recognition: it is not 'improved' to the point of defamation; and when it lies silent beneath the moon on a summer night – but perhaps I may be forgiven for reproducing here a couple of verses written for the *World* some years ago[32] (though many years after my childish experience of it as a passing home).

> In Oban Bay
> *Noon*
> A Shocking place. Too vulgar, dear, –
> Such dreadful people – and so queer, –
> And so outrageous in their gear, –
> Go where you may;
> 'Tis odious all you see and hear
> In Oban Bay.
>
> *Midnight*
> A spot to dream of. Solemn height
> And awe-struck ocean, silvered white,
> 'Neath August moon. Nor sound, nor sight,
> Nor note of day.
> Oh, Heaven, that it were always night
> In Oban Bay!

As my father got his wild shooting and deer-stalking in Mull and often spent a week at a time at Scalastal farmhouse, where he had installed a farm-manager and his wife, hoping to make the farm pay (which it never did), he did not object to the Oban villa as my mother and the rest of us did, though I daresay he was well enough pleased when the following summer it was settled that we should for the time being dislodge Mr and Mrs Sandy Crow, and ourselves take possession of Scalastal.

It was an excellent and commodious farmhouse – for a farmhouse. There was even room in it for the inevitable governess, while the tutor had lodgings in a cottage near; and the summer being an exceptionally fine one on the west coast, nobody minded roughing it a little indoors.

That was the summer of the Indian Mutiny. Who among us older people but can recall that awful time? Every newspaper, every litter filled with its appalling details, and such details as even children could understand and feel the horror of.[33] As much as anything so far away, and so absolutely beyond our powers of conception could, it cast a shadow over our daily life. The sad looks of our elders, and seeing my father once turn away from his untasted dinner after the post came in, made an impression we could not forget.

But of course ordinary life flowed on just the same; and there were the long, light evenings when we hung over the side of the boat with handlines, or even condescended to the 'cuddy-fishing' beloved by the natives of the Sound of Mull; and there was the 'Scringe Net,' which gathered within its deadly folds salmon and cod, as well as whiting and haddock; and there were ascents of the great, dark mountain, Dhundeghu, (the mountain of the two winds), and joyous processions home after a successful deer-hunt; besides the never-failing treat of seeing the cows milked, and trying ourselves to milk, to the infinite worry of the cow – so that altogether we got on very well at Scalastal, and when a full harvest was succeeded by a rush of 'leading in' to secure it, (my two elder brothers, on leave from their respective regiments, heading the carts all through the night), we had finally such a harvest dance as had not been seen before in these parts.

Tom Macdonald, the head shepherd, was the hoped-for partner of every Highland lass. A splendid-looking fellow was Tom, with the figure and the face of a Greek god. To see him striding over the hill-tops was a sight. There was no mistaking who it was: his height and the pace with which he covered the steepest ascents, betrayed him. Painters had tried in vain to beguile such a model away from his simple, solitary life, but Tom was proof against them: they held out no bait sufficiently tempting.

Nor did my brothers, who would fain have brought such a recruit to their respective headquarters, fare any better. Tom only laughed, looked sheepish, and whistled his dogs to heel. Those wonderful dogs, of the purest collie breed, there was nothing they could not do and understand. Tom was a king to them, and his 'Forrit–forrit–forrit' a word of command.

And Tom had his secret aspirations, his vein of romance. It may be that he was at that time a trifle spoilt, (though afterwards he became an excellent and much-respected member of society, married well, and throve exceedingly); but according to nurse Aiky, who was always our informant on such points, Tom in his heydey was very high and mighty towards the adoring females who cast their eyes in his direction.

'He's for nane o'them. He's jist bothered wi' them. He's a' for reading and *poetry*. Mistress Crow says there's a pile of poetry-books i' his bit room that blocks up the window – and he has aye ane i' his pocket when he's oot on the hills.'

Of course this was interesting; we were at an age to be poetry mad, and to spout to each other from Tennyson, Byron, and Scott directly our time was our own. We looked at Tom Macdonald from afar with a sense of sympathy.

And one day, far, far away upon the moor, by the side of a foaming waterfall and beneath a red rowan-tree, we chanced upon a plaid-girt form stretched upon the heather, poring over an open volume. '*Doch!*' exclaimed our Fräulein, and hurried us on. It was not for our virgin eyes to rest upon such a picture.

A crofter in the Outer Hebrides / The Oban Times

Nevertheless, years afterwards – when a certain London Adonis was disporting himself in the Row, the admired of all admirers, and my father, looking at him, muttered, 'Not a patch on Tom Macdonald' – such of us had seen the lonely shepherd lying beneath the rowan-tree on the slopes of Dhundeghu, were inclined to echo the sentiment in their hearts.

Highlanders, both men and women, are often something of readers and poetry-lovers, but though many can recall instances of this, I fancy an experience that once befell myself was exceptional.

In a poor Argyllshire hut, which boasted only a *but* and a *ben*, I saw a small, beautifully-bound book lying open, face downwards, as though someone had just been reading it, and laid it aside at the approach of footsteps. Taking it up idly to look, what was my amazement to find it a copy of Dante in the original!

As there were some painters at work on a cottage close by, I jumped to the conclusion that here perhaps lodged some mute, inglorious Milton feasting his soul – but why feast it in Italian, and old and difficult Italian to boot? This in itself was curious enough, but a fresh surprise awaited our party.

'Who does this book belong to?' we inquired of the good woman of the house, and the response was a bolt from the blue – 'Mysel', I'm gey fond o' readin',' continued the speaker, standing still to twirl her apron and glance lovingly at the little volume; 'and whiles, when I'm no thrang, I get yon oot. I'm frae Glasgy,' she added inconsequently.

'But this language – do you understand it?'

'Oo, ay, I did aince, and I do a bit still. I got yon as a prize at the Normal.'

A prize? It seemed a queer sort of prize, and we were bent on getting to the bottom of the mystery. 'A prize for what?' demanded someone.

'For French, I was heid o' my class for French – it cam easy to me; and then they speired: Wad I learn anither language or what? Sae I said "Italian;" and when I had lairnt Italian, they gied me this for my prize.'

Now we knew, and once again was truth stranger than fiction. This poor, peasant woman, clad in homespuns, with her coarse, worsted stockings and clumsy clogs, plying her daily toil of cooking and washing and sewing on the wild moor, far from the madding crowd, possessed that strange, inscrutable gift for other tongues given to so few, denied to so many, and by its aid could soar at will into other altitudes. I often saw her afterwards, always busy, always cheerful, and am glad to think never in the least sensible of any hardship in the lot which seemed so much at variance with that to which she might have aspired.

The Sound of Mull is a glorious place. From Scalastal, looking south, one can see the dark ruin of Duart Castle, standing out on its bare and lonely headland; then, to the left, the island of Lismore, where many currents meet and foam; while the long chain of the Appin mountains, faint and blue in the distance, bound the view and proclaim the mainland beyond.

Opposite us was Ardtonish, at the mouth of Loch Aline, another rugged pile, but less imposing than Duart; while finest of all, against the western sky, stood out the bold Killundine.

Aros, too, desolate but enduring, brought its testimony to the fierce feuds of other days when every chieftain's home was a fortress.

We learnt to know Aros well, when presently my father added the shootings of Glenforsa, on the other side of the island, to those of Scalastal; and for three years

'The dark ruin' of Duart Castle / The Kylin Archive

we resided every summer, and often late into the autumn, at the little old-world house on Loch Baa, a small inland loch, whose waters flowed for a couple of miles, before emptying themselves into Loch Nagaul, an arm of the sea.

Perhaps of all our Highland homes Glenforsa was the most romantic. It was certainly the most primitive and remote. The posts came but thrice a week, and letters and parcels were not delivered at the house, but were deposited in a rudely constructed box within a pile of stones, at a point a mile and a half away.

As the hour when old Posty went by was also peculiar – between six and seven o'clock in the morning, – and as our elders were naturally impatient for news of the outer world, we younger ones easily obtained leave to ride off on our shelties and fetch the mail. It was a responsibility to be gloried in, – besides which, we were not forbidden to extend the ride, provided it was before and not after our commission was fulfilled; and at the fresh and fragrant hour, when all the shy, wild creatures were still about, and the early mists were breaking on the crags above with their shadows reflected in the loch beneath, it was a joy only to live. I believe we should not have been sorry to go every day; at any rate, I know it was a grief if a morning were too wet – and a Scotch mist can be very like rain sometimes – when another messenger had to be substituted.

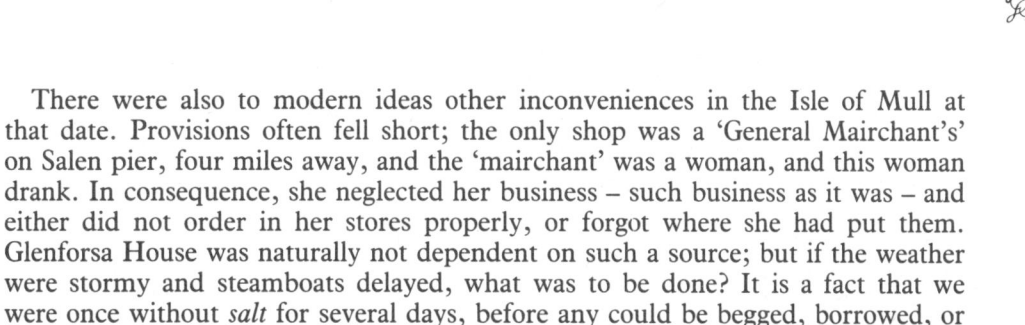

There were also to modern ideas other inconveniences in the Isle of Mull at that date. Provisions often fell short; the only shop was a 'General Mairchant's' on Salen pier, four miles away, and the 'mairchant' was a woman, and this woman drank. In consequence, she neglected her business – such business as it was – and either did not order in her stores properly, or forgot where she had put them. Glenforsa House was naturally not dependent on such a source; but if the weather were stormy and steamboats delayed, what was to be done? It is a fact that we were once without *salt* for several days, before any could be begged, borrowed, or stolen, all our cottage neighbours being in the same plight; and the season being over, and other shooting tenants departed, we had none but cottagers to apply to.

We were also a long way from any church, that at Salen being the nearest.

To meet this difficulty, my father had had what I can only term as a most terrible conveyance specially built – a sort of bathing-machine which could carry six people within and three without. When the door was open there was also a seat on the step, and this was *the* coveted seat in the 'Bus,' which is not to be wondered at, considering it was the only one blessed with a breath of air. No windows were made to open; the heat within was well-nigh intolerable on a summer day, and there was nothing we would not have done, no fatigue we would not have endured, to escape the sensation of nausea engendered – a sensation reminding us only too forcibly of our grandmother's carriage at Park Place.

The 'Bus,' however, came to the door every Sunday morning, and such as could not evade it rumbled off, to change halfway with others who had started earlier to walk. Outside the little port of Salen we all met again, and the 'Bus' retired into obscurity, while a picnic luncheon took place – this being, even to my parents' view, unavoidable. There was only one service, and it was at twelve o'clock, lasting till two. We could not get home till past three, and food must be eaten somewhere. 'Hoots, there's nothing *wrong* in eating out of doors,' quoth my father when the idea was first mooted; and his good common-sense having thus promptly settled the question, the Sunday picnic (though it was never called such) became a settled institution. No doubt it also helped us to endure the service which followed, as to which the less said the better.

But the walk home, gathering as we went the large heavy-headed cotton-rush, the bitter-sweet bog-myrtle, the delicate cup-shaped Grass of Parnassus, besides rare ferns that throve in that soft, moist atmosphere, and moss and bell heather that loved the peat-bogs! Somehow on Sundays we seemed to fill our hands fuller of these than on any other day of the week, and the great china bowl that stood in the hall was always cleared and waiting for its nosegay the night before.

One day we went to Staffa. Staffa was to be seen from our side of Mull, and looked often temptingly close, though in reality it was a good way off in the open sea.

Our party, including several guests, numbered seventeen, and we went in two open boats rowed by our own men, my father and brothers also taking their share of the work. The day – it was the 22nd of June – was one of those 'halcyon' days when earth and sky and sea are alike motionless in melting sunshine, and every mountain peak and craggy headland was mirrored in the loch below. Flocks of seabirds hovered over our heads, and swooped, and soared, and poised themselves aloft, and then, what did we see next? A dark, shining object upon the surface of the water? An object that moved, that turned from side to side, then disappeared, to return soon, in company with another. They were the square, sleek heads of seals.

Seals? We were accustomed to seeing seals by this time, Loch Nagaul being a favourite haunt of theirs; and we often watched them waddling over the rocks, and sportively plunging among the sea-pools of a group of islets barely detached from the shore; but it was a new thing to be thus followed, and at first we could hardly credit the evidence of our eyes, and still less the statement of a boatman: 'It iss the music they're after – oh, yess, indeed, it iss. They do come always to the music.' My mother was playing the concertina, as she often did upon the water, and the seals had bidden each other to the concert. They kept close by for many miles, in fact till we got well out to sea, and far beyond their usual range.

How long it took us to reach our goal I do not know. We were able to put up sails coming home, but had to row the entire way out, as there was not a breath upon the ocean; and a steamer lay of Staffa, re-embarking her tourist passengers, as we approached. No doubt we were looked upon as one of the sights of the day, since rowing-boats rarely venture so far from land on that part of the coast; but the steamer blew her whistle and was soon ploughing her way south, past the 'Ross of Mull' and the 'Dutchman's Cap' – so that our humbler craft could draw in to the mouth of the far-famed Fingal's Cave, and find only its own wild tenants there.

The tide was low, and the rugged pathway to the inmost recesses of the cave not so troublous as it would otherwise have been to light heads. But it was exceedingly slippery, and at the very furthest point within something happened. I was standing still, gazing up into the vaulted roof, my mind filled with the wonder, the glory of the place,

> 'Where as to shame the temples deck't
> By skill of earthy architect,
> Nature herself, it seemed, would raise
> A minster to her Maker's praise,'

when something or someone startled me –   one is easily startled at such a moment – and, losing my balance, I fell.

The fall was nothing; but seeking a handkerchief wherewith to wipe off the traces, I drew back my hand with a scream. It had plunged into – what?

At the same instance, a foul smell – a smell that could only be called a stench – filled the air.

We were at the extreme end of the cave, as I said, where it narrowed to a point,

Fingal's cave 'By skill of earthly architect' / The Oban Times

and there was no escape for the putrid fumes; after a single inhalation and a glance at my tell-tale hand, my brothers and sisters with one accord rushed from the spot, holding their noses. I was alone with a broken guillemot's egg in my pocket, and the huge egg was addled!

With the strength of combined disgust and despair, I tore the pocket from my holland frock – luckily it had already begun to give way under the weight of its varied contents (for it was stuffed full), and, though plentifully bespattered in the process, I did succeed in wrenching it loose and flinging it into a pool. Then after a hasty dabble of the horrible hand, which had to be held at arm's length even then, I hurried after the flying squadron in front, as fast as a poor, frightened, shaking little girl could scramble over the slippery pathway.

They yelled to me to keep back – to keep away from them all!

It was not cruelly meant, I knew; I could hear them laughing as they ran – but still!

Then what did my tearful eyes behold? Someone not going from me, but coming towards me – a friend, a deliverer!

It was only the poor tutor: an uncouth Edinburgh student, whom in secret we laughed at and despised, but whose next action put us – put me in particular – to shame. For this humble Dominie Sampson, who had not been with us in the cave, but who now learnt the shocking tale of what had happened there, instead of turning back, made straight for the hapless, ostracised culprit, filled with pity and commiseration.

'Miss Lucy, let me help you; let me' – and he produced his own clean handkerchief and fell to wiping; 'but how is this? You have surely not left behind a whole pocketful of things? Oh, that will never do: I'll bring them,' and having carefully conducted me to a place of safety, where I sat ruefully alone, but thankful to be again in the sunlight, he disappeared, heedless of remonstrance.

Now there was in that pocket a whole collection of treasures. There was, for one thing, a beautiful little tortoise-shell penknife, with four blades, by which I set much store; and though I forget what else, I remember that the good, kind man was himself amused at their multiplicity when presently he returned, with all intact, and all, even to a pair of gloves (how *could* he do it?) carefully rinsed in sea-water. And he never thought that he had done anything: never dreamed that his gallant act – for so I *will* call it – was to be recorded of him long, long after he had lain in his quiet grave, at the close of a useful and honoured life. My heart warms to thee, even as I write, honest and excellent Liddell.

⁂

The beautiful lines on Fingal's Cave which I have quoted from *the Lord of the Isles*, remind me that it was in this island home of ours that I read my first Waverley Novel.

The event – for it was an event: marked an epoch in my young life – happened on this wise. As we had now two residences of a sort in Mull at one and the same time, and as our sportsmen were even keener on shooting over the Scalastal moor than that of Glenforsa, rooms at the farmhouse were always kept in readiness, and they and others of our party were forever coming and going between the two.

We loved this; it was a delightful change, engendering no trouble, as the humble 'Bus' carried luggage on the top – and there were always volunteers in plenty when the question was raised, 'Who's for Scalastal this week?'

For those left behind, moreover, small indulgences were provided, and one of them was invariably liberty to select a new story-book from the bookshelves wherewith the house was well provided. The owners of Glenforsa must have been readers, for albeit some of the volumes were quaintly out of date, and many were beyond the capacity of young folks, there was abundance of lighter literature of the best quality. Our reading was, of course, supervised by a careful mother, but she was not one of those who ground us down to the usual type of children's books; whatever was good of its kind she did not consider over our heads, provided we aspired to it; and when I took for her inspection a volume with a faded, brown, linen cover and a label bearing the name of *The Talisman*, she smiled.

Most of Scott's novels had already been read aloud in the evenings by my father, who read well; but this was for the benefit of my elder brothers and sisters at a time when I was too young to sit up for it; and it had been my lot to hear only a page or two before the loathed bedtime summons came – always at a thrilling moment.

Now I was older; I was wiser; I hoped for the best – and the best came to pass.

The sister who was to be my companion for the nonce also made her choice – I think, *The Inheritance*, Miss Ferrier's masterpiece[34] – and as soon as we had seen the departure of the rest, we hurried to a selected spot.

This was a little bend of the lake below, fringed by alders, where moss and fern crept down among the rocks even to the water's edge. It was a favourite haunt. There we were safe from intruders, hidden from every eye; and the distant bark of a collie and the lapping of the waters, varied by an occasional 'plop' as a trout leaped and turned in the air, were the only sounds to fall upon the ear. As the month was August – our holiday month – we had the whole day long before us.

Well, that day – has she forgotten it? I never have, and never shall – amidst ideal surroundings, at a time when the mind is capable of being wholly absorbed and the soul stirred to its depths, I fell under the spell of the magician.

I fell headlong. The splendid Saracen, the knightly Kenneth, the noble Richard, and the enchanting Berengaria lived, moved, spoke, suffered and triumphed before my eyes. Hours passed; we were left in peace, for the sultry heat of an August sun was deemed sufficient excuse for what probably seemed torpor in the eyes of others; and except to obey the sound of the gong at meal-times, the whole peaceful, rejoiceful day passed as in a dream. Only the long shadows of evening drove us indoors at last.

But next day found us again beneath our 'Sochen' tree, (our own badge: we always wore a spray in token thereof), and when the last page of the wonderful book – of the two wonderful books, for I must apply a like adjective to *The Inheritance*, and have Sir Walter's own authority for doing so – when this was turned, a silence fell between us, and a grey shade seemed to have descended over the land.

Will anyone in these days believe that such a thing could be? There is so much pleasure, there are so many varied forms of amusement provided for modern juveniles, that it seems to me they are cheated of a lost delight – the power of illusion. Except in rare cases, the boy or girl of to-day is too intensely self-conscious, too critical and competent, to surrender himself or herself wholly to the creations of genius.

Forty or fifty years ago it was different; men and women were not then ashamed to dwell for a while in the realms of fancy, or romance, as the following will show. There was a certain sombre Doctor of Divinity who frequented our house, a dear friend of our parents, and benignant though somewhat unapproachable generally – certainly dry as dust to the world at large. One day we had an argument among ourselves concerning the Waverley Novels, by which we younger ones were by this time fairly besotted, and, carried away by the heat of the battle, we appealed to Dr Veitch for his opinion as to which was the best – the very, very best?

The good man looked from one to another, and wagged his foot thoughtfully – he had long, thin feet at the end of long, thin legs, and when he crossed the latter, they entwined like a vine.

'Which – which?' – we urged, hotly.

The doctor coughed, and pressed his finger-tips together.

We hung breathlessly on his lips; we did not like his sermons, but his judgement on the present occasion would give victory to one side or the other. 'Say *Guy Mannering*; say *Ivanhoe*; say *The Pirate*.' The wagging foot ceased, and a light came into the pale blue eyes.

'If you ask me which, I think when I had read each one I should have said that one; but now, if I were now to say' – he paused, and his voice sank. 'I think – *The Bride of Lammermoor*,' he murmured.

The Bride of Lammermoor? We were scarcely prepared for that; no one among us, strange to say, had selected that – the most sensational, the most emotional, the most terrible of all.

The Bride of Lammermoor? Was it fancy, or did I really see a glance, and a glance full of meaning, pass between my parents, who had hitherto listened in silence? Their old friend came from Lammermoor, had been born and bred among the Lammermoor Hills; was it a memory of his childhood – but then why those softened accents, that momentary hesitation? And his bowed head remained sunk upon his breast – what was passing within? Could it have been that something deeper and tenderer still stirred those dry bones? In the far distant past could there have been some bonnie Scotch bluebell, some golden-haired, sunny-faced Lucy Ashton, who had also been a bride, and not for *him*? Who could say? He had never married, and that spare, bent form was not always bent, nor those scanty, grey hairs always grey. *The Bride of Lammermoor?* Young as I was, I had my own thoughts, and perhaps others had theirs.

⇒) (⇐

As autumn approached, wild weather often set in on the West Highland coast. There would be hurricanes of wind and lashing rain; branches torn from the trees; seaweed flung across the shore roads – flung over the dykes and into the low-lying fields beyond. The gulls would walk about in our garden, pecking fearlessly at upturned potato roots and fallen fruit. 'Spates' from the hills made the trout-burns unfishable; and as the day for our return to more civilised regions drew near, there would be anxious eyes watching the sky and sea, and anxious ears on the stretch when the mountains themselves seemed to moan, and echoes hung about the glens.

For we had a fearsome journey before us, as those who have traversed the Hebrides in those times and at that season of the year will attest. There were no piers for steamers to call at, all along the Sound of Mull, as far as Tobermory; and passengers had to row out in an open boat to be taken on board the *Clansman* or her mate (whose name I have forgotten) – which pair of good, solid boats absorbed all the traffic of the west coast after the summer boats had ceased to run.

Even those only ran on alternate days, and were very erratic, depending as they did upon the amount of cattle, sheep, and herring-barrels to be shipped at each port. Falkirk Tryst, the great market of the north, is held in November, and either not cognisant of this or regardless of its effect upon the Highland traffic, my parents frequently timed their departure from Mull so as to clash with it. This was unlucky, for the *Clansman*, increasing her load at every stopping-point, would often be fifteen or twenty hours behind her time – once she was twenty-four, and we had waited exactly a day and night upon the pier, or in the little smoky, whisky-smelling shop attached to it, ere the long-drawn cry of 'Bo-o-at' was raised.

As she might appear at any moment, and as telegraphic communication, which might have warned or comforted us, was never thought of, it followed that no one durst leave the spot – since the instant the smoke of the steamer was seen, always before she herself appeared, we had to put out to sea.

And it really was 'putting out to sea.' There was but the faintest caricature of a bay, either at Salen or Craignure, (the latter the port of Scalastal), and in the Sound of Mull the waves run high. Worst of all, moreover, was the fact that so many hours of weary waiting had had its almost inevitable effect upon the sturdy boatmen. What Highlander can be kicking without taking 'a glass?' I recollect my father's aside to Sandy Crow, the farm manager – 'For Heaven's sake, Sandy, keep an eye upon them' – and the anxious eye he himself cast upon the group as we embarked.

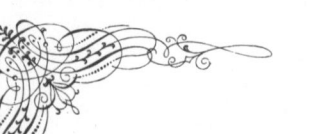

But we got on all right, too tired and sick of our surroundings to care very much what brought relief, and only on one occasion was there any real danger.

The *Clansman* was later than ever; it was night when she appeared, and the night was dark and stormy. Our small boats tossed from wave to wave. A chill sensation kept us all rather silent, and the huge side of the steamer towered above us like a monster. Then – Tom Macdonald missed the rope!

I do not say that he was drunk; the lordly Tom was a sober man, but could 'take his glass' with another, and no doubt there had been a good many glasses going, with but little food to temper them, – the fact remains that the stalwart shepherd, lurching forward to catch the steamer's rope, overbalanced himself and fell back into the boat. The boat was rocking vehemently. Afterwards we heard whispers: 'A near thing – ay, a near thing. *Man!* yon micht ha' been a near thing!' – and we did not ask questions. Another hand caught the rope on its return swing, and we were quickly on board the steamer.

She was packed from bow to stern. Not only were there farmers and drovers bound for the 'Tryst' from every point along the route, but several families who, like ourselves, had waited till now at their various moors, the weather previously having been fine, and sport plentiful; and these with their dependants filled the cabins and saloon. The saloon had to be turned into a sleeping-place. It was hot to suffocation. It was unbearable to our panting lungs – but everything suits somebody. A head bobbed out from under the table, on which our mattresses, or what did duty for such, were spread, and a voice exclaimed cheerfully, 'I'm very comfortable down here. There's no draught.'

No draught indeed! We recognised the broad burr of a Berwickshire man we knew – one who might have been expected to value fresh air; but the head of Mr Tom Horne withdrew, and soon a peaceful snoring proclaimed that asphyxiation, if nothing else, had completed his satisfaction with his cosy corner.

That night *The Royal Charter*[35] was wrecked off the same coast. The wind rose higher and higher, and how we fared can easily be imagined when we came to rounding the Mull of Cantire – or the 'Moil,' as it is called by its inhabitants.

For those who do not know Scotland, I may explain that a 'Mull' or 'Moil' signifies a long, narrow promontory, which usually does not strike out to sea, but runs parallel with the mainland; between the two, cross-tides and currents are rife. The Mull of Galloway is the only other important one on the Scottish coast, and rounding it is as trying to landsmen as the other. A heavy swell from the Atlantic is sure to send its long rollers inwards in either case; and when a gale is blowing, a terrific sea may be on.

The *Clansman* weathered it on the night I refer to, but she was twelve hours late when she drew up alongside the Broomielaw.

It was again a dark night, and a November fog made it darker still, and we had an hour to wait before our train for Edinburgh would start. Anything more unpromising than that hour looked, it would be difficult to describe – and yet even it had its compensations. We were huddled miserably together, waiting for cabs to be brought, in which to drive to the station, when the lights of an open house – a wretched place, a sort of sailors' eating-house – met our gaze; and seated within were some of our steamboat crew merrily at work. We prevailed on our long-suffering Fräulein to let us join them.

Not that we actually sat at the same board, but we partook of the same mutton-pies, hot and savoury; and the poor Fräulein, who, after all, was human and dying of hunger like ourselves, laughed for many a day after over the adventure, protesting that nothing had ever tasted so good as those salty, peppery mutton-pies, she having existed throughout the twenty-four previous hours upon a single peppermint drop!

After this, my mother refused to 'round the Moil' any more. She and my elder sisters crossed by ferry to the mainland, by way of the Isle of Kerrera – and drove thence to Ardrishaig, where they caught the daily boat for Glasgow.

This transit was simple enough, and it was decreed that though we of the rearguard should still take the useful *Clansman* to Oban, we should follow our leaders for the remainder of the journey. The *Clansman*, however, being late as usual, we had but little time to lose, as we had to be at Ardrishaig by noon. About four in the morning we started; and this time, there being no kind servants to look after us – for they went on in the steamer – we had no breakfast, and were in a state to eat anything when our goal was reached.

We had half-an-hour. Much may be done in half-an-hour.

We ensconced ourselves in a good hotel facing the pier, so as to make sure of not being left behind, and fell to work. An elderly man from a table near watched us with twinkling eyes. We heard afterwards that Lord Hill – the Lord Hill of his day – on hearing a certain enormous appetite remarked upon, exclaimed with a chuckle: 'Call that an appetite? *You never saw those young Colquhouns eat herring!*'

Edinburgh, 'attractive to us all, young and old' / The Kylin Archive

Edinburgh Society in the 'Fifties

Several years before this, we had moved to Edinburgh for the winter months. Portobello, as a place of residence, had become impossible, since the elder daughters of the house had now to be taken into society; and 11 Brighton Crescent had accordingly been sold on our going south after leaving Blackhall.

In what was then the furthest west part of the Scottish capital a new district had sprung up, and was looked upon with much favour. It has never, however, extended far, the tide of fashion having turned off at right angles, and Eton Terrace, where my father purchased a house in 1855, still remains pretty much as it was, though gardens have replaced what was then a somewhat bare grass slope, down to the 'Water of Leith.'

In some ways we children liked the change, but there was one drawback – the Dean Bridge.

The Dean Bridge, to some of us, was a nightmare. From its height it was – and we heard whispers of this in the household – a favourite resort of suicides; while we also had our secret terror of either being blown over ourselves, or seeing such a fate befall another, on every windy day.

This may sound absurd; but be it observed the reign of 'King Crinoline' had begun and with every gust that swept down the deep-cut valley below the bridge, the hoops flew about, and could with difficulty be prevented flying over the fair owners' heads.

What a thraldom that crinoline was! Not a kitchen-maid cleaning the doorsteps, not a beggar in the street, but must have *something*, whatever it was, which bulged and swung, and was a source of supreme discomfort, but without which she would not have felt it decent to be abroad. Going to bathe within our grounds at Mull, with merely a *sortie-de-bain* over our bathing gowns, we nevertheless could not venture forth without the inevitable appendage. Once, being only twelve, I tried it, but felt so miserable and ashamed, that I had to run back to the house, and return inflated and happy.

My best frock stood out straight like a Japanese parasol. I used to wonder what the Fairchild family[35] would have thought of it, when of poor Emily, dressed for the archery meeting by the ultra-fashionable Louisa, we learn that 'her skirt was short, fully displaying her ankles,' and the reader is expected to be as shocked as were her parents at such an apparition.

The strange thing was that, so far as my recollection serves me, neither old nor young resented the incubus which had been thrust upon us. We were wedged together in carriages, with hoops billowing up to the roof; we scuttled crab-like through turnstiles; we were unable to pass in gangways; we endured every imaginable form of inconvenience, and heard ourselves derided for it by fathers, husbands, and brothers, and we boldly faced them, vowing that come what might, we would never, never give up our crinoline!

How we jeered at an old beau, a great admirer of our sex, who protested that all beauty of outline was now gone from a woman's figure. We thought him the silliest old fool imaginable. We devoutly trusted that *we* at least should never see 'beauty of outline' thus exposed again – indeed I am sure that we fully believed it never would be so – and when it is remembered that for *twelve years* the infatuation lasted, it will be seen that there was something to be said for conviction.

I have already alluded to the fruitless efforts of my grandmother, Mrs Fuller-Maitland, to oust the parasite from Park Place. Domestic autocrats of the old school who made similar attempts elsewhere were, I have heard, foiled in like manner; while among gentlefolks who chose to make a stand on their own account, I can only recall two middle-aged sisters who had the hardihood to adhere to it.

These were the Misses Macdonnell of Glengarry, sisters of the last great chief of the name.[37] They were not going to do what they did not choose for anybody. They disliked and despised the universal monstrosity; and encumber themselves with it? Not they!

As they had fine, tall figures, and carried themselves very erect, their appearance thereby might not have suffered – indeed they might have been looked upon as the only sane women among a crowd of lunatics, had their clothes been suitably cut and shaped; but as they only went for these to a village seamstress, and as she was unaccustomed to making any sort of skirt to be worn minus crinoline, the effect was unfortunate.

The wide folds fell in about their heels; they had sone grand old tartan silks which were pleated like the philabeg of a kilt; and entirely unaware of anything ludicrous or incongruous, they placidly wore them so that one in particular – the elder and taller of the two – had the effect of a fish walking on its tail.

And she danced, moreover, and danced beautifully – and a more coveted partner at certain houses was not in the room.

True, the round dances which now reign supreme were then in their infancy, and were very long in being acclimatised among the sober-minded. My sisters and I had to sit out whenever a waltz was next on the programme; but as we always had a partner to sit with, and as we were borne up by a sense of virtue – or by a faculty for making the best of things – I expect we did not mind it very much.

Besides we knew we were only dancing at all by sufferance. My mother had inherited the old Puritan repugnance to this form of merrymaking, and had she had her way, never a ball, or even a 'hop,' as the phrase was, would any of her daughters have seen. But, luckily for us, my father, who had a great respect for tradition, scouted the idea. 'The ladies of our family have *always* danced,' quoth he; and put down his foot. When he put down his foot, which was not once in a blue moon, the foot remained down. We had no more to fear.

We went therefore to children's parties as other children did; and were beautifully attired, and had the hairdresser come in the afternoon to curl our hair. Little boys, as well as little girls, had their hair curled on occasion in those days, and I must own were greatly improved thereby. Many a plain little fellow would blossom out into quite a 'mother's darling' under the magic tongs; and, beyond a doubt, it was not only *little* boys who took advantage of this whim on the part of Dame Fashion – certainly those who happened to have straight hair seemed to be few and far between. Hair was divided down the back above the nape of the neck, and brushed well out on each side. When I see an old Crimean veteran with his grey locks thus arranged, I think of how that venerable mode once became him, and am glad he clings to it still.

But if my parents were divided on the subject of dancing, they were at one as to operas and theatres. Scotch people, if they made any pretensions to piety, were dead against the stage fifty years ago.

One is at a loss to understand why this should have been so, seeing that they take first rank among the playgoers of to-day; but I suppose the very hold that music and acting have upon the Celtic mind now that it is open to receive it, was anticipated and dreaded by our forefathers. I recall that on one occasion when a season of opera was being given in Edinburgh, and my parents were speaking with some severity of a desire on the part of some of us to hear for once *Semiramide* or *La Sonnambula*, that the same learned divine who had voted *The Bride of Lammermoor* first among Scott's novels, instead of joining in their animadversions, murmured gently, 'They tell me that Salvini is worth hearing,' and looked – yes, he did – as if he would fain have heard for himself.

Cards were also forbidden us. My mother had never touched one in her life; my father had, and was very silent on the subject. Probably when in the army he had done as other young men did, and gambling stakes were high then as now.

One evening some of us younger ones had been out at a small party – not a large one, when dancing would have been *de rigueur* – and we had enjoyed hugely a game for which prizes were provided in the shape of satin boxes of bonbons. We showed our prizes and described the game – oh, it was such fun! – there were kings, and queens, and knaves, and aces; and you sat at a round table, and the grown-ups took us in charge and watched our 'hands,' and showed us what to do. 'Why, they've been playing cards!' exclaimed my father.

We were struck dumb. Did he then know this wonderful game? At that time we had never heard of it; but as he only looked amused, not angry, we pressed for an explanation. It was given kindly and wisely – and then we learnt the meaning of his whimsical air: 'To think of the good T's playing cards,' he said aside to my mother. 'Well, well, different people have different ideas'; and with this placid summary of the situation, it was dismissed.

It was not till 'Bezique' came in many years afterwards that a revolution took place in the minds of austere people, who then began to discover that 'The Devil's Book' might be a very innocent book in innocent hands; and 'Patience,' which succeeded 'Bezique,' finally and for ever broke down the wall of prejudice.

Despite these restrictions and prohibitions, there was enough of gaiety and variety in Edinburgh life to make it very attractive to us all, old and young. There was a vast amount of entertaining; I remember thinking that our elders were never a night at home during the season, which lasted from the beginning of February to April. How the Church of England people managed during Lent, when most of the private balls and all the public ones took place, I leave it to others to say: we Presbyterians, having no such period in our calendars, had no scruples to contend with. In the daytime there were concerts, flower-shows, bazaars, and 'The Exhibition.' 'The Exhibition' meant the Scottish Academy of Pictures, which was the regular accredited lounge every afternoon between four and six o'clock. Every regimental dandy from the Castle, or Piershill, or Leith Fort, every gay sailor from the man-of-war in the Forth, had his season ticket, and when tired of patrolling Princes Street, turned in to the 'Exhibition,' there to meet his dancing-partners of the past, and secure their promises for the future.

There were also good race-meetings within hail, of which, in our home, we only heard the echoes. Never being taken to one, however, we got along without; and I must add that whenever there were any amusements afoot of which my parents did approve, they neither grudged trouble nor expense in letting such of us as were of an age to do so take part in them. Thus, even when quite young, we heard Jenny Lind sing and Thalberg play, and attended many interesting and impressive functions – of which I recollect two in particular, because when Gladstone[38] and Carlyle were severally installed Rectors of the University, I, though only a schoolgirl, was one of the privileged few who, having no claim to being present, was so, and in a good seat, too. My mother vacated for me her own for the former ceremony, and I must relate how I was in luck's way for the latter.

It was a wet and stormy afternoon, and I was sitting by the drawing-room fire – for some reason or other permitted to be there – when in walked a figure familiar to every denizen of Auld Reekie. The snow-white locks and eagle eyes of Professor Blackie were before me.[39]

Wrapped in his shepherd's plaid and supported by his stout stick, he had braved the weather for the purpose of bringing a coveted ticket for the installation, then the theme of every tongue. My mother, I told him, was unwell, and would be unable to profit by his kindness. He inquired about my sisters? There were only two at home, and they were already provided for.

He grunted dubiously; I eyed him hungrily. He said something; I answered – I forget what. Then all at once I found the ticket in my hand!

Perhaps I had shown, however innocently, something of the breathless hope which had sprung up within; perhaps the good professor thought that a young girl who could so hope and care was as worthy of the honour as an indifferent or callous dowager; or perhaps he was merely disciplined to tramp further afield when here was a recipient ready to his hand. At any rate, my rejoicing ears caught a gruff but kindly, 'Well, well, child, have it for yourself then' – and never did heart leap higher.

There were but twenty ladies to be admitted to the Music Hall on the occasion.[40] Twenty – and all the women of Edinburgh desirous of going! – some, no doubt, from real and intelligent interest in the proceedings, others because it was the event of the moment. Edinburgh being a very small place, there could never be more than one event paramount at a time, and Carlyle was at the height of his fame.

Well, we were early there, we three; and whether disdainful glances were bestowed on such a poor little brat as myself or not, I did not care; my whole soul was on the platform. But though I can still see the rugged face beneath its shock of grizzled hair, all I can remember now of an address of which at the time I lost not a word, is a single sentence. The speaker was surrounded by the first men in Scotland, and the judges in their robes formed an imposing portion of his platform audience. In his absent-minded manner, and homely accent of the broadest Scotch, Carlyle observed tranquilly, 'In my young days, we thought a great deal aboot the law' (pronouncing it *la*); 'but,' with a gentle sigh, 'nobody thinks anything aboot the *la* noo,' – where a great laugh responded from the hall below, and was heartily joined in by all the administrators of the *la* present.

Carlyle, rector of the University / The Kylin Archive

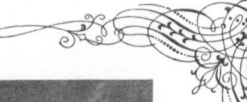

Professor Blackie, who founded a Celtic Chair at Edinburgh University / The Scottish National Portrait Gallery

About this time Dr Caird[41] as a preacher and orator was also at his zenith. The power of his eloquence was such that crowds would assemble outside the churches wherever he was to preach – willing to wait any length of time for the doors to open; and when one sees the queues of to-day at pit entrances of theatres, with their indomitable patience and sturdy resolution, one may take it that these same human beings would have exhibited like qualities outside a church door (at any rate in Scotland) fifty years ago.

On one occasion when Caird preached at St Cuthbert's, Edinburgh, the galleries sank three inches, while many stood throughout the service on the backs of pews, holding on by the lamp-posts. We had been at the morning service – this being in the afternoon; and rather than lose our seats, we sat on, and ate buns by stealth, having brought them in our pockets. We younger ones were offered the chance of going home, but scorned the idea.

The crowds increased, and the police had to be called in to force a passage for the preacher himself. We could just see his small, black head moving slowly, very slowly, up the aisle – and then what a sermon!

It was on St Paul's announcement to the Athenians, 'Whom therefore ye ignorantly worship, Him declare I unto you'; and never perhaps has an audience listened to anything finer than the rush of thought gathered up into the noblest language, when a 'point' was approached in any of this preacher's great oratorical outbursts.

And the fame of them spread to strange places. A railway porter, wheeling his truckload, was overheard, nudging one of his fellows with, 'D'ye see yon wee man?'

'Ay,' responded the other, staring, 'Ay; A see him. Whae's he?'

'Caird; yon's Caird. Man, *he's a gran' wee deevil at the preachin'!*'

We did not know Caird personally; but his still more widely known contemporary, Norman Macleod,[42] was often at our house, a welcome and honoured guest.

One trait I recall of him; brimful of humour, he could control it, of which the following is an instance.

It was then a custom in Scotland to ask a minister, if one were present, to say grace at dinner. One day my father, in his slow, emphatic, and most solemn tones, began his usual formula, not noticing the presence of his reverend guest – then was suddenly enlightened; and it is impossible to give an idea in writing of the ludicrousness of the scene. Try to imagine it. 'For what we are about to receive – *Oh, Dr Macleod, I beg your pardon*!'

Amidst the stares and tittering of a tableful of giddy youngsters, Dr Macleod calmly lifted up his hand and 'asked a blessing.'

When he had finished he observed in a quiet aside, 'That was rather trying' – and changed the subject. We all felt impressed, and, I am sure, regarded the speaker with an increase of esteem ever after.

Our relations the Sinclairs, were naturally much to the front in our Edinburgh life. I have already mentioned their excellence as entertainers and organisers, and now that we had come to reside close by, as it were, we reaped a liberal benefit. Miss Catherine Sinclair, in particular, was never tired of making up parties for this thing and that, and we grew to recognise that the Sinclair carriage at the door meant something good, and probably some impromptu good. My parents, deaf to many another call of the world, could not refuse relations – and thus many a time even we young ones were sent flying to make ready to accompany our kind aunt, who had bethought herself of some gay scheme on the spur of the moment. You may be sure we went in double-quick time.

Aunt Catherine's 'Ulbster Hall Lectures' were also arranged about this time. They were by invitation, and were very smart affairs. No one would have thought of giving a party on the same evening, if they were in the set likely to be asked, and – strange as it may seem – young men and girls were as pleased as their elders to be present.

There were all sorts and conditions of lectures, and when it is remembered what an intellectual centre Edinburgh was once, it will be readily understood that it was easy for a personage like my aunt to pick and choose, and provide the best of fare for her guests.

Though the Ulbster Hall – which she secured and named after her family designation – was small for a lecture-room, it was large for an evening party, and the lectures were brief, and the party stayed on, and there was supper in an adjoining room (I also remember that trays of 'negus' and 'hot jelly' went round beforehand), so that altogether it was very pleasant; and when it came to my father's turn to give an account of Highland sport, and all his family had to be present, we young ones were in the seventh heaven. On that solitary evening did it fall to my lot to attend an Ulbster Hall lecture, for they only lasted a couple of winters (I think), and I was, of course, too young for anything of the kind, unless there were a special reason for making an exception to the rule.

Edinburgh society was not provincial in the 'fifties. There were family mansions, belonging to the best blood in Scotland, regularly opened for the season; while the surrounding country was so thickly peopled that at all the leading social gatherings there was an appreciable infusion of country-house parties.

These outside neighbours entertained in their turn, and kept the ball going; and as my mother occasionally permitted us younger ones to accompany her to make calls of ceremony where they were due, we grew to know and love such places as Hopetoun, Dalmeny, and Dreghorn, among many others. Nowhere are there more delightful and resposeful homes than those in the Lothians, with their large,

Rev Dr Norman MacLeod, who later married Lucy's sister, Helen Augusta / The Kylin Archive

well-cultivated gardens, shady avenues, and views of rich, fertile landscapes on every side.

Next door to ourselves in Eton Terrace was a family from the north, and, as we had made their acquaintance there, we saw a good deal of the young ones, who were our contemporaries. There was one little boy who did not care much for games and pastimes, but whose pencil or paintbrush was rarely out of his hand.

We used to get him to take portraits of our pets, and were such ardent admirers of his prowess that one day he produced and presented to me – (or rather, to be strictly truthful, bargained it for a plate of toffee) – a picture of a kestrel hawk sitting on a bough, with which I flew to my father. He, after examining it carefully, and with corresponding appreciation, wound up his remarks with, 'The thing is – it's *so true to Nature – so exactly true to Nature*,' and permitted the little picture to hang in his own collection of bird and beast portraiture. When I see a crowd assembled before the later production of that distinguished ARA, Mr Joseph Farquharson,[43] I fancy I hear a voice from the past again exclaiming, 'So true to Nature!' The lonely heron rising from the sea would surely have drawn forth his old friend's note of praise.

One more reminiscence of Edinburgh in bygone days. Two caustic Lords of Session – both of whom were well known to us – had had an argument and separated in heat, neither being able to prove his point.

The question, however, speedily solved itself, and Lords D and Y spied each other across the street soon after. The former halted, perhaps a shade more readily than the latter, and, shaking his stick in triumph, bellowed at the pitch of his voice, 'Aha, Lord Y, ye see I was right. Lord Y, I say, ye see I was right.'

'Humph,' growled Lord Y, unable to deny it, then hurried on, firing this Parthian shot over his shoulder – 'Well, Lord D, ye may be *sometimes* right, but ye're *always* disagreeable.'

The retort – well deserved – soon passed into a household word among us; and I have often thought that if those people who pride themselves on being 'right,' at whatever cost to their opponents, could understand how the man who thus feels is '*always*' disagreeable, perhaps he would be less loth to proclaim every petty advantage.

Highlands of Scotland, 'visions of ruddy grouse and purple heather / The Kylin Archive

A Youthful Author

The Highlands of Scotland are indissolubly connected in the minds of most present-day people with visions of ruddy grouse and purple heather; tramps over glorious stretches of moorland; sails over mimic seas; full, jocund country-houses (and still fuller, and more jocund bachelors' boxes); brimming steamboats; competing railway porters; every sort of convenience and luxury for those who can afford to pay, and the longest of long hotel bills for all, whether they can afford it or not.

Such is, perhaps, a faithful portrait of the Scottish Highlands in August and September – their season; and in their season only are they visited, as a rule, by the world at large.

But here and there, in the merry springtime, there is a salmon river to be fished, or moor to be inspected, or a run for health to be made, and a northern raid becomes imperative.

Then how happy is the man who wakes up some sunny morning by the banks of Loch Awe or Loch Maree, to find the whole warm air sweet with the scent of larches from which ring the loud 'Cuckoos,' and to behold on every side the budding and breaking forth of beauties which are usually only seen in their maturity!

In August who reckons on the myriads of sparkling flowerets which adorn the grim old Sound of Mull in May? Who that knocks over the lordly blackcock in September thinks of the fine young fellow strutting forth in his pride, with his following of loving spouses behind him, on a dewy April morn? Who that finds music in the 'Whir-r-r' of the rising wing on a cloudless 'Twelfth,' calls to mind the joyous note of the parent bird, the 'Cock-cock-cocking' by wayside and moorland path, when the nest was full, and the hatching in progress a few months before?

Only those few and far-between adventurous spirits who, as we have said for purposes of their own, resisting the blandishments of pleasure, the toils of ambition, or the tether of custom, have left the madding crowd behind and soared into this aerial world of innocence and delight, can know or picture what is to be found there.

To the delicious, drowsy re-awakening of the mountain solitudes after their wintry slumbers, there are, however, a few drawbacks, for which it would be well for the uninitiated to be prepared. Let me give an instance.

My father, when seeking for a new Highland home, which he did on an average every three years, was in the habit of starting off with an agent's list in his pocket, soon after the days began to lengthen and genial weather to set in.

He drove himself in a light mail phaeton which accommodated three, and once when it fell to my lot to be one, we spent the night preceding Mayday at the little inn above the Pass of Glencoe.

The winter had been severe and prolonged; the frowning heights around were still swathed in snow, from which black and rugged peaks jutted forth at intervals, and travellers so early in the year had not been looked for in that lonely spot. When we drove up – and it had been a long drive by way of Crianlarich, Tyndrum, and the Black Mount – a long, rough drive – and we were spent and weary, we were

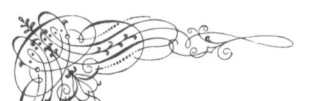

Glencoe, with 'frowning heights and black and rugged peaks' / The Kylin Archive

not welcomed in the usual hospitable fashion. Host and hostess looked blank and bewildered, and it soon appeared why. Their rooms were still shut up; the beds had not been slept in since the previous October; and there was nothing to eat – nothing at least that 'gentry folk' could eat – in the house!

This was frankly owned, but still the case was desperate. Night was drawing on apace, our horse was dead tired, and there was no other human dwelling within range. We laughed aside the scared looks of our perfunctory entertainers, who did their best to recover themselves in consequence, and entered the house.

Owing to improvidence or ill-luck, no food had been tasted by any of the party since an early breakfast; wherefore it may be imagined how appetising would have been the odour of frizzling trout, or savoury ham and eggs, or, in short, almost anything that might have seemed within the range of the solitary inn.

Almost anything? Certainly anything in the shape of buffalo steak, or rhinoceros hump. We sat round the crackling fire in the little peat-reeking parlour, and cheerfully awaited our supper. Whatever it might consist of, we were, or thought we were, prepared for it.

But *braxy mutton*? Has the reader ever tasted, has he ever smelt, braxy mutton? Mutton so called is the body of a sheep which has either died, or had to be killed, when suffering from a complaint which, though hard upon the sheep, is innocuous to the eater. The sheep, having reached an advanced state of *embonpoint*, surrenders to fate, and this mutton is largely consumed, and not at all objected to, by the denizens of the Scottish wilds.

But oh, that first whiff from the kitchen! That puff from the passage! Our sickened stomachs could stand no more; and as the horrible dish was borne in, with one accord we demanded that it should be borne out again.

We tried the eggs. Another anguish of disappointment.

Then the scones. They were damp, flabby, and tough beyond power of thought to conceive: teeth could not rend them.

Lastly, the oatcakes (bread there was none); and the oatcakes, hard as flint, dry, tasteless, and white as a dusty road in a March east wind, proved the only accompaniment to the hot whisky-toddy which helped us to endure starvation.[44]

Perhaps it also saved us from rheumatic fever; for no sooner had we taken off our upper garments in the mouldy confines of an upper chamber than a voice was at the door. 'Out of bed with you, quick! – Oh, you're not in? Well, don't get in! – What? Oh, you *must*! – Lie down anywhere. Hoots! You *must*. Your mother told me to keep an eye on you, and the whole place is dripping. Here – here's some more whisky; it's all I can do for you. Nonsense! never mind if it does'; (the protest may be inferred), 'and mind, wrap yourselves in your plaids, and lie on the floor.'

He was not to be trifled with. Sadly we had to obey, but I am bound to add, soundly we slept; and early, early we were off, fleeing the baleful spot, and devoutly trusting never to return.

But what a Mayday was that which broke as we traversed dark Glencoe, now ablaze in sunshine, with melting, shining sheets of rock reflecting every spreading ray, with the eagle circling round the topmost peak, and the roar of hidden waterfalls on every side!

What a thundering from point to point and crag to crag! What a liberal outpouring of rejoicing birds! What merriment among the lambkins! 'Begone, dull care! Hence, loathed melancholy!' Away with every thought of every evil past, and every lurking fear of ills to come! That smiling scene, wet with its thousand tears, that emergence into warmth and sunlight from the dark tunnel of its wintry tomb, was one to drive from the most insensate breast every lingering regret or apprehension. Even now – now when so many years have rolled between – the whole is as fresh before the writer's eyes as though beheld yesterday; and the beauty, the glory, the majesty of that May morning on the wild mountainsides of Glencoe remain a memory which Time has never effaced nor other scenes eclipsed.

We were not, however, destined to pitch our tent so far north that year. After prospecting in various directions, my father decided upon Garth House, in Perthshire – a country he already knew something of, having rented Kinnaird in the earlier years of his married life, before I, his seventh child, was born. (He had also tenanted Leny, near Callander; Sonachan, on Loch Awe; and other places – of which, for the same reason, I can say nothing).

Garth is a substantial, modern residence, which belonged at that time to Colonel Macdonald of St Martin's, a friend of my parents, who visited us there and elsewhere. It is beautifully situated on the river Lyon, and in addition to the fishing belonging to it, my father acquired that of Meggernie, fourteen miles up the glen.

To reach this we had to past Chesthill, where dwelt two brothers, bachelors, and often saw them together down by the riverside.

One only, however, wielded a rod; and on this being commented upon by a stranger one day, with the inquiry, 'Does not the other Mr Menzies care for fishing also?' – my father made something of an Irish bull in reply: 'Oh, poor fellow, he can't fish; he's blind; he only comes down *to look on*.'

The Lyon not being so rapid a stream as the Dee, we were not cut off from communication from the opposite banks as at Blackhall, a ferry-boat plying to and fro just beneath our windows; and we were thus enabled to climb over the heathery shoulder of Drummond Hill, and drop on to Kenmore, Lord Breadalbane's model village, at the southern end of Loch Tay, while my mother could also drive there by a very slightly longer route.

Aberfeldy was, however, our nearest 'town,' though seven miles off – and even to reach Aberfeldy from the south we had to take the road from Dunkeld, some distance. Long ago a branch line of rail has connected these two last places, but it was not even thought of when we went to Garth.

A trifling incident in connection with this sticks to my memory. The bulk of our party having been despatched from Dunkeld, the rest were awaiting a carriage which had been ordered to come round to the inn-door, when a commotion was heard below – we being in the little parlour above.

We had peered out at the sound of wheels; and now we saw an elderly gentleman, whom the same wheels had attracted, spring up the steps and resolutely seat himself within the carriage.

The host, as well as the stable ostlers, were humbly endeavouring to expostulate; but Sir Robert Menzies was a tough customer to deal with. He alleged that the carriage was his, had been ordered by him, and would not hear of any prior claims to it.

He had red hair and the proverbial temper that goes with it; while my father, good-humoured and easy-going in general, was not without a dash of 'chestnut horse' in him when roused.

He and Sir Robert had been friends in youth, had pulled as oarsmen in the same boat, when challenging other crews, as was then the fashion; but they had drifted apart, and one was probably as disinclined as the other to meet again – under the circumstances.

Two shy, proud, angry men, neither of whom would abate an inch of his dignity – what was the unfortunate landlord to do?

He flew between the two, upstairs and down, pleading and representing, then stood still and scratched his head.

Sir Robert sat in the carriage and called to his womenkind to get in. My father hid in the parlour and forbade his to budge.

He felt secure in having the stronger case, for though we were in the Menzies country, and it was a daring act on the part of the humble innkeeper to thwart the fiery laird who snorted at him from his vantage-ground, on the other hand, the poor wretch had a son, and that son had just entered on a lease of one of the great hotels on Loch Lomond. To flout a brother of Sir James Colquhoun might have spelt ruin to his offspring.

Rendered desperate, he approached the carriage for the last time, and whatever it was he said, it had the desired effect. The irascible baronet bounced out as he had bounded in, and disappeared, when, but not till the coast was clear, we descended, and drove off.

I may add that as Castle Menzies was within easy range of Garth, it was impossible for the inmates of both houses not to behave afterwards as neighbours, and this proper state of things was brought about somehow; but a dead silence was always maintained as to the tussle at the inn-door!

It may have been on the above occasion, or upon another (for we had constantly to pass along the same road), that a fisherman, up to his waist in mid-stream, was pointed out by our driver, who, probably a poacher himself, obviously appreciated the delicate precision with which the casts were thrown.

'Thon's a penter-lad,' explained he, sitting round to see the better. 'He lodges hereaboots. And when he' no pentin' he's fishing,' and when he's no fishin' he's pentin'.'

'He can fish,' observed my father, also eying the swirl of the line; but he did not know then, nor till long afterwards, how well it was for the world that when the 'penter-lad' was 'no fishin' he was pentin',' – for the name of the lad was John Millais.[45]

※

After our prolonged sojourn in the isolated Hebrides, it was no doubt a pleasant change to the feminine elders of the family to find themselves once more in a good country-house like Garth; though we younger ones always loved Glenforsa best, and often on a sunny morning sighed for our early ride to the post-box and the sight of wild Loch Nagaul, with its bold headlands melting away into the blue beyond.

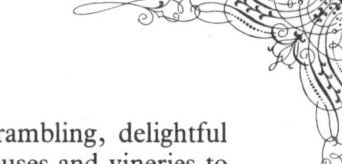

We appreciated the garden at Garth, however – a large, rambling, delightful garden, stocked to the brim, and with a fine range of greenhouses and vineries to boot.

Gooseberries? Can anyone who is not conversant with the Scottish garden, either past or present, know what a real gooseberry is? Those we meet with in the south are not worthy of the name; no wonder they are disdained as coarse and tasteless, only fit for pies in May.

But the gooseberry that is pruned and trimmed and respectfully netted like peaches and apricots – the gooseberry that abounds beneath the shelter of the south wall (though it may be outside the wall), prolific to a degree undreamed of by the Sassenach, with Honeyglobes, Ironmongers, or, best of all, the small round, green, hairy berry, through whose thin skin the seeds show – those are the true products of the soil, and the daintiest epicure can hardly despise them.

They are sweetest on the lowest branch. Perhaps the gardeners' cottages are near, and hens scuffle in the warm earth beneath? Never mind that. Pick and eat the dusty fellows – you will find them worth it.

Even a dog may teach you something in that respect – at least our dog Dash could. Dash was a black retriever, highly sagacious. Either he had been taught in his puppy days to eat fruit, or had found out what was what for himself – anyhow, he would lie panting among the heavy-laden gooseberry bushes on a sweltering August day, then, as the fancy took him, turn up his head, cock his eye, and snap!

He liked to snap in comfort. He never altered his position, nor did he, so far as we know, pay any heed to gooseberries except when in repose – although we often took him for a walk round to see what he would do; but it was an attested fact that, when lying down at leisure, he was sure to indulge his appetite sooner or later, and after what happened one day to one of his youthful masters, my father was sometimes nervous about Dash. Had Dash eaten a gooseberry with a wasp in it, the consequences might have been serious.

But let me narrate the accident to which I refer. It happened to a younger brother, and in an agony of pain and fright he rushed to Aiky, his quondam nurse who was now housekeeper, and mercifully in her store-room at the moment. The tongue had already begun to swell: the wasp – who could tell? – might have left its sting in it – in any case the danger of suffocation was great.

Without loss of an instant, Aiky applied carbonate of soda, and continued applying it. And we all remembered afterwards what the remedy was, for the doctor, who was far up in the glen was summoned, and did not arrive till the peril was past, emphatically stated that the little boy's life was saved thereby, not failing, however, to add that had the sting been half an inch lower down the throat, even carbonate of soda would have availed nothing.

After that we were, of course, very timid about wasps – for a time – and even gave bees a wide berth, though a keeper, M'Craw, cultivated them and could do anything with them.

'Julius Caesar M'Craw,' my father dubbed this man. He held in whimsical derision the practice of tacking on grandiloquent Christian names to common ugly-sounding surnames, and could not resist making these up when opportunity offered, so that we had a perfect collection of them, though I think 'Julius Caesar M'Craw' was the oddest.

'Julius Caesar' had a very sweet tooth. He dearly liked the damaged dates and raisins with which it was his duty to provide the young pheasants, and was invariably munching when we came across him, while his pockets bulged significantly. However, as the pheasants throve, there seemed to be enough for all.

I have said that we often crossed in the ferry-boat to the other side of the river Lyon, and climbed the purple hillside opposite. There it was that an incident– not an accident this time – befell myself. I was running, and fell over a whin-bush, when something, some awful thing, like a volcano, broke loose beneath my nose, and with a mighty rushing sound soared aloft.

The very atmosphere quivered, and the earth shook – or so it seemed. Paralysed, I lay still, while the giant capercailzie – the only one I ever saw at close quarters – vanished among the pine trees. Capercailzies were not common even in those days; I fancy they are almost extinct in Scotland now.

But there were red-deer in abundance on that hillside, and at a certain season of the year we were forbidden to go there. We could hear their 'belling' to each other, and at nights this weird note would sometimes sound quite near, as there was a drinking-place beneath our windows, whereupon, if we were in bed, we rose and looked out. I do not, however, remember ever seeing a monarch of the glen, so probably they waited till hidden by darkness.

Here let me record what I once did see – a sight never to be forgotten – namely, a battle-royal between two noble stags when choosing their hinds for the season.

I had wandered to a lonely part of the deer-park at Cobham Hall, Kent, and was absorbed in a book – must have been absorbed for some time – when suddenly I became conscious of a loud rattling, clattering, and scuffling close at hand. Cautiously peeping round the tree, whose giant stem hid me from their view, I found that a whole herd of fallow-deer had gathered together, and were watching with silent interest a fight between two champions. The fight lasted some minutes – not very long, I daresay; but the antlered heads were again and again locked and loosened before one grand fellow, the larger of the two, after a final and protracted struggle, freed himself, shook his head, and slowly turned round.

He did not, however, quit the field; *that* he left to his victorious opponent; and a pretty sight it was to see the air with which the latter, after a moment's pause as though to make sure of his triumph, selected his fair ones by some telepathic communication known to themselves, and led them away.

In an instant another combat was begun. The vanquished stag was challenged afresh; and so on, till every female member of the herd was allotted her mate, when, as silently as they came, they dispersed, and the tall bracken swallowed them up.

The giant Capercailzie / The Kylin Archive

87

But if we had no encounters with deer at Garth, we had something to endure from venison. With venison we were always abundantly supplied, as, when we had no deer-forest of our own, it was sent in from Rossdhu and other places; and why I remember it at Garth, was because we had there a cook who had her own notions on the subject. She could not and would not roast a haunch before it was thoroughly 'high.' Aiky reported that she could do nothing with Mrs Cook, who, having lived in that capacity in a certain ducal household, was not to be set right on such a point. 'Me not know when venison is fit for the table!' Aiky reported her as saying: 'Me that have sent it up *when the ladies was faintin' all round – and the duke said it it was butiful!*'

In the end, however, she had to go back to her duke, or to someone else who liked 'butiful' meat; for it was the same with all game, and our less exalted palates and nostrils could not stand it.

In especial my father vowed that she fairly chased him out of his den. His den was a small, sunny nook, right over the kitchen, in which he usually spent his mornings, engaged, when not arranging his specimens, in the delicate manufacture of salmon flies.

He never threw a fly that he had not himself tied; and it was a marvel that hands so broad and strong, so fitted to wield the rod and gun, should be able to perform as they did such miracles of intricate, finikin workmanship.

He also fished entirely with a single gut, and strengthened this by strapping it with india-rubber. Perhaps all salmon fishers do the like, but I mention it as possibly typical of a time when methods were more primitive than now.

I wonder if any man nowadays cleans his own gun? I have seen my father in his shirt-sleeves, working like any hodman over a pail of water, and sending for pail after pail too, when the ramrods were fizzing up and down the well-worn barrels. But sport fifty years ago included other matters than the mere filling of the bag.

As for the luncheon! 'Bags that go out full come back empty,' cried the sportsman of the past; and though ponies went up to the moor at mid-day to bring home the morning's luck, the most they ever carried of food and drink was a packet of sandwiches and some bottles of spruce beer. The spruce beer was home-brewed, and had to be made often – we were all so fond of it; but, like the rest, it has fallen out of favour now, I fancy.

Garth House was a memorable Highland home to me individually, because it was there that I wrote my first original work of fiction.

It has been said of me that I began to scribble in the earliest days of childhood. This is not true; I had not even the desire to do so, being far too fond of an outdoor life directly lesson-hours were over. But we had a longer summer holiday than usual at Garth, owing to a change of dynasty in the schoolroom; and perhaps that release from maps and grammars, and perhaps also a growing passion for reading, kindled a new flame.

There was a large sunny room at the far end of the passage which was rarely used, as spare rooms more conveniently situated were plentiful, and we never had many visitors at a time. My pair sister and I dried rose-leaves there, spreading them on newspapers with which we bestrewed the floor; and, seeking a quiet retreat for an enterprise which must be hidden from every eye, I carried thither an exercise-book and pencil.

With these in my lap I squatted beside the rose-leaves – having first spread open a large screen in front of the door. Anyone entering – and there was always an off-chance of someone entering – would only find a little girl busy with her *pot pourri*, and would never think of looking beneath the newspaper.

At night also the book lay safe in its secret resting-place, and silent as the grave was the author about its existence. Even now I doubt if some members of my family will not be surprised to learn that a novel (save the mark!) yclept *Macgregor; or, Our Chieftain*, came into being in the blue room at Garth, in the year 1858; and I am quite sure that no one ever saw it or heard of it then.

As may be guessed, it was a barefaced imitation of the author who was then my divinity – thus much I remember; also that after a couple more exercise-books had been filled with high-flown *Scottese* of the most blatent type, 'Macgregor' – a roaring, ruthless, lawless brigand of the approved order – abruptly perished, and all record of him was destroyed. I think, I hope, I recognised that there was no single merit in the audacious attempt.

Certainly it was not repeated for some years. When we went into Edinburgh, masters for various branches of knowledge, as well as for music, drawing, and other accomplishments, were now substituted for home tuition; and, eager to learn, I obtained permission to study Latin and algebra along with my younger brothers, who had as usual a tutor from the University. The strain of all this was enough, and it was not until in a measure freed from it when nearly eighteen that I tried again my 'prentice hand at composition. Of that, more later on.

Rossdhu, our father's early home / The Kylin Archive

The Colquhoun Country

We went next to Glenfalloch, near the head of Loch Lomond.

This change was liked by none of us except our youngest brother, a little fellow of ten, who had his own reasons for the preference. On being asked whether he liked Garth or Glenfalloch best, he promptly answered: 'Oh, Glenfalloch: I have a ferret there.'

How often have I thought of this since! How often do we hear in effect the same thing said! Some place vaunted, and its graces fondly dwelt upon, all because the speaker has 'a ferret there,' – and if the 'ferret' be some lovable human being, well and good; but if be only some point of luxury, some trifling ingredient fused into the main issue by a vague and undiscerning mind, it must raise a smile. Let me, however, return to the new home.

Such of us as had no 'ferrets' of any kind at Glenfalloch, which was merely a small stone house in a deep glen, whence were no outlets except at either end, found our chief consolation in its proximity to the Colquhoun territory, and in especial to Rossdhu, our father's early home.

Glenfalloch, with a view of Ben Lomond in the distance / The Kylin Archive

Two uncles and an aunt now lived there, and as they were most kind and indulgent relatives, there was constant to-ing and fro-ing between them and us – nothing being easier than the transit by boat between Luss and Ardlui, our several points of embarkation, on the small steamers which plied, and still ply, up and down the loch.

In these our faithful Aiky was constantly to be seen, and had her favourites among the various crews, whom she would address as 'Captain, dearie,' or 'Stewarty, dearie,' one little black-haired steward being her especial '.

'Mrs Aitken' being a personage to them, and dainties from her housekeeper's room very acceptable, she might call them what she chose – and no lady of the land was helped on and off the gangways more tenderly and deferentially; but when she carried her endearing epithets into strange places, we had occasionally to wince. Thus once it was, 'Hey, let me oot o' the train' (in which she was seated on a southern migration); 'I want to speak to the gaird,' and when the guard appeared – 'Eh, noo, Gairdy, dearie, are oo i' the richt train?' in coaxing accents that would have elicited an impudent rebuff from a man with no sense of humour. But happily that guard had, and he simply roared.

At the upper end of Loch Lomond steamers are able to penetrate a short way inland, as the river Falloch broadens into a sort of canal before losing itself in the waters of the lake; and the little saloon steamers thread their way up this as far as Inverarnan, where they come to an anchorage at a rustic pier beneath a huge, wide-spreading elm. When we saw the steam arising from this secluded spot (which we could do from the windows of Glenfalloch House), we knew the boat was there, and ten minutes' walk would take us to it.

Half-way was the boundary between Dumbartonshire and Argyllshire, with a turnpike-gate on the edge of either county. Thus there were two turnpikes within a hundred yards of each other – a queer state of things, which has since passed away.

There being no West Highland Railway at the period, coaches from the north were the only means of conveying tourists and other passengers from Dalmally and Tyndrum to Loch Lomond, Loch Katrine, and the far-famed Pass of the Trossachs; so that every afternoon these came in rapid succession, galloping, rocking, and swaying, down the glen.

There were dangerous corners to be turned; but of course the bulk of the coach-load did not know this, and were innocently happy as they spun past, though we, who soon grew familiar with every inch of the road, were well pleased when they disappeared among the trees on the plain below.

Once when my father was landing a large trout – large for the Falloch, – the driver of the coach pulled up to allow his load – and himself – to witness the spectacle. In their excitement some on the near side leaned over so far that a cry arose, 'Look out, there!' – and for a moment, a terrible moment, a catastrophe seemed imminent. They were right in the middle of a bridge, too – a bridge over a side stream; we wondered how our fisherman could calmly bring his trout ashore;

but he knew nothing, and mercifully nothing happened; we never, however, passed 'The Otter's Inn' afterwards without, I fancy, a vision of what might have been rising before our eyes.

'The Otter's Inn' was so called because a well-known old gentleman-otter, who was in the habit of passing his time between Loch Duchray and Loch Lomond, finding the journey too much for his powers to compass in one day, established a regular stopping-place within a crevice of the rocks about midway – and nothing would have induced my father to intrude upon his privacy. Even if he suspected the 'Inn' to be tenanted – and sometimes it was whispered that the old otter was lying low for a day or two – he would quietly fish the pool below, which was one of the best on the river, and pass on.

There being but few outdoor amusements to be had in this new moorland home, which was also bare of the *entourage* we were accustomed to, we started something fresh. We kept boats at Inverarnan, and we five sisters learned to row scientifically. Hitherto we had only handled an oar now and again as occasion offered, but now my father (himself an expert) regularly trained his feminine crew, one acting as cox. We named the largest boat the *Fanny*, after our mother.

And often we pulled down the loch as far as 'Rob Roy's Cave,' on the Inversnaid side, lit our fire, and boiled our kettle there, rowing home again after tea and a rest. It was a good long pull, but we took most of the day over it. And when presently we lost by her marriage one of our best oarswomen, who feathered her oar with as much 'skill and dexterity' as the young Thames waterman in the song, my father had himself to be cox. That, however, he grumbled at. It spoilt the appearance of the boat.

Of course we climbed Ben Lomond. Not as our Colquhoun great-aunts had done, to dance a reel on the top by moonlight – much as we longed to do this – but in more commonplace fashion. Every now and then a party would be formed for the ascent, which was not a difficult one, and guests from the South were sure to want to go. The late Lord Herschell[46] was one of these, and years afterwards when re-visiting us on Loch Lomond's banks as Lord Chancellor, he would fain have repeated the expedition – but climbers were not forthcoming.

I must tell a comical incident of this later visit. We had accompanied our departing guest down the loch, and made a halt at Rossdhu on the return journey. No one was in residence; but the old housekeeper showed us hospitality, and, in return, the young ones of the party informed her with much *empressement* that they had been allowed in strict privacy to hold the Great Seal in their hands the evening before. 'Did you so? Eh, dear!' responded the much mystified old woman. 'To think of that!' continued she, seeing more was expected, 'and was it – was it – *alive?*'

N.B. This piece of simplicity on the part of good Mrs Sim has, I know, been attributed to others; but there are plenty now living who heard her, and when one comes to think of it, the simplicity was not all on her side. It was foolish to suppose that one of her class, and a country woman to boot, should have any clear ideas about a State matter so far beyond her ken.

A grievance we had at Glenfalloch, which had not fallen to our lot before. My aunt, Miss Colquhoun, took it into her head that the clan tartan was becoming and appropriate clothing for her nieces, especially now that they were so much on their own ground, and proceeded to have webs of it woven at Stirling for our especial benefit.

Having presented a piece, she expected to see it worn, and worn on all occasions – and no one ever knew when she would appear at Glenfalloch. The material was beautifully fine and soft, and a Frenchwoman would have been charmed to see herself turned out so *chic*; but we were shy of being conspicuous, and, moreover, some of us were at the awkward age, when dressing is most difficult. We anathematised our aunt's taste, but we dared not wound her feelings.

Later on, when our kind uncle gave a ball for us, with *carte blanche* to order what we chose for it, including ball-dresses, we did indeed use our pretty tartan with extremely good effect; but bodices and 'peplums' of it in velvet, over white silk shirts, and scarfs of the silk bordered with the tartan, looped up over the left shoulder, might be, and were, much admired, while plain frocks entirely made of the plaid – however, we had to wear them, and I daresay they were not as ugly as we thought.

Dumbartonshire was not a lively county, but occasionally there were functions at which my uncle, as Lord Lieutenant, had to preside. For these the big coach was ordered out, and as Sir James, the shyest man in Scotland, liked to be supported by as many of his own people as possible, we crammed in, three on either side.

Not that it was much of a cram. It was an enormous vehicle, rather magnificent in its way, and it did not heave and swing. I do not think we minded it nearly as much as our grandmother's carriage at Park Place.

Even when very young we were not treated by our father's family as by our mother's. In the latter we were 'children' up to any age; and though, as I have said, very kindly regarded as such, our opinions carried no weight, and we were never asked for them.

Among the Colquhouns it was different. They liked us to talk, to tell them things, to report whom we had met and what we had heard. When our uncle took his tea-cup to his own table apart from the rest – tea was still brought in at Rossdhu about eight o'clock – one of us would fearlessly follow and proceed to entertain him, satisfied if he merely blinked his eyes and smiled in response – elated if his lips moved to emit some slow, shy question or comment. My father was devotedly

Rob Roy's Cave, 'a good long pull' / The Kylin Archive

attached to this particular brother, and we all inherited the feeling more or less.

Accordingly, when seated opposite him in the coach, we prattled of all the doings in the countryside: anxious to please, and tolerably secure of doing so, since there is no more greedy devourer of gossip than the man who is incapable of procuring it for himself. A woman is better off: her maid can cater for her; but comparatively few men chatter with their servants, and my good uncle would have starved in this respect had we not dutifully provided him with choice morsels.

On one occasion we were summoned from Glenfalloch to attend an open-air gathering at Balloch; new colours were to be presented to a volunteer regiment, and a luncheon provided by some Glasgow magnate. The then Duchess of Montrose[47] was to present the colours.

All went well: the sun shone as it *can* sometimes shine on Loch Lomond side, and we young people followed our elders into the luncheon tent, where my sisters were speedily provided with seats; but none was forthcoming for me, and I had to wander miserably round the table till a chair was inserted – I know not by whose orders – between the host and the great lady on his right hand.

Conscious of having no claim to be in company so old and grand, I was sitting dumb, wishing myself anywhere else, when there came a voice in my ear, speaking in the confiding whisper of one school-girl to another:

'Have *you* ever eaten off gold plate before?'

Of course I had not.

'Neither have I,' whispered the duchess, back. Then she made a face and laughed; whereupon I feebly tried to laugh also, and there after, much comforted, endured the situation philosophically.

And in after years, whenever I read of 'Joe Manton's' successes on the turf, I thought of that kind, merry face and reassuring laugh, and my grateful heart hoped that the colours of such a friend in need would always win.

Large dinner-parties were given at Rossdhu during the autumn months, and once when one of these was in prospect, we had an adventure which might have turned the day of feasting into a day of mourning.

My cousin, the late Sir James, then a young man at Cambridge, had some of his undergraduate friends staying at Rossdhu, whom he was anxious should see the beauties of the neighbourhood; and as their time was limited, and wet weather had prevailed before, when a doubtful morning cleared into a glorious summer day, no power on earth could stop his ordering out the launch.

Further, we must go to the head of the loch – though it was represented that we were starting too late for such an expedition, when it was necessary to be back in time for the dinner-party. The hour for dinner-parties was seven, and we girls protested we must be back by six at latest.

As, however, we were all athirst to go, we were quite sure this could be done. Opposition only made us surer, and we persuaded – or bullied – my good-natured father into accompanying us.

Away we went in the so-called launch, about which a word. It was a curious affair, designed by a kinsman, George Boyle, and sold by him to our too confiding uncle, who thought it ingenious and suitable for the loch. He fully believed in its sea-going properties – to our cost, as the event proved.

This amateur vessel was worked by paddles and petroleum lamps – and all at once, when we were far out in the middle of the loch, the machinery, such as it was, broke down and the paddles ceased to work!

We hoped a passing steamer might, however, rescue us, and signalled one before long. Alas! we could not make her understand that anything was wrong. She merely dipped her flag in playful response to ours – when our boatman exclaimed, 'She thinks the chief's on board,' and looked blankly at each other as she held on her way.

Then a little wind got up. Oh, it was nothing – a mere ripple on the surface of the water; but it caught our awning, and we had hastily to take it down. My father, the only responsible member of the party, began to look anxious.

The sky darkened, the squalls from the hills grew more frequent, and a little, a very little, more boisterous. It was time to get ashore. Nay, get ashore we *must* – but how?

We had no oars. By some supreme piece of folly these had been left behind, and we were at the mercy of the wind and water; and though we little dreamed then of the tragedy to be enacted one day not far from the spot whereon we lay helplessly drifting, we realised enough to sober even the indomitable spirits of youth.

Very grave and cold, we sat still and eyed each other for a dreary, indefinite period; but at length a species of deliverance came. The wind, instead of veering about in short puffs, blew steadily from one quarter, and our boatmen, seizing the plank which was used as a landing-stage, contrived to row against it, thus propelling the launch forward, till by slow degrees they brought her to land on the nose of a long promontory about ten miles from Rossdhu.

So thankful were we to be on *terra firma* that what followed was merely food for merriment, albeit it consisted of our borrowing from a farm a mile off, a cart and horse, (the only one available, as it was hay-time), into which we packed – eight of us – one, my brother Roderick, standing up to drive.

No cushions, no straw, nothing but bare cart to sit on, and in – yet we galloped along at the top of that great, gaunt horse's speed, his fetlocks streaming in the wind, (I have never seen such fetlocks since), the thought of our uncle and his dinner-party overpowering every emotion.

Our poor father, now an elderly man, naturally suffered most; but all he said was 'Get on – get on!' – and get on we did with a vengeance. A carriage was in front, and a carriage behind, as we tore up the Luss avenue, distancing both by our headlong speed – for what did we care? We had only one thought at the moment.

And it was justified. A figure stood at the bottom of the long flight of steps beneath the portico. Our hearts beat faster as we recognised it.

There was always something sacred about the person of our uncle – he was never spoken of to us by any other name than 'your uncle' – and that he should be standing there, waiting and watching, in full evening-dress too, equipped for the forthcoming party! The anxiety which drove him thus to depart from his usual secluded habits must have been great indeed; and as he turned and hurried up the steps again, we looked at each other in silence.

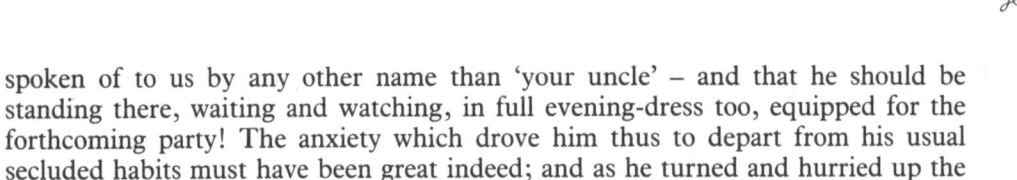

And how we raced to our rooms, and how we flew down when ready! The guests had all assembled, of course, but not a word of rebuke or reproach was said to us; nay, the only reply some stammering syllables of explanation and contrition met with next day was an approving 'You weren't long in dressing,' and this kindness penetrated our very souls.

Will elder people take the hint? I should like to say a word at this point anent a practice more common in my youth perhaps than now – that of scolding the young for a misdemeanour before awaiting a possible explanation of it. My dear mother, with a highly strung temperament, did not always understand the mistake of doing this; and if she had exacted a promise to be back by a certain hour, she expected that promise to be kept at all hazards.

So well was this understood by my father and brothers that they would run a very real risk rather than expose her to the uneasiness of a fancied one. They would pelt home from the moors at the close of a long and arduous day at such a pace that they were often too worn out to eat; and on one occasion my eldest brother fell down in a dead faint on the threshold.

One would be slow to censure the nervous fears of an affectionate parent, but perhaps it would have been better for us all if ours had been a little more philosophical – above all, if she would have been content to sit in a window which did not command a view of the front door!

❦

The china room at Rossdhu was a great delight to us. No restriction was laid on our re-arranging it to suit our ideas, and we spent many happy hours there. A former Sir James had been a collector, laying out money upon this costly craze which his wife considered would have been better applied elsewhere, and accordingly she endeavoured on one occasion to outwit him.

He had purchased for a considerable sum a pair of large Indian vases, a bright yellow in colour, and covered with marvellous designs. By these he set much store, and of course they – or rather one of them – got broken (by whom history sayeth not, nor yet why it was mended); but at any rate, thenceforth the other remained alone in its niche.

Now comes along a pedlar, ready either to dispose of his wares or add to them as occasion arose – and here was Lady Helen's opportunity. She produced the solitary vase, (her husband being well out the way), and trusting to his holding it to be of but little value since its mate was no more, struck a bargain with the pedlar, who gave her ten shillings, and popped his purchase into his wallet.

We may believe that he then hurried off as fast as legs could carry him, for well the wily rogue must have known what he was about – and perhaps he would have slipped aside if he had foreseen whom luck would presently run him up against. But Sir James, a bent old man, in his rough homespuns, probably looked little like a great Highland chief, and there was nothing about him to warn what an encounter might lead to. The pack was readily opened at his bidding.

Now here was the crucial moment. It might have been expected that the familiar features of the Indian vase would at once have disclosed to their former owner his lady's nefarious proceeding – in which case both she and Master Pedlar would have found themselves in a tight place; but either the old gentleman had not looked at his china for some time or his eyesight was dim with advancing years, for all he thought was, 'Here is a chance! Here is a match for my Indian vase!' – and proceeded to haggle with the pedlar, eventually buying the vase for ten pounds.

The question next arose, how to get the money out of the house, and the purchase into it? But the laird's strongbox was in his private sitting-room on the ground floor, and down the same passage was the china room. The two men – we could see them as we hearkened to the tale! – stole with stealthy steps inside through a back way, and both feats were soon accomplished, when again, and this time finally, the succcessful trickster vanished, and his dupe hastened to enjoy his triumph.

And here the story ends, but the yellow vase still stands alone in its corner at Rossdhu.

Of this Lady Helen, after whom the town of Helensburgh was named, a sister of the first Earl of Sutherland, and a beautiful woman if fairly represented by her portrait, many stories were told; one being that which elicited the well-known reply anent Dr Johnson,[48] who, on his tour round the Hebrides, paid Sir James and Lady Helen Colquhoun a visit.

Her ladyship was, for those days, a fastidious woman, and the doctor's manners displeased her. She muttered aside, 'What a bear!'

'A bear, it may be, madam,' retorted one of the great man's followers; 'but if so,' he appended wittily, 'it is *Ursa Major*.'

Lady Helen was also an autocrat, and a determined one. She ruled with a rod of iron and took practical measures to have her behests carried out – as is attested by a relic still to be found at Rossdhu in the shape of a ring which she had had made for a housekeeping purpose.

No hen's egg which could pass through this ring was deemed fit for consumption by the frugal dame; and as all retainers within hail were expected to bring their eggs to her for sale, these were regularly subjected to the ordeal, and woe betide the seller whose hens often failed in their duty.

One more word about this lady. She was one of the first flax-spinners of her day, and the present writer is now in possession of her beautiful little satinwood spinning-wheel, being the only one of her descendants who has acquired and cultivated the obsolete art. It was in consideration thereof that the wheel was presented to me, and, needless to say, it is one of my treasures.

⇛ ⇚

A small but valued heirloom still to be seen on a table in Rossdhu drawing-room has a peculiar interest attached to it.

My father, when a young man, was bathing in the bay, when his attention was caught by a glitter beneath the pellucid waters, responding to the sunshine overhead. He dived, and brought to the surface an old, enamelled box, which had however no lid.

Considering that the lid might be somewhere about, he dived again, and again brought up something, which still was not what he sought. It was a small silver box, in the shape of a heart.

Elated by success, he descended a third time to pursue his quest, and a third time came up with a reward for perseverance in his hand – not indeed the lid of the enamelled box, but of the silver one – proving to be the most precious find of the three, since on it was engraven a name, that of Humphrey Colquhoun – beyond doubt that of his ancestor 'the fierce Sir Humphrey,' of whom many a bloody tale is told in the family annals.

When properly cleaned, the little group looked like the laird of Cockpen's wig; 'as guid as new,' bearing no traces of their long immersion; but, often as their discoverer searched the spot thereafter, he found no further relics of the past. Perhaps it was rather wonderful that he had found these.

Although it is to the discredit of a forefather, I must tell what happened on one occasion at Rossdhu, as it explains what has often puzzled readers of certain novels and poems.

We Colquhouns have been asked over and over again, 'How is it that there is scarcely any mention of your family in Scott's famous novel *Rob Roy*, which is cast in your own country, and wherein the best scenes take place on your own lands?'

The same inquiry has been made respecting *The Lady of the Lake*,[49] wherein the solitary reference to us is scarcely polite, and certainly not true. 'Glen Luss and Rossdhu' are *not* 'smoking in ruin,' nor do 'The best of Lomond lie dead on her side'; but Sir Walter had his own reasons for putting such statements into the mouth of our hereditary enemies, the Macgregors.

When engaged on the novel – which preceded the poem – he travelled down to Loch Lomond-side to collect material and obtain local colour, and presented himself at the then Sir James Colquhoun's door, confident of welcome and assistance.

But he had reckoned without his host. That Sir James was my grandfather, and as stupid a country magnate as existed, though perhaps it is not for me to say it. Truth, however, will out; and we descendants of the worthy gentleman – and no one more than his own son, my father – had cause to rue his pride and pompous stupidity as regards the famous author.

Who and what was a mere Edinburgh lawyer to the Chief of Colquhoun? Mr Walter Scott – he was not yet 'Sir Walter' – might be a clever man of letters, but he was a person of no consequence, as Sir James esteemed consequence, and he slunk out by a back way to avoid an intrusive, prying body, having ordered *the butler* to show him round!

Such an affront was never forgotten nor forgiven; in *Rob Roy* the Colquhouns were absolutely ignored, and the scene of the *Lady of the Lake*, originally intended to be laid on the banks of Loch Lomond, was removed to Loch Katrine!

Sir Walter Scott, 'a person of no consequence' / The Kylin Archive

As Sir Walter himself made no secret of the why and the wherefore of this, and as my father often referred to it with much regret, I have no hesitation in stating it as a fact.

❧ ☙

Sundays at Rossdhu were as strictly kept as in our own home – rather more so in fact: for though we were allowed to receive any *letters* that came by post, (the bag being put into the carriage at Luss while we were at church), none of its other contents were doled out.

Our uncle, on reseating himself within, would solemnly unlock the bag and scrutinise every envelope before handing it either to the recipient or the recipient's representative; but every newspaper, book, or parcel was put back again, to await a 'lawful' day of issue.

We had, however, certain amenities during the service. We sat in our own loft, and in the centre of the loft was a fireplace, which in cold weather contained a fire – although I have not often mentioned it, we were often at Rossdhu in the chilly months of autumn and spring, it being the custom for our relations there to invite such of the family as did not take part in the annual migration to Park Place – consequently we were very glad of that church fire.

When the text for the sermon was given out, we turned round our chairs – huge red and gold armchairs which had been in family use for two hundred and fifty years – and settled ourselves with our toes on the fender; and at least once, and sometimes twice afterwards, our uncle would rise and put on fresh coal – a proceeding always watched with the greatest interest.

And I think we liked being prayed for as 'the family that is held in highest distinction amongst us' – though there came once to Luss parish a modern young minister who did not, and prevailed on my uncle to let him omit the clause, it being obviously out of date and appropriate only to feudal times.

My uncle was quite agreeable, but the people were not. They decided that the modern young man was seeking to belittle a worthy family from whom many of their blessings flowed, and indignantly demanded that he should do as his forbears had done. He had to give in; and though, with the growth of Time, there came a certain change of feeling and removal of ancient landmarks, the tie between the Colquhouns and their people has always remained a strong one on both sides.

My dear uncle was beloved on his estates. He was 'as gentle as a lamb,' we were often told, and could an old man or woman but reach his ear with a petition, it was attentively hearkened to and promised consideration. Nor was the reaching difficult, for this truly good landlord, who never entered the house of a compeer except under a sense of *noblesse oblige*, was a frequent visitor among his poorer friends, and kept a patriarchal eye on all their concerns.

He did not indeed make up marriages between them, as his own father had done to their satisfaction – ('Aweel, Sir James, if ye'll bring it aboot,' had been a frequent response to the latter's 'I'm thinking, John – or Peter – that Mary – or Maggie – So-and-so, would make you a good wife'); but he was always pleased to hear of a wedding, and invariably attended it. In other matters, I say advisedly that appeals were 'promised consideration,' since my uncle was not an impulsive man, and he had to consult the factor, Mr Wyllie.

As I write the name of 'Wyllie' I can hear Scotchmen of a former generation exclaim, 'Wyllie? I know! I remember those Wyllies. All sons of a father who was a factor, *nascitur non fit*.[50] There was a Wyllie in every part of Scotland in my day.'

As my uncle had been lucky in securing the services of a specially able and upright member of the family, it was no wonder that he acquired the habit of referring all matters of the estate to him; and my father, who was sometimes a little restive on the subject, and could say what he chose to a brother with whom he was on the most free and affectionate terms, would sometimes have his jest at 'the omniscient and infallible Wyllie.'

His 'What does your paragon Wyllie say to it?' or 'You have to get Wyllie's consent, of course,' would, however, be taken in perfectly good part, and once the laugh was turned against himself.

At Glenfalloch he had unearthed a nice little cottage, hidden deep in a moorland glen, and precisely on the boundary line between the Breadalbane and Luss estates.

Having carefully prepared his little trap, he soon had our uncle within sight of the hut, and pointing to it with his stick, casually observed, 'Whose cottage is that, I wonder,'

The wonder meeting with no response, he put the question straight, 'Whose cottage is that, James?'

'I don't know,' said James, simply.

'Why, it's *your own*, shouted my father, much delighted. 'It's your own; and I thought that you wouldn't know, and I bet you Mr Wyllie – '; but the words died on his lips, for behold! there was Mr Wyllie emerging from the cottage door! It was some time before he jested at the latter's expense again.

The household at Rossdhu was almost invariably recruited from homes on the estate. Boys and girls were brought thither for inspection as soon as of an age to leave school, and if they inclined to domestic service, a niche was found for them in the pantry or kitchen, whence they gravitated upwards, or were drafted onwards as the occasion offered.

At a later period than that of which I write, I had a pleasant and touching experience of the feeling sometimes – we may hope often – engendered by this, and may perhaps be pardoned reproducing a little account of it jotted down at the time under the subjoined heading.

'Freddy: A Touch of Nature.'

'He was a gorgeous creature, and he sunned himself like a great bird on the steps of a Mayfair mansion. His coat was pink, a rosy pink, well set off by the under plumage, so to speak, of jet black and snowy white. Shoe-buckles finished him off and glinted ravishingly as he struck out his toes and eyed them from time to time. One word more: powder crowned his top-knot, and the smoothness of the cheek beneath and the unruffled outline of the features were only redeemed from beauty by an all-pervading expression of profound and unfathomable inanity.

'The hour was five o'clock – calling time. Suddenly, in the midst of the glittering equipages which crashed in ceaseless kaleidoscope around, there stopped, beneath the gorgeous creature's nose, a humble little vehicle with a solitary occupant.

'The creature's eyelids dropped; he did not approve of victorias for the afternoon – moreover, the lady inside was old enough to have known better. Had she been very young and very smart? – but as it was, his descent of the steps was a protest in itself – slow, supercilious, vengeful. As much as he could hate anything, he hated that victoria, root and branch; his soul – he hadn't much of a soul – but such as it was, it sickened at the thought of taking in cards from so mean a source. Then all at once something happened.

'The lady was busy with her cards; the footman – Good Heavens! can it be that this crimson, quivering, palpitating, *human* face belongs to the stucco image of the doorstep? Its very nostrils are working with excitement. They breathe, entreaty, expectation.

'The lady sees nothing – goes on shaking off the little tissue papers which fly about; there is a sort of gasp at her side.

'Still she takes no notice – why should she? To her a footman is but an automaton; and she will be gone and never know; in sheer desperation he breaks convention's fetters.

'She starts, looks at him confusedly for a moment; then all at once, with an electric shock of recognition – '*Freddy*!'

'A mist swims before Freddy's eyes; for he sees, and knows that she sees, not the great, pillared houses blazing in the June sunshine, not the fluttering crowds and champing horses, not the pride and pomp and artificial grandeur and luxury of it all – but a brown hillside, and a blue loch, and a heather-roofed hut by a wimpling burn.

'And the resplendent Frederick of Mayfair is a mountain laddie again, running to tell his mother that "the ladies" are passing on the road below; and now, with shaking fingers, he flies for refuge to the modest carriage-wrap they would have disdained to touch five minutes before; and as he smoothes and tucks for appearance' sake, his trembling lips can hardly find words to reply to the gracious and, oh, so prized inquiries.

'He has got a very good place, ma'am, thank you, ma'am: he is doing very well, ma'am, thank you, ma'am; his old mother is alive and well, ma'am, thank you, ma'am – thank you very kindly, ma'am for asking after her: she will be pleased to hear, he will write and tell her: and if you please, ma'am, he hopes the family is very well, and the little misses very well, (and everyone else very well that Freddy can think of); and though the whole only lasts a few minutes, spin it out as he may, when it is over, and the little carriage rattles cheerfully off, Frederick the Magnificent stands quite still, with the cards in his hands, looking after it as if all the light had died out of his sky.'

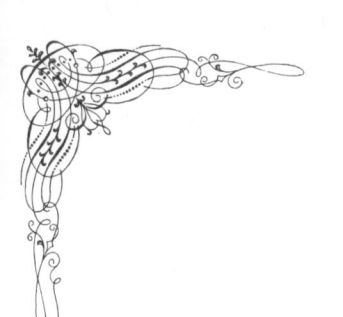

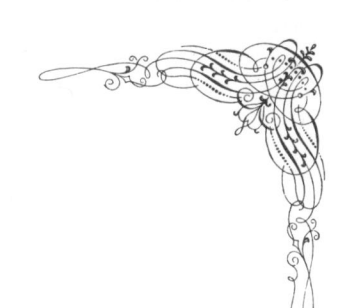

Personages and Personalities

While summering at Glenfalloch, we had changed our winter quarters, sold No 6 Eton Terrace, and bought No 1 Royal Terrace, at the other end of Edinburgh.

The house being in process of erection at the time of the purchase, my father had it finished to suit his own requirements, which comprised two bathrooms, then an almost unprecedented luxury! It also had an inner as well as an outer hall, so that his little collection of British birds, beasts, and fishes could be well accommodated.[51]

In other respects the Royal Terrace house was not nearly so large as its predecessor; but our family was now lessened, and it was big enough. We did not miss, or rather missed pleasantly, two extra flights of stairs, and it was indeed a relief for us younger ones not to have to toil up to the top of these to our bedrooms.

Royal Terrace was not then, and is not now, a fashionable quarter; but this, I suspect, was not reckoned any disadvantage by our parents, as the whole of Edinburgh being on such a small scale as compared with other cities, it neither prevented our going anywhere nor having anyone come to us, while yet no one could go out and in without meeting an acquaintance at every step. Shy people, and both my father and mother were shy, appreciate such freedom.

The former, nevertheless, was reminded that he could not even at that end of the town always escape encounters, and his retort was characteristic: 'Hoots, there are only the Milne-Homes, and I never mind *them*; I can always find something to say to *them*. They have queer birds down at their place on the Tweed.' I might add that, though doubtless cemented by the birds, the friendship with their owners then begun has been carried down to this present day.

Our Royal Terrace house, to be sure, faced the north – a drawback – though there was a fine view of the Firth of Forth from the upper windows; but, on the other hand, there were many sunny rooms at the back opening into a little garden, which again opened into larger and beautifully kept gardens above, and the Calton Hill sheltered the whole in a kind and comfortable way. This house still remains in the family.

One of my early impressions of it was the following. We girls were busy one day with our various avocations, when our pleasant morning-room, which was made over to us entirely, was suddenly invaded by a younger brother, crying in high excitement, 'Who's for the first sight of the Channel Fleet?'

He then hurried off, such as would go, to a high bank in the upper gardens, commanding an extensive prospect; and we had scarcely established ourselves there, and fixed our eyes on the blue horizon, when its smooth, straight line began to exhibit a curious undulation. We were all gifted with long sight, and cried, 'There – there!' at the same moment.

The undulation quickly resolved itself into seven distinct specks – hardly even dark specks, so far off were they; but they were at regular distances from each other, and never for an instant was it to be imagined that they could be anything else than the seven men-of-war expected that day to cast anchor in the Firth of Forth.

We were right. A slight breeze just rippled the sea, just sufficed to fill the sails, and on they came, the grand three-deckers of old – a sight never to be forgotten by any who beheld it.

By noon all were duly ranged between Inchkeith and the mainland, and the next thing was a ring of our doorbell, and the announcement that Lieutenant Wilson was in the drawing-room. There had been some mistake, and no one had told us that this sailor cousin was on board one of the Fleet vessels (as First Lieutenant of the *Warrior*),[52] and we had never met him, though his mother was a Fuller-Maitland – a sister of our mother – so that it was a complete surprise and proportionate pleasure to find ourselves thus promptly sought out.

Nor shall I be deterred by fear of offending the modesty of a certain grey-haired admiral from saying that we were charmed with our kinsman, and more than charmed to accept the invitation to an afternoon dance on board his ship, with which he came charged.

For one glorious moment it seemed as if we were all to be allowed to go. Our cousin would hear of no refusals; he saw three sisters, all to him much of an age, and he did not understand the etiquette of being 'out' and 'not out.' But, alas! I was 'not out'; I was on the verge – the worst place possible; and with a sinking heart I heard my doom pronounced: the *Warrior* dance was not for me.

And now comes the point of the tale. It might be supposed that poor Cinderella, thus left behind when the gay party started forth on the following afternoon, would weep and wail in secret. She did nothing of the kind. She had a consolation little dreamed of by others, and, the first pang of disappointment over, found it – as it has proved many a time in after life – sufficient. She had begun to write.

Four years had passed since *Macgregor; or, Our Chieftain*, had found an early grave in the wastepaper basket at Garth, and he had no successor up to the present time. But shortly before the Channel Fleet's appearance in the Forth, various discursive efforts had been the result of a something – I could not tell what – which

HMS Warrior, the first British Ironclad warship, finished in 1861 / The Kylin Archive

burned within my breast, and with one of them on a larger scale than the rest, though modest as compared with the dare-devil *Macgregor*, I was now busy.

It absorbed me; I heard the dressing and fussing preparatory to the start for the *Warrior* without emotion, nay with indifference, and directly the front-door shut, locked myself into the empty bedroom wherein all the debris lay about, and thought only of the luxury of having it to myself. Not a sigh did I waste upon the revel of the quarter-deck.

Yet of this second literary attempt, all-engrossing as it was, I have again no record, and am glad to think I thus recognised as before its lack of all merit except the bare fact of existence. 'Sir,' said the mighty Johnson of a dog walking on its hind legs, 'it is not that it is well done, but that it is done at all, which is remarkable.' Whether 'Remarkable' should be applied to a crude effort on the part of a girl of seventeen may be questioned, but let that pass.

The tale was named *The Moderator's Breakfast*; and to those for whom the words have no meaning I would explain that during the month in which it was written the Church of Scotland was holding its yearly 'General Assembly,' presided over by its 'Moderator' (a clerical 'Speaker' – annually elected by his brethren from among themselves). This congress is held in Edinburgh, and every day during the fortnight in which it take place, the Moderator entertains a party of several hundred people to breakfast at his hotel.

Of course, most of my readers know all about this; but some may not, and may never have realised what festive scenes take place during the merry month of May in the old Scottish capital.

Princes Street is gay with black coats – if such a thing may be. Holyrood, with a Lord High Commissioner in residence, is red with soldiers. At night black and red fuse; and the grim old walls echo with music and dancing.

Dinner-parties and supper-parties are everywhere; and the gardens, blossoming in their spring beauty, and the crags, hanging with early green, which separate the Old Town from the New, are alive day and night with flying feet, either hurrying up to the Assembly Hall to attend the sittings there, or hurrying back to fulfill social engagements.

All of this I had seen from my youth, and though, naturally, I had not participated, imagination had been at work. Mentally I pictured this Paradise to ministers' daughters, perhaps brought from the ends of the (Scottish) earth; I used to note their happy faces, their new frocks and bonnets, and their special air if a young blackcoat – or any coat – were in attendance.

It did not follow that this last was a cleric. He might be anything. A laird, or the eldest son of a laird, was frequently an elder of his parish church, and as such, would represent it at the General Assembly. Young Scotsmen rather liked this distinction.

The regiments, too, as I have stated before, at all times supplied Auld Reekie with a rather unusual amount of the sterner sex, and these were joyously ready to make hay while the sun shone in the flirting line, – so that opportunities on every side were promptly responded to, and all went merry as a marriage-bell.

For the main theme of my tale, then, I chose a love-story based on these lines. I depicted a lovely daughter of the manse, all innocent of the world and its arbitrary distinctions of class, meeting her fate in the shape of a too attractive young nobleman and elder of the kirk, who loved and rode away, leaving her to watch in vain from her far home in the wilds, to which she had had perforce to return when her dream of bliss was over.

He not only never followed her there, he had never meant to follow her – and in *that*, to my mind, lay the pathos of it.

In piling up the agony I revelled; but it was not altogether badly done agony – it could not have been, since the tears streamed down my face as I wrote. Our dark-eyed sailor and the *Warrior* dance were very far away at such a moment.

Although this new attempt at authorship shared the fate of its predecessor, it was not destined to be followed, as before, by a cessation of further efforts.

I had tasted something of the joy of creation – but a taste, yet how divine the flavour! – and was soon again at work.

This time, however, I was off on a new tack, and came down from my high horse with a run. Surely it was a leap from a Scottish romance to a *Parable from Nature* in the style of Mrs Gatty,[53] – yet, strange to say, the parable lived, while the romance left not even its ashes.

The parable was a quaint little performance, obviously an imitation, both in conception and construction; but it was at least unpretending, and treated of things within my youthful range. I printed it carefully out in a brown morocco album, and with an eye firmly fixed on Mrs Gatty proceeded to illustrate it as she did hers. Others of its kind followed, and soon the album was full – whereupon I bought another.

In the second was a story, *The Merchant's Sermon*, which marked a new departure; it was virginal; it had no Mrs Gatty in it. Indeed, I never afterwards reverted to the methods of that delightful writer; unique in her own way, but followed my own bent, with the result that more and more my leisure hours became absorbed and preoccupied.

Luckily for me, those were the days of albums and manuscript books. We transcribed music, poetry, passages from favourite authors. Little, ladylike compositions of own own in prose and verse were also common enough – sometimes in the shape of riddles, or such trifles as arose out of 'Cross Questions and Crooked Answers' and games of like nature; so that although my rough drafts were often hurriedly scrawled in the bathroom, of all places, kneeling by the edge of the bath! – I could make a fair copy of them without provoking ill-timed curiosity. Thus I continued to write *sub rosa* and by fits and starts for the remainder of my life before marriage.

But life on the surface was a very different affair. Although there was now no school-room proper in our house, my sisters and I continued to have masters for various accomplishments, and to pursue them with an ardour which was then very much in vogue. We had Garcia for singing, Lichtenstein for playing, Ferrier for water-colour drawing, and last but not least, Mr Thomas M'Glashen for dancing.

Mr M'Glashen was not merely *facile princeps* as a teacher of Scottish dances in Edinburgh, but a *character*; and we used to think he could not but amuse our young princes and princesses at Windsor Castle, whither he was annually summoned, as much he did us. My father, in particular, would often stay in the room during our lessons for the sheer pleasure of a talk with him, while we rested between one 'figure' and another. His shrewdness and sagacity, as well as his wonderful tact, would be commented on afterwards. He was a past master in the art of bringing his pupils on, whether by spur or pat on the back – they learned to dance somehow, one hardly knew how.

Once after skipping, fiddle in hand, before his little class, to the tune of

'Loudon's Bonny Banks and Braes,' which he played with equal delicacy and spirit, he paused for breath, (and to furtively mop his forehead, for he had the figure of a barrel, though wonderfully light upon his feet), and signed to us to follow his example.

The little class obeyed. It consisted of a sister and me and our youngest brother, who at the close looked hopefully into his teacher's face; but we girls, who had seen him hopping about, feared.

M'Glashen, however, rose to the occasion. Slapping his thigh with the bow of his fiddle, he had all the air of paying a compliment, and his whole face beamed as he pronounced, 'Two ladies quite right; one gentleman – *nearly so.*'

One day my father put the inquiry, 'Does Mr So-and-so dance well?'

'No, sir, he dances like a dancing-master.'

'What?' cries my father. 'What? You to say that, Mr M'Glashen! It's an ill bird that fouls its own nest, you know.'

But the sturdy Terpsichorean was not to be daunted. 'I will tell you what I mean, sir. It is necessary for a teacher to *overdo* the part, for if he does not, a pupil will *underdo* it. *We* have got to dance like dancing-masters, but a *gentleman* never should.'

'Only a clever man would have thought of that, and only a candid one would have acknowledged it,' quoth my father afterwards.

One winter M'Glashen instituted a series of small and select gatherings for the purpose of practising reels and strathspeys. We went in for various recondite forms of these, and there were experts among us. One, a very young and pretty one, was a favourite pupil, and to the surprise of her master, he saw her one evening standing motionless, while the 'Hoolichan' was in full swing.

'Miss Ina, what is the matter? Why are you not dancing?'

She replied that she could not think of a step.

A step? and she knew twenty!

Perhaps a charming duchess of to-day will say this not true – but at any rate it was so reputed, and M'Glashen loved to tell the tale.

Our dear little drawing-master, Mr James Ferrier,[54] whose landscapes were the delight of lovers of Scottish scenery, was of another sort. Having a large family to provide for, he supplemented his income by teaching, and his lessons were eagerly sought for.

His method was his own. He never spoke; he sat at an impromptu easel, and we clustered round and watched. When he had finished for the day, he produced his watch, murmured, 'Good morning, ladies,' and was off. By that day week, each member of the class produced more or less faithfully a copy of what had been done before her eyes; but even then, I think, he hardly passed a comment; he simply went on with his own work.

In the end an exquisite little picture would be presented to the pupil who had best deserved it (or from whose crude sketch it had been produced), and thus at the close of the annual course we possessed two or three of these, any one of which was a gem. I have since thought – though I am sure neither he nor we considered it in that light at the time – that we ought not to have accepted such valuable gifts. We had, however, an opportunity of showing our gratitude later on, when sickness and trouble overtook our friend. He had a stroke of paralysis, and was laid aside for years, it was thought that he would never handle the brush again – but behold! there suddenly appeared exhibits as beautiful as ever. James Ferrier had learned to paint with his left hand.

Of our other teachers, Herr Lichtenstein, the Hungarian, will still be remembered by Edinburgh people, and his pupils owed him much; but it was always with a mamma, or elder person in the room, that he gave his music lessons. He was altogether too personable, too agreeable; it was known that he had been in the army, and it was whispered (as I write of so long ago, there can hardly be any indiscretion in recording this) that he had been obliged to fly his country. In plain terms, he had been a spy. Be that as it may, he took very kindly to Edinburgh, had himself naturalised, lived in comfort, died respected and regretted, and we never learned if the 'spy' story were true or not.

<hr>

Let me mention a few of our friends of those days.

Miss Walker of Dalry[55] or, as she was more often called, 'Miss Helen Walker' belonged to the type of old Scottish lady which has now almost entirely passed away. She did what she chose, lived as she chose, dressed as she chose, and said – in old high-class Scotch – very much indeed what she chose.

Her sayings were always flying about, like the curls of her 'front' – and both were of the corkscrew order. But it served nobody's turn to take offence, seeing that the little old lady stood secure on her feet, and, although by no means ill-natured, cared not a job for sensibilities that clashed with her own. If she liked you, well and good; if not, you were outside her pale – and somehow people did not wish to be outside her pale.

Miss Helen was *the fashion*; she entertained continuously, though one could hardly say largely, for her small house (in Lynedoch Place) was *very* small; and yet it would be frequented by guests whom many of her richer neighbours tried in vain to allure within their doors. Her form of invitation, like herself, was arbitrary and unconventional – a pencil scrawl on a dingy visiting-card, which looked as if it had been dug out of a pocket stuffed full of other things – but the recipient of that 'Come on such-and-such an evening, at such-and-such and hour' invariably went.

Women were careful, moreover, to wear smart clothes: Miss Helen would have pounced ruthlessly on any fancied disrespect; and once I caught an aside in the cloak-room: 'No, I am not going to a ball, but I simply did not dare to come shabby,' which summed up the situation. Shabby the old lady might be herself, like a rag-bag, if you chose; but it was noted that her sister, Lady Hall of Dunglass, whose visits were always occasions for parties, would be magnificent – at the other end of the dress scale. It was obvious that 'Leddy Hall' knew what pleased the queer, little, old hostess.

And she would stand by her side too, woman of the world as she was, and never turn a hair whatever Miss Helen said or did, though the latter's remarks were often of a kind to raise a titter, and once at least her ladyship must have been sorely tried. I can see that scene now.

These primitive little assemblies were 'small and early,' and if the giver did not name their limitation as to hours, it was only because she forgot it. Most people, however, knew to be punctual and were so.

But a certain young hunting laird, very pink, very smart, and terribly ill at ease, as a young man from the country is apt to be when off his own beat, came tip-toeing up the stairs an hour after the time appointed, and the hostess had left her place. She wheeled round as he was announced; she transfixed him with her eye, and she almost spat with contempt: 'Weel, Tom Christie! Weel, here ye are!' Then, snorting rapidly: 'Ye're very fine, and ye're very fash'nable, *but ye'll have to go away at eleven o'clock all the same.*'

Needless to say, long before the fateful hour the unfortunate 'Tom' was nowhere to be seen, nor did he ever thereafter reappear at Miss Helen Walker's parties.

One word more about Miss Helen. She was a rabid teetotaller, and, to the grief and mortification of her highly respectable old manservant, would not permit wine or spirits on her table, whoever might be her guests. On one occasion he was at the end of his patience – but revenged himself.

His mistress was entertaining two elderly bachelors of position, Mr Ferguson of Kilkerran[56] and another whose name I forget. For their benefit she had lain in *four bottles of soda-water*, to which indignity they had perforce to submit; but as their coats were being helped on in the hall previous to departure, a sadonic whisper, we will hope, consoled them: 'Ye'll hae nae heedaches the morn frae *yon*!'

Could Miss Helen have heard her faithful retainer, she would soon have reduced his grin of scorn to one of penitence; but the two maltreated men chuckled as they walked away.

⇒) (⇐

Another old lady of the same order, vigorous, eccentric and masterful, was Lady

Ruthven. She had a beauty in her youth, and even when I remember her was handsome, with a fine Roman nose, and curved chin – the latter denoting her character. She ordered about everybody; but as her warmth of heart and general excellence were acknowledged, her whims were submitted to, and she was very well liked.

Over her household she ruled with a rod of iron, and as those were the days when old ladies – including even my pious and society-hating grandmother at Park Place – personally inspected the legs of prospective footmen, and had their calves measured, her ladyship was not perhaps singular in keeping her Donald of that ilk well under her thumb.

Donald dared not call his soul his own, let alone his wardrobe. His mistress supplied him with but one suit of livery – he had himself to supplement it with other garments – and only wear it when she ordained. But there came a day when he had forgotten to take her orders or she had forgotten to give them anent this – and there was a dinner-party in prospect, and the afternoon was waning. The old lady was engaged with visitors, when the door opened and an agitated head was thrust in: 'Is't ma ain breeks, or yer leddyship's breeks, I'm to pit on the nicht?' Report had it that her leddyship, without alteration of a muscle, decided in favour of *her* breeks.

Lady Ruthven was extremely deaf – a fact of which she took no account when herself speaking, – and as she had a very deep and powerful voice, which she never dreamed of modulating, the results were occasionally disastrous.

One of my sisters, when a guest at Winton, had an experience of this. It was on a Sunday morning, and she had accompanied her hostess to the parish church, where the service was long and dreary. When one remembers that the Presbyterian form of worship is writ in no book, but depends both for its length and strength on the minister who conducts it, one can sympathise with a deaf member of the congregation who loses patience if it is carried on beyond due limits; but no one was prepared for what followed a period of uneasy fidgeting on her ladyship's part.

Suddenly she leaned forward, and in stentorian tones, distinctly audible to all around, demanded, *'Is he near done yet?'* shooting out her trumpet for the response as she spoke. At the same moment the deerhound who always accompanied his mistress to church and lay at her feet, started up; auditors on every side stared and tittered, and the sermon without more ado stopped short. The 'he' referred to never afterwards occupied the pulpit at Winton.

A still more embarrassing frankness occurred in an Edinburgh drawing-room.

A musical reception was in process, and the old lady, who, despite her infirmity, could enjoy and appreciate good music, was seated in the front row of chairs, where she applauded heartily as long as it pleased her. But presently a young gentleman of her acquaintance (and of nearly everyone else's acquaintance present) began to sing, and the scene changed. Oblivious of the proximity of Mr H's relations, she 'glowered,' she muttered, she waxed more and more wroth, till at length as the performance continued – and songs were lengthy in those days – she caught a young friend by the skirts, exclaiming loudly, 'Miss Makgill-Crichton – Miss Makgill-Crichton?' But the singer sang on, and Miss Makgill-Crichton affected not to hear.

It was no use; the next moment came the tap of a huge fan followed by the well-known, bassoon-like voice: 'Miss Makgill-Crichton, my dear? Do sing again! Do give us that song again! What? Oh, you must!' Then, with ringing emphasis: '*Anything* to stop that bawling.'

The Misses Makgill-Crichton – afterwards respectively Mrs Fletcher and Mrs Chetham-Strode – were lovely singers, quite the leading amateurs of the Edinburgh musical world, and everyone was delighted that the above despotic command should be obeyed; but the young lady herself afterwards alleged that between mirth at the very uncomplimentary form it took and terror lest a worse thing should befall her if she hesitated, she could hardly bring forth a note.

Lady Ruthven,[57] however, beamed, and then and thereafter was serenely unconscious of having done anything beyond breathe a hint of her wishes in her young friend's ear.

Another familiar personality of old Edinburgh days was Mr William (afterwards Sir William) Fraser,[58] the antiquary. His genealogical lore was great, and there was scarcely a charter-chest in Scotland he had not at some time or other rummaged for muniments, when compiling his histories of ancient families. These tomes, handsomely printed and illustrated, comprised, among others, *The Red Book of Menteith*, *The Scotts of Buccleuch*, *The Earls of Cromartie*, *The Book of Calaverock*, and *The Douglas Book*. There were about twenty in all, and I presume that each, like our own *Chief of Colquhoun*, was limited to an edition of one hundred and fifty copies, and printed for private circulation only. Hence they soon became valuable, and if one ever came into the market, it was snapped up at a high price.

But Mr Fraser, as I recall him, had other aspirations beyond being known as a scholar and antiquarian. He was a middle-aged bachelor and, though plain and badly marked with small-pox, still fancied himself something of a beau.

As this was occasionally inconvenient, not to say annoying, I fear that a shock to his vanity which took place at our house one day, did not meet with the sympathy it should have done.

My mother had an afternoon party – the first, I think, I had attended as a 'grown-up' – and I was officiously proffering tea and coffee to the guests as they entered the dining-room before going upstairs, when in came Mr Fraser. I had rather hoped he would pass the door, but he did not.

He began to make himself agreeable. I offered him iced coffee; the weather was warm, the iced coffee good – I was not prepared for what followed. One mouthful the poor man took, then emitted a screech which made every head turn round, and rushed from the room! The icy mixture had found out a tooth wherein a raw nerve lay; and what, as he afterwards explained, he had mistakenly supposed to be 'nice' coffee, caused a blending of surprise and agony unendurable.

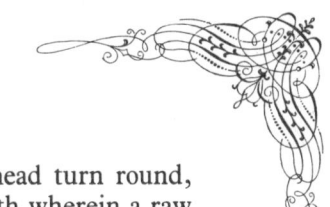

And although the victim of this unintentional practical jest subsequently endeavoured to laugh it off, it was clear that he never forgot such an exposure of his infirmities, especially of his lack of self-control in emitting the screech. He assumed a fresh attitude towards young people, left off philandering, and relegated himself to the shelf. We all liked him infinitely better so, and he remained our very good friend to the end of his days.

It pleases me also to record that at his death it was found he had bequeathed the whole of his savings, which were considerable, to found a Chair at the Edinburgh University for the benefit of students poor and struggling as he himself had been in his youth, and whom perchance a helping hand at the right moment might enable to rise as he had done.

Among others also with whom we had much pleasant intercourse were Sir Noel Paton[59] and his charming wife. Both were extremely attractive-looking, and knew how to dress. My mother, who had a weakness for filling her rooms with ornamental people when she entertained, liked to see the Patons come in.

She would also bestir herself to visit them, though they lived far away in the Old Town – but not only were they worth in themselves a journey, but their quaint house in George Square was worth seeing. It was full of treasures especially of old armour, which the famous painter introduced into his pictures.

Sometimes he would tell us about them, describe how they grew in his mind, and take opinions as to their names. He was quite simple and frank. There was none of that silence on the subject, which, whether intentionally or not, relegates the ignorant and unlearned to such a distance. None of us knew anything about art, but we could talk quite happily with Sir Noel Paton.

One day he pointed to an old helmet, and observed with a smile, 'You will see that fellow in the next Exhibition.' Of course we begged to hear more, on which he told us that the evening before, as the setting sun was pouring its last beams into the 'Armoury,' he turned at a slight sound, to behold his little son (a lovely, fair-haired child) gazing into the depths of the helmet, which had been left by accident on the floor. The little boy's golden curls were all lit up – and as the *painter* awoke within the *father*, and he was contemplating the picture before him as a picture, he heard a soft, small voice pensively murmur, 'I wonder who lived in there?'

That was enough. 'I am at work on it now,' subjoined Sir Noel, with his happiest look.

Sir Noel Paton, 'a most courteous, kind-hearted and sympathetic man', in his studio / Scottish National Portrait gallery

A few months later all the Scottish artistic world was saying, '*I wonder who lived in there?*'

Sir Noel was very desirous of having my eldest sister sit to him for his portrait of the angel in his famous picture *Mors Janua Vitae*, but my parents, who shunned publicity in every shape, would not consent. Amazed indeed would they have been to see the almost universal change of sentiment in this respect to-day, while even then, no doubt, there were some who failed to comprehend such reticence. However, so it was, and the angel had to be sought for elsewhere.

And one other recollection of our old friend stands out to memory. He had a house for the summer on Loch Long, and one day some of us found him alone far up on the hillside above. He was sitting on a wall, intently watching a flock of sheep, who were being herded down from the heights by a shepherd and his dogs. He rose and came towards us, and we saw that he had a Bible in his hand. 'Oh, I'll go home with you now,' he said cheerfully; 'I have been here long enough; but I was just getting a picture.' It was his picture of *The Good Shepherd* – one of his finest efforts.

I have already mentioned Professor Blackie, see page 72 but am tempted to insert here a quotation from a letter of my own which has since been put into my hands by a married sister who had preserved it all these years.

After detailing that some of us had been making a round of calls with our mother, which 'did not afford us any entertainment,' I proceeded, 'except one at Professor Blackie's, which indeed was enough to compensate for all. He was sitting with Mrs Blackie and Miss Wylde at tea, most comfortably attired in a blue-and-red dressing-gown, and Chinese-worked, turned-up slippers.'

A sketch of the Professor was appended, with his opening salutation, 'Here comes Mrs Colquhoun, with her beauties behind her' – which is a specimen of the odd but kindly greeting we usually met with from our eccentric friend.

Quite recently I was laughing over the above with one who knew Old Edinburgh well, and she capped it with an experience of her own. 'He was sitting in that very Chinese get-up when we went in one day. After a while he rose, went out, and returned attired as a sailor – loose blouse, open neck, flapping pantaloons, and bare legs and feet! Not content with this transformation, he vanished again; and this time reappeared in the imposing garb of a Spanish grandee, a huge sombrero crowning his snow-white hair! Thus in the short space of half an hour, we were treated to three apparitions, each more extraordinary than the other.'

Yet with all this gaiety and *daftness*, 'Daft Blackie,' as he loved to call himself, could be serious on occasion. He came to our house one evening in the gloaming, to find only two of us younger girls sitting by the fire, and immediately began in his usual merry vein.

But presently his mood changed. He gazed into the glowing coals with a new expression; we all fell to talking thoughtfully, and somehow, we knew not how, it seemed natural to talk of other things than the mere topics of the hour. Exactly what our visitor said I have long ago forgotten; but I know that he discovered a wonderful tact, that he did not intrude upon our inner feelings with any of that freedom which so shocks sensitive youth, that he asked no questions and excited no fears – that he just talked gently and easily of what constitutes true happiness in this world and the world to come – and at length that he went quietly away with a 'God bless you, my dear girls,' which left us solemnised and still. We had not been preached at, but we had been taken into a truly good man's confidence.

Dr Maxwell Nicholson, of the Tron Church, in the Old Town of Edinburgh, was of all our friends the most valued and intimate. He prepared us all for our first Communion, and held a footing in the house similar to that of the beloved 'curé' in a French château. We flew to tell him whenever anything good or ill had happened, relying on his affection, sympathy, and counsel on all occasions; but as there is nothing to relate of one who, however great his influence in his own sphere, always shrank from publicity, I will confine myself to telling of a very remarkable sight we once saw close by the Tron Church, to which we were proceeding one Sunday morning.

To begin with, we saw a crowd – what seemed a huge crowd in those days – and, following the direction of their eyes, beheld the ruined wall of a house fifteen stories high – one of the historic old tenements of Edinburgh – which had collapsed in the night!

Empress Eugénie, travelling as Countess of Pierrefonds, visited Scotland in 1860 / The Kylin Archive

The night had been calm and still – there was nothing to account for the catastrophe; but the fact remained that without a moment's warning down came the entire building, burying sixty people beneath its ruins!

No one escaped; not one was living when disentangled; and there, on one of the topmost walls, a canary was singing in its cage, unharmed and rejoicing in the sunshine.

A number of clocks had stopped at a certain hour – about two in the morning, I think – which seemed to indicate that as the fatal moment. The whole was a sight never to be forgotten.

Of Dean Ramsay, Dr John Brown, and other Scottish notabilities who came and went at the Royal Terrace house, I have nothing new to say – so much has been said already by others; but I may perhaps be permitted here to mention a star of another magnitude, who rose but for one brief moment on my horizon, yet who created an indelible impression.

A sister – the sister who was my invariable companion – and I were returning homewards one day from another part of Edinburgh, when we perceived a crowd collected in St Andrew Square, through which lay our route.

The crowd was in front of the Douglas Hotel; and as we drew near, wondering what it meant, a lady stepped through an open window on the first floor, and stood in the balcony.

A deep-breathed murmur of 'That's her – that's her!' ran through the assemblage, and then the cheering broke forth. We did not need to ask who 'her' was; we were looking on the lovliest face we had ever seen!

In the year 1860 the Empress Eugénie,[60] travelling as the 'Countess of Pierrefonds,' visited Scotland, that being the first time a royal lady of France had done so since the days of poor Queen Mary. She had undertaken the trip in an endeavour to recover her health and spirits after the death of her only and beloved sister, the Duchess of Alba, and her beauty was enhanced by the deep mourning in which she was clad.

The enthusiasm of the crowd below seemed to please her; she bowed and bowed with a wonderful, undulating grace of movement that nothing could surpass, while a smile played upon her lips. Finally, a little fluttering handkerchief was waved with an enchanting gesture of dismissal, and the beautiful, dark figure withdrew – turning, however, more than once to wave as she went.

My next sight of the Empress Eugénie was among the woods of Cap Martin five-and-thirty years afterwards.

Regimental balls in Edinburgh were exceptionally brilliant the year I came out – and this I do not say because of the glamour cast upon them by the eyes of eighteen, but by reason of the prosaic fact whose testimony is indisputable. Their sumptuousness and extravagance had reached a point to which the authorities demurred.

The cost to a young subaltern when his regiment, quartered at Piershill, or the Castle, or Leith Fort, proposed to return the hospitalities of Edinburgh people by a ball, was absurdly great, often out of all proportion to his means – though, of course, he would sooner have died than say so. If my memory serves me right, – and I *think* it does – a ball given by the Scotts Greys – of course the fine old 'Greys' were determined to be second to none on their own ground – mulcted every host on the occasion no less a sum than forty pounds. We happened to have a distant cousin in command at the time, and my brothers, I suppose, got this out of him; otherwise I do not see how we could have heard it – and of this I am sure, we did hear, and heard also of the fuss made at headquarters.

Headquarters pronounced the luxury supposed to be necessary for such affairs excessive, and instructed commanding officers in future to put it down with a high hand.

But it was not put down when I went to my first ball, given by the 72nd Highlanders, then stationed at Edinburgh Castle, which ball took place earlier in the season than that by the famous 'Greys,' and in point of brilliancy and splendour there did not seem to be a pin's point to choose between them.

Many ballrooms have I seen since; but I can honestly affirm that as a spectacle a regimental ball in the Edinburgh of forty years ago was not to be surpassed. The flowers, the music, the polished floors (into which a kind of yellow wax had been rubbed till they shone like gold), the rows of gorgeous chaperons, brave in diamonds, lining the walls, – the multiplicity of uniforms and bejewelled kilts (scarce a black coat to be seen) – most of all perhaps the gossamer-like attire of the girls, which had an ethereal elegance far above that of the present utilitarian dancing-frocks – (you may stare, my dear young ladies of to-day, but if we did get torn and ragged by the end of the evening, and if the floor were bestrewn by flowers from the garlands encircling our skirts, we were worth looking at, even in ruins) – all of the above combined to create a scene dazzling to behold, memorable to look back upon.

Hapless subalterns might have to pay the piper – or their share of the many pipers – but they enjoyed themselves hugely at the time, and casting vile care to the winds, proudly escorted their partners about to admire the banks of flowers (blazing as though it were June, not February), and to dip their handkerchiefs in fountains of eau-de-cologne rising and falling in silver-gilt basins, as though no such things as aftermaths of bills existed.

One adornment of the ball given by the 72nd was, I fancy, unique of its kind. At either end of every long supper-table (there were, I think, three) a peacock sat in state upon his own pie – no doubt incited thereto by old Sanderson, the bird-stuffer – with the tail spread. The peacock is the crest of the regiment. The effect was very fine.

As there were – I should say 'are' – two dancing-rooms available on these occasions, with a corridor and abundance of sitting-out places between, it is possible to have music in both without any echoes of either band reaching the other. This was a source of special satisfaction to such of us girls as were prohibited from joining in the round dances looked askance upon by strict parents, for the custom was to have these in one room and 'squares' or reels in the other, simultaneously and alternately. What I mean is that in the Music Hall a waltz would be going on, and in the Assembly Room a reel or lancers. At the close of these the waltz or polka would strike up in the latter, and the reel or lancers in the former; quadrilles were no longer to be seen anywhere, but we thought 'lancers' quite modern. By these means we and such as we could dance on without intermission, and as it was of course only at such balls as commanded twin rooms so happily placed that we could do so, this may have been one reason why we found them so agreeable.

And shall I win any sympathy if I tell what befell a sister and me on one sad occasion? Recollect that we did not go to a tithe of the entertainments we were asked to, that our parents were most terribly particular as to which we did attend – and then, only then, can you appreciate what follows.

It was a year later on, and the regiments at the Castle had been changed, the

74th Highlanders having succeeded the 72nd: and with the former had come a cousin of ours, belonging to the Stonefield family, of whom I have yet to speak.

One evening he gleefully informed us that he and his had agreed to give a dance – a dance, not a ball – and invited us to it then and there. Owing to some cause or other, we did not see him again in the short space of time which intervened; but that was nothing. We heard of others going to the dance, and confidently awaited our note of invitation, and – it never came. Every hour we looked for it; but the fateful day itself arrived, and still no orderly in uniform marched to the door, and no large, crested envelope was handed in.

Our parents, old-fashioned and self-respecting people, peremptorily forbade any move on our part, even to a mention of the affair, lest it should appear that we were being slighted; and we were powerless to do aught but watch and watch from the drawing-room window, – at which, I am bound to say, we spent most of those anxious feverish hours.

Again and again we would exclaim 'There – there!' as a kilted Highlander came into view – and naturally there were plenty of them about; so, albeit they usually came in pairs if bearing a message from the Castle, we were willing to believe in a solitary one, if only he would stop at our door – but alack and alas! he never did.

Our maid inquired if our ball paraphernalia was to be laid out? We said 'Yes' eagerly; we could not and would not give up hope. And we had our hair dressed – an elaborate process in those days – and congratulated ourselves on having done so whenever the door-bell rang.

But it was all to no purpose. At ten o'clock my father said, 'I wouldn't take you now, whoever sent. *My* daughters don't fly in at the last minute to any open door' and we ourselves felt proud and hurt, and sadly, sadly went to bed.

Next morning, of course, the mystery was cleared up, and a miserable, spiteful, little twopenny-halfpenny mystery it proved to be.

Our cousin called early. Why had we not come the night before?

Our retort was prompt: Why had he not sent our invitation?

Sent our invitation? He had *given* it. What was more, we had accepted it.

He then proceeded to explain. He was 'most awfully sorry,' but thought we knew that no other than verbal invitations had been issued, with a view to making the affair as smart and select as possible. Everybody who was anybody had been there; and the fact that it took place under the rose, as it were, and that the great bulk of undesirables had been weeded out by a trick, gave a special zest to the evening.

'I nearly came along to see what had become of you,' appended my cousin. 'But I had been away for the day, and was very late in getting to the rooms, when somebody told me you were there – or were coming. When I realised you weren't anywhere it was too late. I took it for granted something had happened.'

It was long before we could bear to think of that evening.

Kames castle on the Isle of Bute, / The Kylin Archive

The Gay Isle of Bute

Our tenancy of Glenfalloch having come to an end, we made a raid further west, and the shooting of the north end of the Isle of Bute being to let, together with the old Castle of Kames (which had belonged to Robert the Bruce in the twelfth century), my parents went down to inspect it, and took me with them. We put up at Rothesay, three miles off, and drove out one bright February morning, when the Firth of Clyde lay still as a millpond, and the white caps of the Arran hills stood sharply out against a blue sky.

We found an ancient tower, covered with ivy almost up to the battlements, whose romantic outline amply atoned for a certain barrenness of surroundings.

It was weird, it was strange; it was unlike any other abode we had ever dwelt in. Its stern, storm-beaten aspect might have repelled some people, testifying as it did to the warlike times in which it had been built, and the vicissitudes it had gone through; but I stole a glance at the faces of my elders and was satisfied. The venerable walls, the tall narrow windows, the simplicity and solidity of the whole, was no less attractive to them than to me, and though my father now and again looked round with a quizzical eye, eventually he decided to sign the usual three years' lease. 'If you can stand it, *I* don't mind,' he said to my mother; and as we were assured that divers small matters should be attended to, and the whole place put into thorough working order before we took up residence there, we went down in June, full of hope and expectation.

Alas! the shock! 'The ivy-mantled tower' was no more! In their zeal to do things handsomely for a tenant of sporting fame, the trustees of the then Lord Bute, who was still a minor, had had all the beautiful, leafy covering, the growth of ages, torn up by the roots, and the entire building whitewashed from end to end.

We looked at it in despair. The fine old relic of the past had disappeared; Kames was not a good, habitable, would-be modern dwelling – and only its massive walls and the noble arched roof of its 'Baron's Hall' attested to its former grandeur.

It looked smaller too – infinitely smaller, when thus perked up, white and new. I felt ashamed of it – I, who had inflamed enthusiasm by my glowing reports. I had now to sustain indignant looks and undisguised scorn: they were sceptical even as to the Bruce, – and I think, I *think*, they asked if there were no traces still to be seen of the historic spider?

Ah, well, we bore up. Although to the imaginative the exterior of the ancient structure was hopelessly despoiled of romance, a flavour of it still lingered within. There were winding stairs, narrow passages, odd nooks, and everywhere the deep-set windows. I hesitate, but I believe some of the tower walls were eight feet thick, and I know that it was dangerous to make any remark not meant for the public ear, until every separate recess in the 'Baron's Hall' had been explored.

Once, before we grew cautious, this was most unfortunately brought home to us. We had a guest of whom we were sadly tired, while yet he was not for the world to guess it. He heard, he could not help hearing, a voice demand, 'When *is* he going?' – as, unseen by the new-comer, who paused to emit the ejaculation, he sat reading in the nearest recess. He was not allowed to go the next day – he had too much tact and good breeding to insist upon it; but *he* knew, and *we* knew, and I doubt if either of us ever forgot.

One of the boasted improvements of Kames was the installation of gas; but the gas, which had to be brought from some little distance, was either indifferently laid on or revolted from its unnatural surroundings. After sundry playful little threatenings, it went out – went 'black out,' as the vulgar say – all over the house in the middle of our first dinner-party.

As our youthful landlord, Lord Bute, was present, with whom the responsibility for such behaviour might be supposed to rest, the mishap gave rise to plenty of laughter and badinage, and if anything rather added than not to the general hilarity; but to one person 'without the gate' it was gall and woodworm indeed.

Deluded by the prospect of gas – a luxury to which we had not hitherto been accustomed in the Highlands – old Aiky, now a feminine major-domo, had for the first time in her life left behind in Edinburgh the state candlesticks, of which we possessed an exceedingly handsome set, and those that had now to be hurriedly collected from garret and kitchen were of the meanest description.

And the candles? Tallow candles, neither more or less – till during the evening a few of a better kind were procured from 'the shop,' the one shop within hail, – and those barely sufficed to light an ordinary room, so that the lofty ceiling of that in which we were assembled, remained sunk in gloom.

Next day the poor old woman was found rocking herself to and fro, her chin resting upon her hands, her back hooped. 'It wasna the gas,' she whispered hoarsely; 'but' – and a shudder ran through her frame – 'but *thae* cannelsticks! Wow! that I suld ha' lived to see *thae* cannelsticks upon *our* table!' Never afterwards did an emergency of the kind find poor Aiky unprepared; but, of course, with the usual irony of Fate, never again did a like emergency arise.

Despite our first disappointment, we soon grew very fond of Kames. The old castle is charmingly situated close to the entrance of the Kyles of Bute – those narrow straits which here wind their way between one inland sea and another – while the wild Loch Striven, with precipitous banks and overhanging mountain peaks, lies directly opposite. There are parts of the Rhine whose ruined fortresses stand out upon their rocky headlands at every bend of the river, which remind one of the Kyles of Bute; but even the renowned vineyards of the Rhine cannot surpass in beauty the purple confines of the Kyles.

On the other side of the island, which narrows at this point, lies Ettrick Bay – surely a wonderful bay – with its long stretch of smooth, yellow sand, its flocks of sea-birds, and its uninterrupted view of the craggy Arran range. So little was this part frequented in our time that we often escaped thither to bathe from a low cluster of rocks, secure of such privacy as was denied us in our own waters.

We had a bathing box there, and a footpath through the grounds led to it direct; but though the box had a species of fastening, as had the little gate of the path, it was no infrequent occurence to find that the former had been used as a night lodging by trippers (with whom the place swarmed in July and August), and that others had invaded the premises behind, and bedded themselves in the long grass there. Sleepy and dirty, they would bounce out – or up – on our approach; and what could be said in answer to muttered excuses?

In our hearts we secretly felt for the marauders, who, after all, had done us no harm, and to whom the warm, still summer night under the stars must have been Elysium after stuffy workrooms and sweltering attics; and we never – I am glad to think of it now – we never were hard upon them, nor lodged complaints against them.

But we preferred Ettrick Bay – at any rate, while the 'Glasgow Week' lasted. We drove over in an Irish car – a recent importation, despatched by my eldest brother, who was quartered in Ireland – and a more excellent little conveyance for this purpose, as also for moorland use, could not have been imagined. It carried all the paraphernalia and got down over the sands to the very edge of the water. Then, if the tide suited for an afternoon dip, how heavenly it was! – the sun so hot above, the sea so salt beneath – (it rolled in straight from the Atlantic) – and there were anemones, purple and yellow and pink, to be found in the limpid depths of the rock-pools; and though there were no seals, as in Mull, there were cormorants and puffins and the long-winged tern darting hither and thither – while every now and again our ears would catch the sound of a dull thud, as a solan goose from Ailsa Craig, which had strayed thus far from its native place, spied its prey from a height, and swooped.

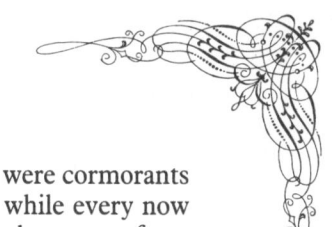

The mild climate of Bute, which fosters a luxuriance of vegetation similar to that of Devonshire and the south coast of England, was a new experience to us, as though it might be supposed that a similar wealth of foliage and blossom would be found in all the Hebridean islands, the fact remains that it is not so – doubtless the learned know why. Even in the days I write of, Bute was fast coming into favour as an all-the-year-round place of residence, and as my mother found it salubrious and attractive, and my father was delighted with the woodcock and snipe shooting, which he had never before enjoyed to a like extent, we remained at Kames during a great part of every winter.

This again was something fresh: we had not remained in the country for Christmas since the Blackhall days, and, truth to tell, at first the young among us did not take kindly to the prospect. But we were soon reconciled on finding that the greater part of our neighbours were stationary also, and there was no need to fear we should be left stranded. Indeed, the little island was always quite gay in a small way, and there was no regular social interregnum as in most parts of the Highlands.

Dancing was the order of the day – perhaps I should say of the night! Everyone danced, old or young. As we were a large party of ourselves, we often danced even when not reinforced by outsiders, and while the 'Baron's Hall' resounded to the 'ring of the piper's tunes,' humble folk from the little port close by, would steal up and plant themselves along the low terrace which ran round the tower, and was on a level with the windows.

We could see their faces, hear – although they did not suspect it – their voices; but it was quite customary in old Highland houses to admit members of the household to galleries and doorways when the gentry were amusing themselves; we did not mind the eager eyes of our friends outside, even if they were a little near the seat of action.

Reels and country dances are, it must be owned, better worth looking on at than their arbitrary supplanter of the ballroom, however much the waltz may be preferred by those taking part in it. Waltzing, indeed, we had; but it was usually kept for more ceremonious assemblies – and it may interest the curious on this point to know that the step we practised then, and the only step we knew, the 'Deux-temps,' is the very 'Two-step' of to-day; but in the 'Long Line Hoolachin,' the 'Triumph,' and other forgotten and forsaken but once glamorous romps, we had our chief delight, and our humble friends outside their spectacle.[61]

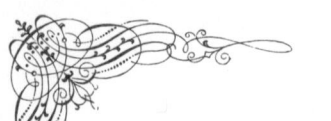

Our cousins, the Campbells of Stonefield, were also great dancers, and now that we had come to reside in their part of the world, there were constant summonses from one house to the other.

Stonefield was an ideal Highland home. Its gaiety, its boundless hospitality, its maintenance of old traditions on the part of the elders of the family, united to a readiness to march with the times on that of the younger, made it the perfection of a meeting-place for all.

The white-headed, ruddy-cheeked, keen-eyed laird – health, goodness, benevolence, stamped upon his countenance – was as a father to all the cadets of the house. They came to him from school for their holidays; from their ships, or regiments, later on. They were not bidden to come; they did not even ask themselves: they came. They were expected to appear. The keepers and watchers anticipated their arrival as regularly as that of 'The Twelfth.'

Nor was it in the handsome suite of brimming guest-chambers that they would be accommodated; no, they were *at home*; each had his own nook. Ah, if other heads of families would bethink themselves of what it is to young lads passed out into the world – and it may be a cold world – to be thus engrafted back into the parent stem when perchance their own branch of it has snapped, there would be many happier hearts in the world!

Old and enfeebled relatives were also an institution beneath that kindly roof. Some were nearly always to be found there, unobtrusively content within the mullioned recesses of the windows, or pottering at their own pace about the grounds. They, too, were *at home*. They crept hither and thither as the spirit moved them. The days slipped by; and, peacefully oblivious of time, they were never reminded of it by word or look.

For they had come to *stay*, it was shown that they were meant to stay; others might come and go, but like the brook, they went on for ever; and old age loves thus to snuggle down in the dear familiar haunts with memories. In such sunshine, outward and inward, collateral branches of the house of Stonefield could freely bask.

Yet were they not neglected – far from it. I have seen them on their frail old feet when the dance was forming, proud and pleased to be begged to join it. I have seen them conducted to seats of honour when weary, tenderly helped into the cosiest corner of the close carriage for church, made to drink the best claret. Albeit a young and thoughtless onlooker at life, I saw all this, and felt the beauty of it even then.

The Highland steamers which had played us so many scurvy tricks in the Mull days, were at it again now that we were once more within their grasp. As we went and came from Stonefield by water – (and there were also Southall, Knockdhu, and Glendaruel only thus to be reached) – it was often of vital importance to us that the *Iona* or *Mountaineer* should be 'on time' – and in the herring season, which was unluckily the Argyllshire visiting season also, they rarely, if ever, were so.

How could they be? Piers everywhere, large and small, would be choked with barrels, as well as blocked with cattle; and though the transference of them would be mainly accomplished by other vessels of the tramp order, in times of pressure, passenger traffic must of necessity be disorganised also. Herring ruled the roost when autumn set in.

Then what agonies did we undergo, waiting and waiting on Port-Bannatyne quay – our point of embarkation, the little port being close to Kames – and what succeeding ecstasies when, after many a hope deferred, the red funnels were actually and unmistakably there! Thud – thud, the paddles beat the water, and the dear, kind, good boat, to whom all was now forgiven, would throw out her gangways. Hurrah! we were on board – all was well.

Stonefield was our best goal – no place like it in our eyes. Up the Kyles there would be more herring, more cattle, and more interminable delays; every port humming, and every port bent on detaining us. Then pitch and toss round Ardlamont Point, and a wildish crossing to Tarbet Harbour; but that little seaport once in view, what relief, what joy! For there would be the carriage and the cart – how long soever they had waited, they were there, not gone, as the croakers among us loved to predict, but stationary as though time were of no account; and there would be the scarlet cloaks and pretty faces of our girl cousins, (the men were, of course, on the hills), and soon all was a tumultuous hubbub of welcome, and bursts of information, and thrills of anticipation – and – and – oh, they were *fine*, those old days! Don't suppose, you girls of to-day, that you have it all your own way, even though we did live in those prehistoric ages.

※

And on one occasion the recalcitrant *Iona*, of which we had so often to complain, did us a good turn.

This time we were departing from Stonefield, our merry three days' visit over; the last farewells had been said, and we were deposited bag and baggage at the little Tarbet Inn, there to await the return boat from Ardrishaig to Glasgow.

We had been begged to stay longer; but my parents were old-fashioned people, formal even with relations, and 'The rest day, the dressed day, and the pressed day' was enough for them; they were not to be moved either by the entreaties of their older hosts, who really wanted us, as an impromptu dance was in prospect, nor by the wistful looks of the younger. Here we were then, so far on our way.

'The boat will be late, sir,' Such was the announcement at Tarbet.

'Late? how late?' – was demanded.

'Oo, late. Jist late. Mebbe a guid bit late. She was late i' the byegaun.'

'Humph!' My father disappeared into the inn, frowning.

He did not relish the idea; but, after all, he had got away from the house. He had dismissed the coachman and horses, and no one could now, he thought, force him to put off the return journey. Here I must say that country-house visiting was at all times obnoxious to him; that he only went anywhere under pressure, and was out of his element under any roof but his own; so that the above indicated no ill-will towards kinsfolk for whom he had a very real affection, and against whom the utmost he could allege was that the bounding exuberance and effervescence of their fine, old, clannish house was less congenial to him as an older man than it would have been as a young one.

He now settled himself down to read the newspaper, and we girls sat in the windows, sunk in sad reflections.

Hours passed, and still there was no smoke above the headland, no sign of the approaching steamer, while the dusk of a November afternoon began to gather outside.

Suddenly we saw a sight. Not the loathed steamer – which, however, we could almost by this time have welcomed, so sickening was that weary watch, with nothing to hope for, – but the carriage – *the* carriage – descending the opposite hillside, and what could it be coming for but – us?

Someone, too, was inside, 'Stonefield' himself!

He was not to be gainsaid; he overruled all objections. What? Spend the night at this wretched place, when they were dying to have us? He was so kind, so cordial, so insistent – while my sister and I listened with beating hearts – that in the end his triumph – and ours – was complete. Fate was too much for even my parents' resolution. Our reappearance was hailed with enthusiasm, and we never afterwards cherished a rankle against the good steamer *Iona*.

We had our dull epochs at Kames. It was a cheerful place, and we were a cheerful party, but occasionally – let me narrate what once happened to intensify the dreariness of a certain dreary month.

A beautiful Japanese peacock, together with a couple of swans, a Nile duck, and some geese of sorts, had been presented to us by our friends the Keith-Murrays of Ochtertyre, who, having seen a piece of ornamental water lying fallow at Kames, kindly bethought them of furnishing it with occupants from theirs. The peacock was, of course, an extra; but he was a lordly creature and could trail about upon the bank, and we were delighted with such an addition to the party.

Not so the gardeners. It must be confessed that 'Joseph' – so named for his coat of many colours, – soon despising the water and the waterfowl, took his airings further and further afield, and complaints arose that he was 'ruining the kitchen garden.'

How often these were made I cannot say; but one fine morning we were greeted by the news that our beauty was no more, had been found defunct in a corner of the garden where he had no business to be. The head gardener, professedly grieving, pointed out that 'the poor bird' was in the habit of browsing on certain herbs grown there, and was sure that these had 'done for him.'

Not being learned in peacock lore, we accepted the suggestion for lack of another; but scarcely had we ceased to mourn for Joseph when the Nile duck followed suit with an equally sudden demise, and the Nile duck never went near the herb corner. M'Phail, however, framed a fresh solution of the problem, and again we had to be content.

But now more mysterious deaths occurred in rapid succession. A favourite cat, a rabbit, and at last – and this was the murderer's undoing – two valuable dogs, a pointer and a setter. He had poisoned them all.

What he might have gone on to poison, who can say? for on being discovered and arrested, he avowed that he had at first had no intention of killing anything but the 'nasty peacock,' but that, finding it 'no that deeficult,' he had proceeded to exterminate any creature that 'vexed him.'

And my father, albeit greatly chagrined at the loss of his good dogs, and horrified at the cool unconcern with which this wretch gratified his spite whenever it was provoked, was yet humane enough to intercede for a mitigation of his sentence when it was pronounced after the trial. 'A poor ignorant creature. I did not want him to get more than he would have done, because the Sheriff felt for me,' he said. Sheriff Orr was a fellow-sportsman, and sympathetic; he said afterwards that he had been much struck with this sense of justice and mercy combined.

Now, trivial and unimportant as the above may seem in the retrospect, what dwellers in country houses but know from experience how such an episode may fill every thought, if it happens at a time when nothing else is happening.

Such times, such flat, dull, eventless periods come to all, and usually, if not invariably, in bad weather. The old year is waning, or the new one has just begun, and except perhaps in hunting districts, where the sound of the horn and the hound cheer up the dismal landscape, there is a lack of outdoor interests as well as of indoor conviviality – a certain stagnation without and within.

The arrival of the post, especially the afternoon post, assumes the character of an event. And just because it does so, letters are few and uninteresting: if they contain any news at all, it is bad news – yet not bad news of an exciting and stimulating character.

That could be borne; yes, it could; for human nature is human nature, and something to talk about and think about would *be* something at any rate; but news of a disagreeable, disconcerting sort: an investment is not reported of very favourably, a suggestion is nipped in the bud, a promising young friend or relation is hardly fulfilling expectations – without being cut to the heart, the recipients of such intelligence feel that the gloom has deepened around them.

The front-door bell is never rung. Where is everybody gone? What has become of all the faces that were so familiar of late?

Perhaps, however, there is a peal – a loud clanging demand – and what music in the sound, what hurry-skurry to catch a peep over the banisters - what breathless straining of attention - what hopes, what fears, what sharpness of dismay as the door shuts, and there is no result!

The cruel servant – they are all alike, men and women – dallies in the hall, quite aware of the burning impatience which, for dignity's sake, cannot have vent. It is pleasant to him or her to feel that no one else has as yet the key to the mystery. Why not prolong the pleasure?

But, of course, in the end there is a would-be careless inquiry – a casual 'Who was that, John – or Mary' – and the truth has to come out.

Only someone come to the wrong house! Only some simpleton who has tricked and mocked its inmates! Deeper than ever the gloom falls.

>) (<

I have a distinct recollection of just such a season at Kames, and that, as drenching skies and stormy seas continued day after day to shut us in from the outer world, we had no distraction for our thoughts when the cruel M'Phail and his murderous propensities absorbed them. I may add that though the passed and the sun shone out again, the pretty duck-pond remained empty, for the swans flew away – flew out to sea – and, though twice recovered and brought back by fishermen, eventually settled, it was said, at a spot on the mainland, where there was a swannery – for they were seen in our bay no more.

Before all these catastrophes took place, however, and while yet Joseph and his brethren were flourishing, a letter received from a little middy who had been at Kames – and from whose home the above Joseph & Co. had come – afforded us some little amusement; and, having just unearthed it from among relics of those days, I cannot resist quoting its concluding sentence:

> 'Please give my love to all. To Joseph – to the gooseberries, to Auk, (the black retriever) to the Hawks, two Swans, one Nile Duck – to the other 18 ducks, to the ducks' eggs by the side of the Pond – to the broods of chickens, and to the stray Cocks and Hens – to the bent pocker and the dear Rat, and to the Family. – From your affectionate friend,
> *Archie Keith-Murray.*'

Why some of the favoured creatures are honoured by having capital letters to their names while others are not it is not for me to say; but I dimly recall that the 'bent pocker' refers to a certain poker which Master Archie had himself battered in the heat of battle – cause unknown – and which thereafter was elevated to be a cherished memory.

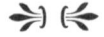

>) (<

We twice saw waterspouts[62] when at Kames; and on each occasion they were travelling rapidly between the south of Bute and the Isles of Cumbrae, where eventually each broke. I have had waterspouts pointed out to me since – in the Mediterranean and elsewhere; but they were nothing like the dark, whirling pillars that stood out so markedly and impressively against the foaming Firth of Clyde. And why each should have pursued precisely the same track, when they were visible at entirely different times, cannot be explained.

The Isles of Cumbrae lie within easy distance of the south of Bute, and when tempestuous weather is abroad, the bells which ring out for prayer from the college in Cumbrae, founded by our cousin, George Boyle,[63] (who afterwards succeeded his brother as Earl of Glasgow), can be distinctly heard. My mother, larger minded than some, loved to hear them.

Her feelings, however, were not shared by the humbler population of Bute, for when Mr Boyle, who was a truly pious man, stood for Parliament, he was widely objected to on the score of his religious opinions. A Port-Bannatyne elector grumbled that he was a *Fuchsia*. What a *Fuchsia* might be was a puzzle; but inquiry elicited that it stood for 'Puseyite'!

This was something to go upon; but again what did a simple, unlettered fisherman know about Puseyites?

The unlettered one hesitated, a shade uncertain as to what he really did mean. 'Come, on' quoth my father, encouragingly.

'Aweel,' rejoined Donald, turning his cap in his hands, 'aweel – I'm no saying – it's no *me* that says it; but' – with a burst of confidence – 'there's them that says the like o' they disna gang to the kirk'; and, whether from this cause or another, the *Fuchsia* failed to win the election, and it was believed that the Port-Bannatyne fisherman turned the scale against him. 'They ne'er thocht he micht hae a kirk o' his ain,' quoth Aiky, very superior.

If, however, the fisher folk were ignorant and prejudiced, if they stood out against a candidate they did not know and for whose repute they did not care, they could be fervently, almost passionately, loyal where it seemed to them that loyalty was due.

There was one among them, (their eyes would kindle as they spoke), if *he* would have gone to the poll, Port-Bannatyne would have gone with him to a man.

That was his house – they would point to a large, opulent-looking villa on the hillside. Those were his lodge gates – another impressive point of the finger. Then, with a final burst, and turning in another direction, and *that* was the bit cottage in which he was born.

We were then regaled with a little story – this happened at the beginning of our stay, while we were yet ignorant of the lie of the land, – and the story was to this

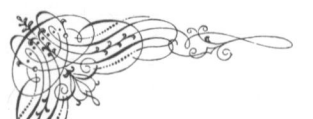

Dark whirling pillars stood out against the foaming Firth of Clyde / The Kylin Archive

effect: that some fifty years before there had been born among the people of the port, of village parents like themselves, a boy who by a stroke of good fortune had been raised high above their heads, but who, unlike so many others thus ascended, instead of shunning his native parts, where he was known to all and related to many, chose still to dwell in their midst, claiming them for his friends and kinsfolk – here the speaker would clear his throat, and mutter softly, but with a thrill in the tones, '*Weel may we be prood o' him – him that's no ashamed o' us.*'

If more were encouraged, more flowed apace. Mr Smith had done more for Port-Bannatyne than anyone had ever done before. No one knew *what* he had done – and given. He was in the front and at the back of everything – big things and small, public and private, high and low.

There wasn't a wedding or a christening, or a funeral that he wasn't there. Never too grand, or too busy – indeed, if away at the time, he would often come back on purpose

The bride, or the baby, that was of his blood, had a hundred-pound note from him – or leastways a note of some kind – it was all 'according' – and always more than could have been expected, or would have been thought of by anyone else.

The minister was forever at his door. *The* minister! All the ministers. His heart and hand opened every way.

As for the gentry, they were as 'daft' about him as the rest. There was his lordship: he couldn't keep away from Mr Smith, and get Mr Smith over to Mount Stuart he would by hook or crook. And there was – and a list of well-known names followed. 'They're a' his freens – a' his freens,' summed up our informant, waving an encircling arm.

But it was only after we ourselves became acquainted with the subject of this eulogium that it had any interest for us new-comers. He was absent for some time after we arrived at Kames, and, truth to tell, we were bored by the constant reiteration of his name, and the chanting of his praises. We felt inclined to say, 'Oh, do let Mr Smith alone!' when people of our own class began to join the chant. What was this unknown, uninteresting individual to us! He lived close by – but that was all.

It was impossible to idealise him. Imagination could not cast a halo over an elderly, commonplace personage, with a name that was hardly a name at all. When at length it was announced that the paragon was actually within our own drawing-room, it was difficult to get anybody to go down to him.

By this time I wonder if any reader of the above guesses why it has found its way into these pages? Mr Smith? Who was he, what was he, that his existence should not have been long since forgotten? Why should I seek to rekindle the ashes of the past? There he was – a short, stout, grey man, with nothing in his appearance or manner to arrest attention or call for comment – nothing except – ah, well, I have said it all elsewhere; and though it was some years before the idea arose of bringing *my* 'Mr Smith' before the world, the hero, if hero he can be called, of my first novel stood before me that summer day at Kames.

A letter I wrote at the time thus cavalierly disposed of him: 'The Port-Bannatyne swell has appeared at last. He is quite harmless – indeed rather nice. And Mama says his driving up in a solemn carriage and pair was in very good taste. She was sure it was meant for respect; but why he could not have stumped up on his own two legs, *I* can't think.' That was all – for the moment.

One by one, however, little things happened. Week by week our new neighbour grew upon us. We no longer needed to be hunted out and reluctantly driven downstairs when he called. When our father returned the calls, he was sorry if Mr Smith were out, had plenty to say about him if he were at home. When his first invitation to dinner arrived, there was a competition as to which of us young ones should go.

Aiky was invited by Mr Smith's housekeeper to 'see the table.' A brougham was sent for her, and, after tea with Mrs Sanderson in the functionary's private room, she returned brimful of news.

It was true that Mrs Sanderson was Mr Smith's sister, and the way she spoke of her brother it was 'just wonderful' to hear. Her husband was the butler. He waited behind his master's chair when there was company, but when alone they were one family and lived as such.

They both 'fair worshipped' Mr Smith – the brother-in-law as well as his wife could talk of nothing else.

But I must no longer linger over this congenial topic. As I have said, it did not at the time occupy such thoughts as I gave to literary effort, which were busy producing certain little sketches, afterwards to see the light in a small volume. Of these *Polly Spanker's Green Feather* and *Will Darling's Cross in Love* survive, though *The Merchant's Sermon* was the first to appear in print. All, however, were rigidly hidden from view while at Kames, and the brown albums which contained them were stowaways in the trunks, when we departed thence in the spring of the year 1866.

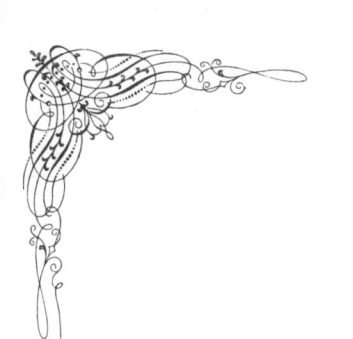

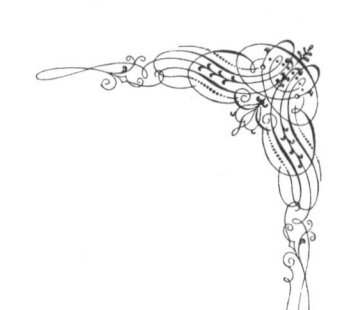

My Marriage

We were at Stonefield one day, when our host suddenly thus addressed my father: 'John, Ballimore is to let. How would it do for you? Let us go and have a look at it!'

No sooner said than done. A large rowing-boat was ordered out, and the tide being propitious, it took something under two hours for four sturdy boatmen to pull us across Loch Fyne in a long slant, when we landed in a small creek below Ballimore House.

No one being in residence there, it was not necessary to go as far as Otter Ferry and make a ceremonious entrance by the lower avenue, and accordingly we marched straight up from the shore by means of a steep, little footpath – how well we grew to know that path! – and, emerging from a belt of wood, found ourselves among grassy slopes surrounding a solid-looking, grey-stone mansion with a handsome portico.

A nice enough place, but still! Naturally it was not at its best, with shuttered windows and no signs of life about; and it had none of the fanciful charm of Kames, none of its historic associations.

On the other hand, it was pleasantly secluded among sheltering woods, and had all the appendages of a comfortable country house. The youthful brigade looked at their elders anxiously.

And the elders were critical, suspending judgement; finally, we started on a tour of inspection.

How long that tour seemed! – how endless the things we had to see! – how tiresome the numerous inquiries! how slow and halting the replies! Little we cared about stables and kennels, drain-pipes and water-pipes – all we cousins thought about was to escape being torn from each other when Kames should be given up; and as this was more than likely to happen, from my father's known taste for contrasting a new sporting-field with its predecessor, we were now on tender-hooks lest any fatal stumbling-block should arise to dash our hopes to the ground.

All, however, went well in the end. After a few more preliminary ups and downs, the usual three years' lease was signed, and we went down to begin our fresh Highland sojourn in the following July (1867).

It was rather later in the year than usual, but we had been in London for the season first. And here I may just remark that it must seem strange in these days that when a break so often occurred in our annual routine, it was never taken advantage of for foreign travel. The truth is that though there were plenty of adventurous spirits among the young ones of the family, no representations could prevail against the rooted disinclination of the higher powers to move aside from the path their feet had trodden for so many years.

It had become a rut, and they loved their rut. My father had never crossed the Channel – never would, and never did, to the end of his days. My mother, before her marriage, had once been taken the conventional, continental tour in the ponderous barouche (courier on the box, servants and luggage behind – every sort of pompous convenience and inconvenience, as aptly described by Thackeray in *The Newcomes*), and that once was enough for her. She would sometimes talk of her solitary experience, but never wished to repeat it.

And, of course, modern facilities were unknown and undreamt of in those days; and we were considered exceptionally lucky by our contemporaries in that we moved about as we did, while our yearly migrations south were always a source of envy. Very, very few of the Scottish gentry, however well able to afford it, took their families regularly across the Border, unless there were particular reasons for doing so, and certainly we should not have gone but for our English grandmother's forethought, and material aid – for, if I recollect aright, she always bore the full expense of the trip. She was a very rich woman, my father only a second son, *et voilà tout!* Everything else then being out of the question, we went cheerfully down to Ballimore at the time appointed.

⊱ ⊰

It was July, as I have said – when the long, light summer evenings are at their longest and lightest; and for once a hard-and-fast rule of the house – that of never going out of doors after dinner – was set aside in consideration of a new kind of sport. This was fishing with hand-lines in the sea loch just below; and as it could be indulged in most successfully when the sun was declining, and as my father was as keen as the rest to try it, he pooh-poohed objections, and headed a procession down to the bay as soon as dinner was over. We still dined at half-past six, so had plenty of time before us.

All around a breathless landscape would be sunk in golden haze; the brown sails of the herring-trawlers would be stealing out from behind point and promontory to take up position whence they could begin their work directly darkness set in – (trawling was still illegal then), – the curlews would be crying, the gulls wading and chattering – all would be beauty and animation, and all would be more than appreciated from the fact that it was in a way a stolen joy.

Only in August, when our sportsmen were too late on the hill to admit of the terribly early dinner-hour being adhered to, were we ever free to wander forth at sunset – though I ought to add that we often, nay usually, had fine views from the windows of the drawing-room wherein we were expected to assemble. But at the time we could perhaps hardly be expected to see with my mother's eyes, and understand that she wished to inculcate habits of refinement, and feared our losing them if allowed to run about too wild during the impressionable days of our early youth.

These were over now – and we felt – but no matter. The law was there, fixed as that of the Medes and Persians, – and a temporary escape from it was all we could look for.

How delightful it was! Old Tom Currie, the fisherman, would be in waiting at the water side; and soon we were hanging over the fishing-bank, one boat vying with the other, and on good nights drawing in almost as fast as we threw out. Codling, whiting, flounders, and 'Goldies' were the usual take; but occasionally a strong, fighting nibble would send a shiver of excitement through the veins, only to be succeeded by ineffable disappointment and disgust as there presently rose to the surface at the end of the line a horrible dogfish, with something like a grin of defiance upon its ugly, cruel face.

Old Tom would then out with his knife. The dogfish was no use to us, but it should not be suffered to depart in peace and go on working its wicked will below.

'Here's the last o'ye, ma freen,' the old man would mutter viciously, ripping up his 'freen's' belly as he spoke, – 'ye'll no eat nae mair o' better folks' food'; and a second twist of the knife would take off the head – after which plop would go the corpse overboard. 'A lesson to the ithers,' – Tom would nod, returning the instrument of vengeance to his pocket, and seizing his discarded line again.

We soon shared his hatred of the dogfish. There was an indescribable ferocity and intelligence in its loathsome countenance, which made it hardly seem that of a fish at all; and great was our amazement when one day my eldest brother, who had an original and independent mind, refused to allow an unusually large 'freen' to be flung back defunct into its native element, alleging that he saw no reason why the flesh, properly cooked, should not be good to eat.

Accordingly he himself bore it to the kitchen, and presided over the cooking – which, I believe, resembled that accorded eels. First it was parboiled, then boned, cut in slices, and fried; after which the self-constituted chef triumphantly awaited its appearance in the dining-room.

To please him, I, who admired everything he did, took a helping on my plate, and swallowed a mouthful.

It was eatable. Eatable – that was all that could be said. On a sudden a remembrance of the horrid, grinning, intelligent face came over me, causing such a revulsion of feeling, that what disastrous effects a second attempt might have met with, history sayeth not, for my good brother carried away my plate – and his own!

At another hour of the day, and when the sun was shining in his strength, we had another kind of sea-sport – namely, that of flounder-spearing.

The bay at Ballimore abounded – abounds still – in large red-spotted flounders, locally termed 'dabs,' which in the autumn months, when they reach their maturity, often turn the scale of a weighing-machine at three or even four pounds apiece.

These frequent the flat, sandy bottom of the bay, skimming from one spot to another so lightly as to pass just under the surface of the sand, their eyes alone protruding above. Thus a sandy shape alone is seen.

The tide must be low, and the water absolutely still, for the spearman to have his best chance – nay, even then he can only hope for success by approaching with the utmost caution, no oars being used. He stands in the bow of the boat, his long pole with its barbed spear in his hands, elevated at an angle whence it will strike the water slantwise, when the right moment arrives – and he is propelled by a confederate, gently pushing from the stern.

Even the shadow of the oncoming boat will sometimes alarm the timid flounder, which then darts from its retirement, raising a sandy dust that obliterates its movements for the time being, and it has to be sought for anew. If the direction has been noted, however, this is not a difficult quest, as it seldom flits far before settling again.

We will now suppose that it is lying still; the spearman spies it, and lifts an indicating finger – he never speaks – and the boat sidles noiselessly in the required direction.

Down comes the death weapon – *well* down, just behind the eyes if possible – and up it comes with the flapping, twisting, brown-and-white flounder firmly attached, the barb on the spear preventing its dropping off when lifted out of the water.

Once acquired, the art of flounder-spearing is not easily lost. After a lapse of thirty years, I took a spear in my hand one day at Arrochar on Loch Long, to try if any remnants of ancient skill yet remained, and accounted for – as Jorrocks[64] hath it – the first five flounders we came across.

Yet again, in ten years after that, I had similar luck in the old Ballimore Bay. I may add that the flounders in the latter place had so increased in numbers that Major Macrae-Gilstrap, the present owner of the estate, draws them in with the scringe-net – a form of fishing not introduced there, though practised in other places, at the time I write of.

※

And the oyster bed, which was so prolific (in a small amateur way) during our sojourn on Loch Fyne, has now disappeared. To us it was a source of endless pleasure; and as it was not of sufficient importance to attract the notice of authorities, we had the whole fun of the fair to ourselves.

In the same sunny bay frequented by the flounders, oysters peacefully rocked to and fro with every motion of the water, and were easily to be discerned at low tide. As they never troubled to detach themselves from rock or shingle, even when laid bare, we often collected two or three dozen without going beyond the water's edge; but if, more adventurous, we waded in, or, more luxurious, dredged with a hand-net over the boat-side, the catch was proportionately greater.

As, however, this sport was precarious, we presently constructed on the shore a small enclosure below high-water mark, and deposited therein a consignment of captive oysters, which could be drawn upon at need – and there are some who yet remember the oyster suppers with which the dancing evenings closed at Ballimore in those merry days.

Of course, the Stonefield party often came over; and on one occasion our old Aiky exclaimed, shading her eyes as a boat shot round the point: 'Eh, see – thonders the wee bishop wi' them the day!' and there was the then Bishop of Bangor (Stonefield's younger brother), a 'wee' man, it is true, but sturdy, pulling his oar with the best. Although no longer young, he had not forgotten how to row on a Highland loch.

The Ordes of Kilmorey also came to us by boat, and we went to them – and whatever Kilmorey may be now, it was a curious place full of surprises and oddities in the time of the well-known old Sir John.[65]

One of these, the first to be encountered, was of a somewhat alarming character. Supposing you drove up to the entrance gates, you did not pause to have them opened in the usual fashion – you might wait long enough if you did; your horses were expected to dash straight ahead, when the gates sank of themselves out of sight! By some ingenious, mechanical contrivance, the horses' hoofs, striking a sheet of metal stretched across the road, effected this result; and as soon as the carriage had passed through, the gates, again without any extraneous aid, resumed their normal position. What would have happened had the machinery gone wrong, as machinery has a happy knack of doing, was a constant source of speculation; but I must own we never heard of any accident. In the house every door had its own mode of opening peculiar to itself, while the windows resembled the portholes of a ship.

The whimsical Sir John had also a taste of his own in the matter of his driving apparatus. Having been a sailor in his youth, he had naturally a high opinion of *ropes*, and testified to this by using them in lieu of harness – so that a familiar sight upon the roads would be that of the jolly baronet perched aloft on a vehicle of unique construction (at one time I believe the seats for himself and his attendant were nothing more nor less than a couple of *saddles*, on which they rode as if on horseback; but I never saw this, so can only speak from hearsay). What I did see many a time and oft was our eccentric neighbour driving tandem with harness composed entirely of ropes, and flourishing a whip like no other whip ever seen before or since.

To this may be added that he invariably drove at a breakneck pace, and bawled salutations right and left as he passed through Ardrishaig, or any frequented place.

Of course, strangers and tourists stared delightedly; while the aborigines, with whom their original neighbour was popular enough, readily answered questions and supplied information – esteeming, indeed, a sight of Sir John and his queer turnout one of the assets of the place – a fact of which he was fully aware, and did not in the least resent. He seldom failed to put in an appearance when the midday boat from Glasgow brought its complement of passengers to the entrance of the Crinan Canal, *en route* for the north – and as often as not, would be there again to meet the returning freight discharged by the small canal steamer. He had many friends, and was continually being hailed on both occasions.

We, on the other and lonelier side of Loch Fyne, had no such daily excitement as that provided by these comings and goings over the way. We were 'out of it' at Ballimore – could not have been more completely disregarded by the main stream of traffic if we had been a hundred miles off; and I fancy that my mother at least had hardly realised, on going to this species of backwater, what it would be to have no landing-stage nearer than Tigh-na-Bruaich, fourteen miles off, and no drivable road except the one up the loch side.

A pier at Otter Ferry has since been built, which would have made a vast difference to us; but as it was, we had to do without it, and my poor mother to get over the hills as best she could in the Irish car.

She also lamented the 'sailless sea' beneath her windows, which really was singularly devoid of life in those days; and I think we all felt a little stranded and isolated when the 'red and sere' leaf of November began to drop from the trees, and the steady drizzle of the west to shut out the landscape on every side.

Nobody could then get at us, and we could get at nobody in an easy, informal way. Every kind of neighbourly intercourse could only be brought about by effort and premeditation, and even those were continually being thwarted by untoward conditions. Neighbours there were in abundance: Campbells to right of us, Campbells to left of us – (it was something to have a name of our own amidst the bewildering numbers who could alone be distinguished by their territorial designations); but of what good were they on the other side of a stormy loch?

On our own side we had only one family within hail, consisting of a retired physician and his son and daughter; and we liked the Nicols of Ardmarnock very much. But Dr Nicol was an old man, his daughter delicate, and his son often away – add to which Ardmarnock, a nice, cosy, little place, was between seven and eight miles off. Seven or eight miles of a rough-and-tumble hill road is a considerable barrier.

We met regularly once a week, however, at church on Sundays – Kilfinan Church was almost exactly midway between us – and it will be admitted that we all contrived to turn that weekly meeting to good account. The Nicols had a lobster fishery; we, our oyster bed. On Sundays, while their masters and mistresses were attending to their devotions within the little whitewashed kirk, or chatting in the kirkyard without, their servants on both sides effected an exchange of sundry hampers, with the result that presently each party trotted merrily home with a treat for the Sunday evening supper.

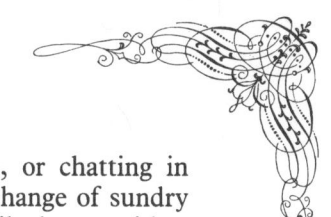

Occasionally, too, we dined and slept at Ardmarnock, and Ardmarnock did the like at Ballimore. How odd it sounds! Nowadays motors fly between – backwards and forwards, several times a day, if desired. No one thinks of consulting the state of the roads or the sky, or is tethered and hindered and bothered in a hundred ways as we of a bygone generation were; they jeer at our primeval torments, – ah, but the oysters are gone, and I rather think the lobsters are too!

❧ ☙

No post arrived at Ballimore till five o'clock in the afternoon – and, to be candid, it was rather wonderful that it should have arrived safely even then. Old Posty was blind of an eye, lame of a leg, and bereft of an arm – having been blown up in a powder-mill – and obtained the situation in consequence. Not only was he entrusted with our leather bag, but with the entire mail of Otter Ferry; and not only did he contrive to satisfy Otter Ferry as to his capabilities, but wooed and won a damsel there, and made her his wife. We were told she married him for an 'establishment;' but whether or not, the union proved a good business arrangement, since when the poor man could no longer hirple along, Meg succeeded to his place. This was not, however, in our day.

There was a recess in the hall to which the post-bag was brought while tea was going on – we had advanced to afternoon tea by this time, – and though I suppose no one would be willing to go back to that solitary mail-delivery at that late hour of the day, it had a certain charm. Leisure and tranquillity prevailed; no one was on the rush, eager only to know if there were anything for him or her personally – snatching up what there was, stuffing it out of sight on the way to the door, and forgetting all about it when next met: contrariwise, at the Ballimore tea-table, every letter, every circular, every bill or receipt, had its full value meted out to it.

Not always desirable, you say? Well, no, I cannot allege that it always was; there were occasional awkward moments, uncommonly awkward moments, as to which a veil had best be drawn; but, in general, the jumble of the bag, stuffed to overflowing as it often was, played a beneficient part. We were furthermore a harmonious family party, and one would always screen another at a pinch.

So that I really think that quaint postal hour grew to be liked among us, and that we missed it when returning to civilisation, like the Vizier of Morocco. (Perhaps my readers may not have heard of that dignitary's tribute to his own country after a stay in London for the last Queen's Jubilee? Impressed, as he avowed himself, by all he saw, he wound up by affirming that though England was a very fine country and London a very fine city, he was not sorry to be going back to *civilisation*).

One great source of pleasure we had at Ballimore, the library. Everybody could find books in it to read – not merely to possess and look at. Of these last, indeed, there was a fair proportion; but of course we young people let them severely alone, and ransacked the more inviting shelves.

My mother, who was both a reader and a thinker, was in the habit of recommending each of her daughters as she emerged from the schoolroom and could call her time more or less her own, to sit down every morning directly after breakfast, when the mind is clear and vigorous, for an hour or so's study of some classic author. She did not select the author, nor any particular subject – which I take to have been the secret of her success in this matter.

Naturally, we had all different likings and dislikings; naturally, too, we were not all students. Yet I know that even those who have not since applied themselves with any remarkable assiduity to the pursuit of knowledge, read *then*, and for myself I can never aver that what I read then has been a gain to me in all after life. One hour's solid reading a day does not sound a very severe strain on mental energy; yet steadily adhered to, week in, week out, it does amount to *something* – it must leave *some* mark; I would fain commend the practice to those who have not tried it.

There was also a quiet period towards the close of the day, which at Ballimore began to be with me a reading-time – either by the side of the shaded lamp in winter, or by the mellow light of the sinking sun in summer. At that hour the old library was deserted by its usual occupants, and one of my sisters, who was a musician, was apt to resort thither to play and sing, untrammelled by an audience – at what time I also would steal in by another door, and sink into a deep armchair unnoticed.

But it was not tough old Gibbon[66] or Rollin[67] that invaded those peaceful moments. They had been fairly dealt with, and now – shall I confess it? – I was making acquaintance for the first time with a writer who was to exercise an abiding influence over all my own future efforts. *Pride and Prejudice* and its fellows had hitherto been unknown to me.

How delightful I found them! How quickly each well-defined and exquisitely worked-out character impressed its image on my mind! How vivid were the scenes – how irresistible the humour – how natural and lifelike the whole panorama! In short, I had reached the best age for appreciating Jane Austen's wonderful studies of still life, and when my devouring of them and quoting from them – for how could I hold my tongue? – presently provoked some good-natured ridicule, was there not a ready retort? Had not the great Macaulay himself said he esteemed it a test of a person's capacity, whether or no he could appreciate Miss Austen?

Bulwer Lytton's novels were also to me pastures new; but Bulwer Lytton[68] was too prolix, too grandiloquent, and wrote too much of a world I knew little about, to be easily assimilated, while few of his characters, to my view, breathed the breath of life. This may have proceeded from the audacity of youth and ignorance; still, the subsequent neglect of an author at one time widely read would seem to endorse it; certainly it is not generally considered that *My Novel*, admirable of its kind though it be, is a book for all time, while the rest – where are they? However, I could read them at Ballimore, and in a manner enjoy them.

I also found a number of old sporting books, of which I was then – and am still – very fond;[69] Scrope's *Days of Salmon-Fishing*, Scrope's *Days of Deer-Stalking*, *Colonel Thornton's Sporting Tour*, and a most thrilling narrative by a big-game hunter (name unknown), *Tales of an Old Shikari*, were among my special favourites, one chapter of the last, yclept, 'The Man-Eater,' being conned almost by heart!

Added to these, were shelves of poetry and the drama, all of which had their turn, Sheridan's plays – tell it not in Gath! – appealing to me more than Shakespeare's, for I enjoyed the smartness, the epigrammatic piquancy of the dialogue; and the charm of this and all the rest were enhanced by the quiet room, the reposeful chair, the pleasant sense of fatigue, (we were far afield most afternoons), and, above all, my sister's sweet voice singing in the distance. It was an ideal combination: I can see, I can hear, I can feel it now.

⁂

At this time, too, we were all much taken up with drawing in water-colours, the scenery around tempting the brush at every turn, and the spring succeeding our first term of residence at Ballimore I had two pictures in the Scottish Academy – or 'The Exhibition,' as it was called – one being hung upon the line. It was also noticed in the first review thus: 'Miss L Colquhoun's *Herring-boat becalmed in Mist* is very clever, though the mist is rather solid.'

We were sitting in our morning-room at 1 Royal Terrace, when my father appeared in the doorway with a newspaper – probably the *Scotsman* or *Courant* – in his hand. He waved it at me: 'Here! What d'ye say to that? A monkey like you! But I had a kind of feeling there would be a notice in this paper, and – '; but I heard no more.

Such a little thing to mean so much – a mere kindly word – yet how I treasured it! The previous day I had indeed had a great moment, when, armed with my own complimentary season-ticket, and escorted by my proud and pleased parents, I had found my way to the *Herring-boat* (what a long way off I saw it!); but its being included in the first notice filled my cup to the full!

Being so long ago, I may perhaps also add that a purchaser – we never heard who – desired to buy the little picture, but was promptly informed it was not for sale. My parents had old-fashioned notions on the subject.

For several successive years I exhibited; then stopped abruptly, a new world having opened; but it was the success of these endeavours in one direction which emboldened me to reveal attempts in another. To explain this we must return to Ballimore.

It may be remembered that no one as yet knew of, or at least took account of, any writing proclivities on my part. As we all more or less dabbled in album literature, it provoked no notice; but at last, at long last, the desire came to confide my secret to one – that one from whom I could hope for most sympathy and also for best judgement, my mother.

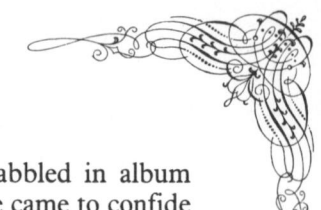

It was a great step; one to cause infinite trembling and shrinking; but an opportunity suddenly offered itself, and, scarcely daring to breath, I approached her sofa – from behind. I could not look at her. Over her shoulder I put the brown albums into her hand, and, after a brief and stammering explanation, fled.

But now she had them! She had in the kindest manner promised to read them, and to read by herself, and tell me the result – by ourselves.

All the remainder of that day I was in ferment. I wandered about alone (for the rest of the party were off on a long expedition), and, while hoping and longing to be sent for, could not summon up resolution to present myself unsolicited before the arbiter of my fate.

Accordingly, prepared for anything, I was as much non-plussed as the expectant Scrooge when no ghost appeared – I was unprepared for nothing, and it was 'nothing' that transpired. The others came home; the time passed as usual; night fell; and nothing had happened.

Next day it was the same. I hung about expectantly, anxious, fearful, and hopeful by turns; but again the hours went by, and bore no fruit. Suspense at length became intolerable, and, taking my courage in both hands, I made for the sofa once more – my mother was usually to be found there – and broached the awe-inspiring subject.

And now I am almost afraid to write it, lest I misrepresent that dear parent who was ever so affectionate and sympathetic; but truth will out – she had forgotten the brown albums altogether! There they lay – my heart thumped at the sight of them – beneath her pillow, where they had slipped unobserved after the first interview, and where no doubt the housemaids had replaced them, presuming it a selected hiding-place.

Ah, well, I had no cause thenceforth to complain. Her contrition and self-reproach were far, far beyond what was warranted by so trifling an offence, which she was now all eagerness to atone for. Once again I left the albums, and retired. She was to read them at once – *at once*: what could I wish for more?

I had yet to learn what. The promise was kept, but it was not plain sailing even then. My poor mother, now full of the subject, and eager to discuss it further, laid down the books by her side, awaiting my reappearance; and as luck would have it, there they were, staring not only me in the face, but a bevy of others who entered at the same moment by another door! In an agony I whipped them out of sight, feeling sure I was betrayed at last; but at last my dear accomplice understood. Thenceforth she and I were bound together by a new tie, and, her interest being now fully aroused, we had many and delightful confabs upon the subject.

She praised, but with discrimination; she stimulated me to further effort; she

'My husband', a pencil drawing by Mrs Walford
The Kylin Archive

pointed out wherein I failed; and when I had done my best to profit by her criticisms, she went beyond my hopes, for of her own accord she put one which she considered the most suitable of the little tales, into the hands of her old friend, Sir James Simpson, whom she knew to be on intimate terms with an editor of repute. His reply was immediate. He had handed the MS. over to Dr Blaikie with a request that he would read it *soon*.

And soon came another note. Dr Blaikie had accepted *The Merchant's Sermon* for the *Sunday Magazine*. Need I say how happy we both were?

About six months elapsed; then came the proofs, and in May of the following year I first appeared in print.

But another event of still greater significance to me was just about to happen. This first literary venture, upon which so many thoughts had erst been fixed, did not create quite a stir in the household, or even within my own heart, as it would have done at another time. It was a day's wonder, and quickly passed. For why, I was on the eve of my wedding!

We were in the third and last year of our Ballimore tenancy (and wintering in the Isle of Wight, where we had a sort of swallow's nest house on the Undercliff) when I became engaged to Mr Alfred Saunders Walford, and the marriage took place within a few months – namely, on the 23rd of June 1869, at St John's Episcopal Church, Edinburgh.

As, however, my husband and I gladly gave my parents the same promise that had been given by them on their wedding-day, there was no very stringent severance on my part from the old Scottish home, for every year found me there, wherever it was, accompanied by one welcomed and beloved by all.

I can, therefore, continue to write of it as before.

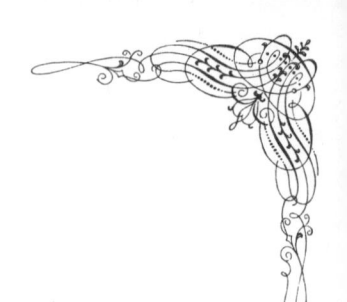

Wanted: A Hero

My father had now been for six years without any salmon-fishing of his own, and an occasional cast over strange waters did not satisfy him. He looked about, and pitched upon Kirkhill, near Girvan, in Ayrshire, as his next country home – though not sufficiently enamoured of it to sign a lease for more than two years.

Although there was good, mixed, low-country shooting, more easy of access than that of Kames or Ballimore, it was the river that was the real attraction. Despite its hideous name, good sport might be expected on the Stinchar, for the fish therein ran to a considerable size, as was presently attested, for my second brother, after playing one for four hours, landed him, and he turned the scale at thirty-one pounds.

When it is added that the noble fellow was only hooked through the back fin, and played on a single gut, it will be seen that this was something of a feat. He was stuffed, with the hook still firmly embedded in the fin, and is now in the museum which was lately tranferred from 1 Royal Terrace to Rossdhu.

A salmon of twenty-eight pounds weight was afterwards caught by another brother in the same water, and the size of all the fish caught whilst we were at Kirkhill was far above the average. The Stinchar therefore did its part.

But the surroundings of our new abode seemed to us dull and tame and after the fine scenery we had long been accustomed to. Ayrshire may be a pretty county. Burns, we know, has sung its praises – but it does not do after the Sound of Mull and the Kyles of Bute. Even the coastline, whose rugged beauty no one can deny, cannot atone to those dwelling inland for lack of purple moor and craggy height – and we were two miles from the nearest sea point.

Moreover, Kirkhill itself was a poor little house, on the edge of a poor little village. The only thing really to be admired about it was the ruined castle within its precincts, and the other ruined castles, gaunt and grim, which dotted the neighbourhood.

These were striking as foregrounds, but where was the background? No folding, fading mountain-range – no stretch of gleaming water; all was cheerful, pastoral cultivation: even Tigg woods, frequented by the roe-deer, although of interest to our sportsmen, added nothing to the landscape.

There were, however, pleasant neighbours at Pinmore, Knockdolian, and Daljarrock; also my mother enjoyed the many and varied drives about the countryside after her enforced abstinence from these at Ballimore. But we never really settled down at Kirkhill. There was always a feeling of being only there for a time, awaiting developments, and this sense of unrest was fostered by the shorter term of tenancy.

Who does not know what it is to have an hour taken off the end of the day – say by dining earlier than usual – and being conscious of it through all that day's varied stages? It may not really in the least affect other doings – it may be quite immaterial as regards *some* at least; but it begets a sensation of hurry and abbreviation. There is something to be remembered which is forever being remembered – and again forgotten. This has a disturbing effect. We experienced something of the kind when having a two instead of three years' lease, and no desire to extend it.

As I have so little to say about Kirkhill, therefore, I may perhaps be pardoned for narrating what was going on in my own little world, during the last part of my parents' stay there.

Two years had passed since the magazine story, *The Merchant's Sermon*, found its way into the pages of the *Sunday Magazine*; and it had not been followed by any fresh literary attempts, though it and a few of the other contents of the brown albums had been incorporated in a small, a very small volume, brought out by an Edinburgh publisher, whose name need not be given.

This venture was a mistake. The little book was unnoticed – though all its contents were subsequently republished separately, and did well; but as a matter of remark, I would caution all young writers against making a first appearance in too modest a form. For better or worse, strike boldly, if you strike at all. A feeble, hesitating bid for public favour rarely meets with any response, as I found to my cost, when instead of my poor little volume bringing me in either money or reputation, there was a loss of nineteen pounds over it, which I had to make good, having foolishly published at my own expense.

Such an experience was mortifying enough; vexed and ashamed, I resolved never again to run a risk of the kind; and what other resolution might also have been formed, or nearly formed in the first moment of dismay, may be guessed. Fate, however, intervened.

I was now far away from the Scottish home during the autumn months, which, with their sombre skies and misty landscapes, had always been those chiefly to arouse imagination and invention, and as my husband was obliged to be absent for the greater part of each day, I had much time to myself.

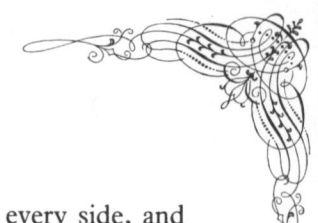

Soon the old desires began to be at work again.

In solitary rambles a new world began to spring into being on every side, and its denizens talked with each other, as it were, over my head. These ghostly companions were often very funny, and I had to laugh aloud, though outwardly alone.

And then a great deal in my new mode of life offered a remarkable contrast to that left behind. My eyes were being constantly opened afresh – as was natural, considering how very limited my range of vision had hitherto been. I now came into contact, easy, sociable, contact, with all sorts and conditions of men and women; and habits and ways of thought revealed themselves of which I had had no previous experience. I was forever being surprised, interested, amused.

It was, therefore, hardly to be wondered at that, instead of recurring to what was familiar – too familiar at the time to impress itself with any vividness on the brain, – I should wash in upon the canvas a picture in all respects different from those supplied by memory, when unable longer to resist the renewed promptings from within.

Write I must – but what? Subjects teemed on every side; but I needed a central figure, and a plot, – and scarcely had this conclusion been arrived at ere the former at least was forthcoming. The central figure was to be the hero of the humble Bute fishermen – later, our own dear and honoured friend, Mr Smith.

It was a mild November afternoon, and I was wandering happily about the Cheshire lanes, pilfering ferns and ivy from the hedgerows as I went along – when all at once the first idea of *Mr Smith* – the book – arose.

That morning had come tidings of the real Mr Smith's death; and, with the inclination we all feel to recall on such occasions whatever we have known of an endearing nature in the friend thus lost to earth, I had been dwelling on his goodness, his kindness, his pleasantness – on the mingling of strength and sweetness, of nobility and simplicity, which made him at once reverenced and beloved; on his beautiful everyday life, so unconscious of any virtue in itself – in short, on all that made this man apart from other men.

Musing and pondering thus, I was turning homewards when a question flashed before my mind. Would it be possible to make a hero out of this 'short, stout, grey man' who was externally nothing, internally everything? Could anything of a romance be constructed around such an unromantic figure? His personality might be all that I and others knew it to be; but could I depict it – could I make anything of it?

I feared and doubted; and, stumbling home in the dusk, continued the inward debate with ever-increasing fervour – inclination pointing one way; prudence, the other – till, hastily pushing aside the tea-tray over which the battle had finally raged, I spread in its place a sheet of foolscap, wrote down the name, and almost without a pause covered both sides.

Before dinner-time a large portion of the opening chapter of *Mr Smith: A part of His Life*, almost precisely as it now stands, was written.

My husband alone knew of this: I did not even confide in my home people till the book was complete – and this was not for about nine months.

The useful typewriter not being at that time in existence, the manuscript, written and re-written, corrected and revised, had to be transcribed for the press – if it were ever to reach the press – entirely by my own hand; and, as I never hesitated to write a whole page afresh, if there were more than a very few erasures in it, it took me six weeks to do this alone, writing at the rate of four or five hours a day.

And here again, I must digress for a moment. It has been my lot many a time and oft to be asked by a young aspirant in the fields of literature to look at a first effort, submitted in terms humble enough; but when, deluded by mock modesty – for such it proved to be – I have suggested amendments and pointed out defects, concluding by a recommendation, couched delicately, to recast or, at any rate, to rewrite the whole, I have been met by such thinly veiled vexation and amazement as betrayed the would-be author's real estimate of him or herself.

He or she really cannot 'worry' more over the 'horrid thing.' It has cost 'drudgery' enough to make it what it is – etc., etc. Reproachful and indignant looks accompany the outburst. Finally, the 'horrid thing' disappears, to be seen no more.

When such is the case, be very sure it is no loss to the world. To the youthful beginner, the task – if task it can be called – of correcting and revising should be one of pure joy. The pen should be loth to quit the page, should hang fondly over every paragraph, pause over every word which, however good, might be altered for the better.

Nor should the sheet be laid aside till it shows fair and clear to the reader's eye, and is no blurred and blotted mass, to be deciphered with doubt and difficulty. How can an editor or publisher judge the effect of a scene or dialogue which he can barely comprehend, because conveyed in an illegible scrawl, with half the words perchance scored out and reinstated?

This may, indeed, be all very well when the author's name and the quality of his or her work is established; if such as one likes to send in the scribbled foolscap full of erasures, or if, as is probably the case, it has become a necessity to do so through over-pressure, it is of small importance; but to those whose step is on the first rung of the ladder, suffer me, after thirty-seven years of busy authorship, to offer one word of counsel: Grudge no time, no strength, no trouble which you can by any means bestow upon the preparation of your work, before it passes from your hands into those of others. If the work be worth doing at all, every iota of pains thus taken will repay you a hundred, nay a thousandfold.

Long as it took to complete, the manuscript of *Mr Smith* was ready at last, and the secret of its existence confided to the two families most concerned. My father's first remark was uttered in some perplexity of spirit: 'If only your poor Aunt Catherine' (Miss Catherine Sinclair) 'were alive to tell us what to do with this!'

But she had been dead for some years, and, in default of any other experienced relation or friend to whom we could apply, we came to a bold decision. *The Moor and the Loch* had fared admirably in the hands of Mr John Blackwood,[70] that 'prince of editors and publishers'; and, albeit in some trepidation, we decided to submit to him the unknown bantling. We agreed, however, that in order not to put in him any awkward position should he regard it unfavourably, its authorship should be withheld.

And, indeed, I had already determined to appear before the world, if I appeared at all, under a pseudonym, and had written upon the title page of the novel, 'By L

Mr John Blackwood, publisher / The Kylin Archive

Wynn.' This was even printed before Mr Blackwood prevailed on me later to alter it, urging that the only reason he could ever see for concealment in such a case was when the author wished to write what he or she was ashamed of – 'and *that*,' he added, 'I am sure your father's daughter would never do.'

To return, Mr Blackwood received the MS., courteously acknowledged it, and we awaited the result with what patience we might.

Mine, I own, was exhausted at the end of five months, and having long before then returned to my southern home, I wrote to my father. He wrote to Mr Blackwood, and – and then followed a wonderful time.

I forget what explanation of the above negligence was given; all I recall was that in the kindest manner possible the celebrated publisher not only at once accepted *Mr Smith*, but predicted for it a great success. When I went north to join my own people in August, I took with me the first batch of proofs.

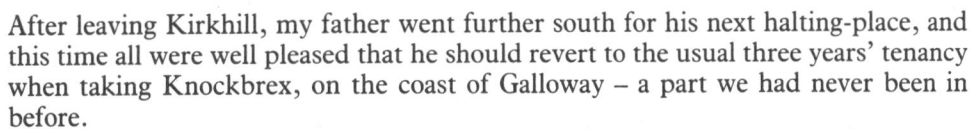

After leaving Kirkhill, my father went further south for his next halting-place, and this time all were well pleased that he should revert to the usual three years' tenancy when taking Knockbrex, on the coast of Galloway – a part we had never been in before.

The impression it made was delightful and instantaneous. We drove from Kirkhill along the banks of Loch Ryan, singing 'The Rover and Loch Ryan' as we went, slept that night at Stranraer – then unthought of as a point of embarkation for the north of Ireland, – and on the afternoon of the second day arrived at our destination.

Knockbrex was the dower-house of the Selkirk family, and, though unpretending, was very much the kind of house we liked. Every window had a view: on the one hand, of a wild and storm-beaten district, wooded after a fashion on the hillsides, with the hills rising into mountains beyond; while on the other was the famed Solway Firth, across which we could at times distinguish on the far horizon the faint outlines of the Isle of Man.

There were quicksands in the neighbourhood. There were also tales about them, sad enough to hear; but the rocky bay beneath Knockbrex and all the thundering shores between it and Kirkcudbright, were safe enough, the pools among them clear and teeming with life. We promised our mother to leave alone the 'shifting sands,' as they were locally called, and if another personage had done the same, it would have been the better for him.

This rash adventurer was a shark, whose end, however, was not due directly to the sands – among which he had been seen, doubtless tempted thither by curiosity – but to his entangling himself in the fishermen's nets at their entrance.

We had been only a few weeks resident at Knockbrex when this event took place; and, with the astuteness of the Scot, the captors – whose nets were ruined, torn to pieces by the rolling and plunging of the monster – made a handsome present of him to my father, whose hand in consequence had of course to be in his pocket, in a generous dole, which went some way towards making good their loss.

But what on earth was my poor father to do with such a gift? It would never do to seem to despise it, however he might see through the simple wiles which saddled him with such an incubus; he must think of some plan to please all parties. Accordingly he started to inspect the shark – we all did – as it lay on the shingle, the tattered nets shrouding it like a pall, and a happy idea struck him. He wrote an article for the *Times*; this was copied into the local paper; the fishermen were satisfied, and the shark was buried. We never heard of another's appearing in the same waters.

Curiously deformed and stunted were the little belts of trees around our new home. Flat as a table, the topmost boughs all bent one way, testifying to the power and persistency of the sea wind; and sometimes the entire roof, so to speak, would overhang the ground on one side with no support from beneath, while on the other would be the stem, bare and bent, holding it at arm's length. In autumn, however, these strange woods, forming a compact and ruddy mass, had a beauty of their own; and I, for one, greatly loved them.

And the piece of marshland between us and the sea, dotted with Galloway cattle, and haunted by snipe and wild-duck, was full of attraction. The mushrooms – I must tell a tale of those mushrooms. They were especially prolific everywhere during our first year at Knockbrex, and so covered the ground that at last we scarcely took the trouble of picking even fine ones, while others were of course beneath contempt. One morning our faithful Aiky, with a twinkle in her eye, met us in the hall as we emerged from the breakfast-room – Would we please look into the stable-yard?

As we always did 'please' to do whatever Aiky decreed, we followed her in a body straightway, and there was a sight indeed! A small cart, filled to its highest height with mushrooms! Mushrooms, not in baskets, not 'in' anything, simply stacked like hay, and overflowing like a hay-wagon!

The household, headed by a youthful butler and still more youthful footman, had risen at crack of dawn, harnessed our good little Alpin (the sole survivor of the Shelties we rode as children) to the light cart he now drew wood in, and, for sheer fun of the thing, brought in that vast army of mushrooms. I may add that a brew of ketchup resulted, which was not exhausted for many a long day.

※

There were beautiful country places in our new neighbourhood: Cally, Cardoness, Earlstone, and others further off; and as there were no fewer than three recently made brides among the various families, we came in for lively doings.

One evening we were dining with the Murray-Stewarts at Cally, and it was announced that next day there would be an impromptu otter-hunt, Captain Clark-Kennedy of Knockgray having suddenly arrived there with his pack of otter-hounds.

Of course everyone was eager to go, and the ladies as eager as the men. Accordingly we were bidden to return to Cally at breakfast with our hosts and adjured not to be later than 6.30 in making our appearance. The hour was ghastly; but we thought nothing of it – at least no one did but I, who alone of all the sisters happened to be at the old home at the moment. It was not only that it was nearly midnight before we returned home from the dinner-party, and all had gone to bed except the servant who let us in – but I had a shrewd suspicion that neither my mother nor Aiky would be best pleased with my turning out again so early and for such a purpose.

However, the four brothers (all of whom chanced to be at home together) combated the idea with such vigour that – oh, of course, it was all *their* doing, it was *they* who argued down misgivings and overcame scruples – it was not my own intense desire to go – oh, no. With the first glimmer of dawn one spectral figure summoned me to rise, another brought me his own cup of tea, for their wants could be attended to, though mine could not at such an hour – and, shivering 'twixt cold and excitement, I hurried on my war-paint.

Should we be overheard? Should we be stopped? But we were off; we left the still hushed and darkened house behind, and as the mists rose sullenly from the shadowy earth, we turned into the beautiful grounds of Cally.

Here all was bustle and preparation. A concourse of wild looking creatures was assembled in front of the house: keepers and boys holding together a cluster of yelping hounds, the gay little master flitting in and out amongst them, new arrivals appearing every moment from every quarter – the whole presenting a weird scene but dimly discerned beneath the pale, trembling light of the heavens overhead. This is what an otter-hunt looks like – before it begins.

As the sun rose over the hilltops, we started. I was the only representative of my sex to go. On hearing that no carriages could follow, every other feminine heart failed, but again the four brothers supported their doubtful and vacillating sister, and she went.

For hour after hour we walked, we ran, we flew this way, we flew the other, we followed the pack now on this bank of the stream, now on that; we consulted and separated, we met again and consulted again – and it was all in vain. It was high noon at last, and the otter, where was he? He had vanished off the face of the earth.

Splendid it was, the whole thing, as a romantic sight and a glorious chase; but evidently we were doomed to disappointment as regarded its primary object, and were resting dejectedly beneath a clump of trees overhanging the stream, debating the question of further pursuit or not, when all at once, within a few yards of us, a dark head rose to the surface of the water!

One wild halloo, one responsive yell, and in plunged the hounds; there was a fury of onslaught midstream, and *the death*!

No doubt this was a very ordinary otter-hunt, no doubt it was only because I had never taken part in one before that it impressed me so deeply; but, as it has always lived in my memory as one of the days of my life, I may be pardoned for recalling it. N.B. – Perhaps also for reproducing it in *Cousins*.

But when we had driven home, (carriages were waiting at a point a mile off,) and had lunched, and were about to depart to our various homes, I underwent an unexpected ordeal. In a lull in the conversation, a voice suddenly demanded the name of my forthcoming book. Now, although proofs of this were coming in daily, they were still, so to speak, contraband, and it had been by sheer accident that knowledge of them had leaked out; accordingly the easy interrogation, a mere piece of civility, stabbed like a knife.

The otter hunt, 'a concourse of wild-looking animals was assembled' / The Kylin Archive

I faltered forth, however, '*Mr Smith,*' and next moment could have bitten my tongue out. If only I had laughed aside the inquiry and held my peace!

For there ensued a dead silence – a silence that spoke – and it was accompanied by blank looks and forced smiles; not all the patter of politeness that followed could deceive me as to the real feelings of my auditors. They had never heard of any title so stupid, so meaningless, so uninteresting; for a full hour afterwards I hated it myself.

❧ ☙

We had another expedition that summer which was not one to be easily forgotten. My eldest brother, who, as has been said, had a mind always on the alert for anything of interest, had arrived at Knockbrex full of the wonders of a sea cave containing fossil remains said to be of great antiquity, of which he had heard as being in the neighbourhood.

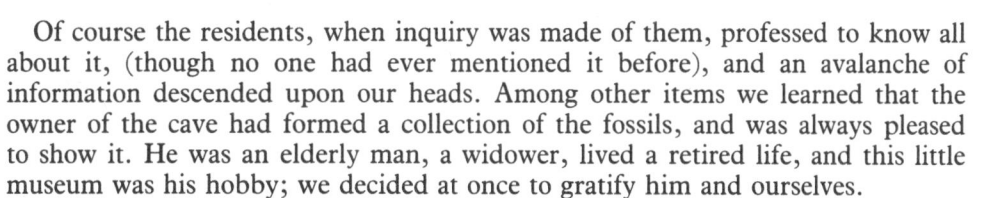

Of course the residents, when inquiry was made of them, professed to know all about it, (though no one had ever mentioned it before), and an avalanche of information descended upon our heads. Among other items we learned that the owner of the cave had formed a collection of the fossils, and was always pleased to show it. He was an elderly man, a widower, lived a retired life, and this little museum was his hobby; we decided at once to gratify him and ourselves.

Accordingly we chose a fine afternoon when there was a garden-party in the same direction, and started early in gala attire (why I mention this will presently appear), so as to have time for our investigations before putting in an appearance at Earlstone.

After a long drive we turned off the highroad and pursued our way along a somewhat rough and lonely track, which, however, was well scored by wheelmarks. Evidently the recluse had had plenty of visitors of late; we congratulated ourselves on following their example; the cave and its relics must be well worth seeing.

Still more convinced of this were we, when on approaching the house – a common little house, but no matter – our eyes beheld not one, nor two, but half-a-dozen carriages – real carriages, not gigs and carts – standing in the stable-yard. There must be an overflow, and the coach-house must be full; we were greatly impressed.

The front door flew open at our approach, and there was – or seemed to be – a hum of voices from within, while quite a small army of menservants stood about. It was all so cheerful, so festive, so different from what we had been led to expect, that we advanced gaily – my sister and I inwardly congratulating ourselves on having on smart new frocks for Lady Gordon's party, and our menfolk, I daresay, not sorry to be in their best kilts.

Conducted by a solemn and irreproachable butler, we filed across the hall into a room beyond that seemed to be cleared for company, only to find there a solitary occupant – one, moreover, who started from the depths of an armchair, and frankly looked frightened to death. Having hoped for a group of learned savants, or, better still, a detachment of lively Americans, lured thither by the same bait which had drawn ourselves, we conjectured that these might be actually now exploring the mysteries of the cave, and essayed a polite remark to the startled little man before us. He was a minister by his garb, so ought to have some response at command; but no – he merely breathed hard and shook his head.

At the same moment the door opened to admit another minister, then two more, and two more; finally, the room was full, yet no one greeted us, nor seemed concerned to entertain us. Where was our host? Why did he not appear?

If this were a Presbytery meeting, as we now surmised, the business was obviously over, and we had not voluntarily intruded; but whenever we endeavoured to explain this, we were met by a mumble in the throat and a shake of the head, while the blackcoats from time to time gazed helplessly at each other. What was to be done? The cave – the cave – if only they would let us go off to the cave. But a motion to that effect was promptly negatived. In fact I am not sure that some of our strange companions did not bar the door – and we were still at a deadlock when, at last, came the end.

A slight lad, solemn, bashful, and not without a touch of dignity in his bearing, stood before us. He also was apparently a minister; but we had no time to wonder afresh at this (combined with his extreme youth), for with one accord the whole body of others started forward, pointed at him, and exclaimed in melodramatic tones that would have done honour to the stage, '*This is the owner of the cave!*'

Grotesque as the scene was, we were mercifully withheld from laughter by an inkling of the truth – and what was the truth? The poor boy had just buried his father – it was the funeral 'ge we saw in the stable yard – the spruce servants were undertakers' men – the 'ministers' were mourners!

Now that the murder was out, and there was no longer any need of their help, the tongue-tied gentry were ready enough to be garrulous; but we could not forget their previous absurd behaviour, nor that of the idiot who let us in when we were so obviously a jarring note in the mournful procedure of the day. We fled indignantly and precipitately; nor did we once give way to mirth till far away and out of sight.

But we never saw the cave, then or thereafter. No one ever had the hardihood to risk a second attempt, when the first had met with such a fate.

In a bookshop at Kirkcudbright I found one day a curious volume, yclept *The Scottish Gallovidean Encyclopedia*. It was written in the year 1824, by a queer, clever, conceited 'buddy' – a 'buddy' of the worst type; but probably a superior personage would not have constructed half so good a book. It is a wonderful book. It is absolutely exhaustive. There is not a phrase, not an idiom, a custom, a superstition, a sentiment of the old 'Gallowa' country left out; one breathes the salt of the sea-foam, hears the booming of the caves, sees the shorn woods, the red moss, and the black cattle.

Ballads are also freely introduced; but, alas! they are nearly all by the would-be poet himself, and I fear are not to be commended. There is, however, an occasional shrewd touch, as in one on the parish of Borgue (ours for the time being):

> 'Borgue lads are fain to wed wi' lasses bonny,
> But scorn to look fra hame in search o' ony.'

Very nice of the Borgue lads, I'm sure; but the result is perhaps not all that could be wished: the Borgue lasses being about as uncomely as can be seen anywhere.

The poet goes on with fearless lack of connection:

> *'Wi' shore and caves whaur gurly wunds do blow,*
> *As by Nockbrax and ancient Carlines Co.'*

What the final 'Co' stands for it is not easy to conjecture; but 'Nockbrax' is certainly Knockbrex, and the then Lord Selkirk, who was our landlord, said he could remember it being spelt so.

Lord Selkirk was a character. A fine type of the old Scottish gentleman, well-bred and well-read, it nevertheless pleased him often to affect a homeliness of demeanour and shabbiness of dress – especially when tramping about on his own lands – which deceived strangers. Thus he had many adventures, which he loved, and as time passed he lived more and more his own quiet life at the beautiful St Mary's Isle, and settled more and more down into his homespuns.

One afternoon he passed our windows, making for the front door. 'There's old Posty,' cried I; for the Knockbrex postman was the counterpart of the Ballimore one, and unmistakable – or so I thought, – round of back, bent of head, and with a scuffle in his walk.

My father rose as I spoke. 'Old Posty? No; that's Lord Selkirk. And now I'll have to go in to him,' he added ruefully, 'for he's seen me. I caught his eye as he went by.' Otherwise he would have fled, as was his wont; he never could abide callers.

Nevertheless, he liked the old lord and rather enjoyed his company – as did I, his daughter; for subsequently he re-appeared in my novel, *The Matchmaker*, under the name of 'Lord Carnoustie.' Kind, friendly old gentleman, he has long been dead and left no descendants, so it can do no harm to confess this now.

'Lord Carnoustie' has been said to be taken from my uncle, Sir James Colquhoun – or, again, from my father; but this is not true. I never attempted to portray my uncle, and my father was, a I avow later on, the prototype of 'Sir John Manners' in *Cousins*.

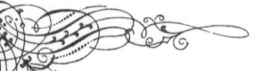

Lucy Walford, authoress of 'Mr Smith' / The Kylin Archive

Publication of 'Mr Smith'

Mr Smith was published on the 10th October 1874, and I question whether any youthful author ever experienced such a 'mingled scene of joy and woe' as I did over it.

One day I would be exalted to the heights, the next plunged into the depths; the warmest epistolary encomiums would arrive cheek-by-jowl with the most contemptuous disparagements. By turns I was joyful and downcast, elated and mortified. I never knew what to expect, nor how the wind would blow from any quarter.

Roughly speaking, however, on the one hand were Mr Blackwood, the critics, and the general public; on the other, the bulk of my relations, and a considerable number of new friends who fancied themselves or their belongings shown up in print. *Mr Smith* seemed, really seemed, to draw out all that was once kindest and cruellest in human nature.

Let me begin with the critics. They were almost unanimous in his favour – so much so that I felt genuinely surprised and quite a little hurt when a provincial paper of acknowledged high status observed that the new novel might be all very well if compressed into a one-part magazine story, but that it was 'made to meander with sickening prolixity through two mortal volumes.'

This made me feel very flat – *how* flat only a palpitating young beginner, moved by every breath of praise or blame, can realise; and perhaps I could not recount it so gaily even now, if twenty years later the same high-class weekly, when doling out laudation of a new novel with no niggardly pen, averred that 'with it all, nothing by Mrs Walford will ever come up in our estimation to our first friend, the incomparable *Mr Smith*.'

Little does the lordly reviewer think how a careless phrase, thrown off in a moment of peevishness or boredom, burns itself into the brain of the sensitive young author, – or, contrariwise, with what ecstasy he or she repeats to him or herself, the choice, discerning, altogether excellent paragraph, (no matter how long it be,) which is to guide the intelligence of their readers.

It was owing to the vast importance my husband and I attached to our reviews that we were enabled to 'tick off' the little slip narrated above; for was not every one of them carefully cut out and pasted into a book, to be read – I am not ashamed to say – over and over again? That early enthusiasm is not a thing to be sneered at. In the nature of things it does not last; review-albums ceased with us after my fourth book; but I fearlessly aver that any affectation of indifference to newspaper criticism has never been and never will be mine, and that it has often proved a source of instruction by which I have gladly profited.

As, however, 'Press Cutting Associations' either did not exist in the days of *Mr Smith* or did not come my way, it may be supposed that only a very small amount of the above reached me in my quiet country home – in fact, that I should only see as much of it in proportion to the whole as one sees of the iceberg whose true bulk is concealed beneath the water.

This was not so. Owing to the kindness of the Blackwoods, and the not invariable *kindness* of others, I really do not think any press notice of the slightest consequence was suffered to escape us; but, multifarious as they were, of one thing I am sure, we never knew who wrote them, and I mention this because the fact seemed very much to surprise a well-known man of letters to whom I told it some dozen years later.

It chanced that at one of Miss Jean Ingelow's literary dinner-parties[71] I was sitting by Sir Frederick Locker,[72] and the same day there had appeared in the *St James's Gazette* (of which Mr Greenwood was then editor) an article on novels signed by Coventry Patmore. It began thus:

Coventry Patmore, a distinguished reviewer / The Kylin Archive

'The wealth of this country in prose fiction is scarcely yet appreciated. The number of novels produced from the time of Walter Scott to the present day which are really works of art, and which deserve, and will probably obtain, a classical proportion, in literature, is surprisingly great; and the fact is curiously little recognised ... To call a book a "novel" is to stamp it at once with an ephemeral character in the minds of most readers; but it will probably be found that while by far the larger portion of the poetical and historical writing of the present century which is looked upon as "classical" will prove to be ephemeral, a large mass of that writing which is regarded as almost by nature transitory, will take its place in the rank of abiding fame with the fiction of Fielding and Goldsmith. No generation has known so well how to paint itself as our own ... Among living writers are two – one well, and one at present comparatively little known – whose work of this kind can scarcely be surpassed: namely, Thomas Hardy and L B Walford ...'

'You have seen Coventry Patmore's article in this evening's *St James's*? inquired Sir Frederick Locker; and, after a little more added, 'I suppose even if he had not signed it you would have known – or would soon have known who wrote it? Oh, really?' – as I disclaimed any such knowledge. 'But I thought – is it impertinent of me to say so? – but I certainly thought – I am sure Miss Ingelow has told me she generally knows something of her reviewers – reviewers of note, I mean.'

To this I had but one answer. Miss Ingelow lived in the literary world. Despite her modest, retiring nature, it sought her out and buzzed around her; I was different; I scarcely knew a writer, certainly not a reviewer. We discussed the subject in all its bearings, but I fear that even to the last he regarded me as a solitary exception to the rule.

※

Mr John Blackwood did not confine himself to sending me press notices of *Mr Smith*, however numerous these might be. Like a truly busy man, he had time for everything: he wrote often, and seldom without enclosing other letters – letters from friends whose opinions were worth having; while there was a warmth and generosity of feeling in his own tributes which touched me to the heart. I cannot write, I cannot think, of that kindest of men and wisest of counsellors without a glow of pride in the reflection that he thought me worthy the time and trouble thus bestowed.

And how gently, how delicately, did he hint at an amendment, with what diffidence suggest an alteration in the page! It would be – 'I am not altogether sure if your meaning is sufficiently intelligible here. Very likely it is my stupidity, but perhaps you would read it over and see what you think? If you decide to let it stand, please just do so.' Or, again – 'If it is not presumption in me to say so, the scene between the lovers might, I think, be amplified with advantage. It is so good that readers would like a little more of it.' Or, on the other hand – 'I have been thinking over your last chapter, and it occurs to me that though it seems a pity to cut it down, the interest at the point is so great that your excellent description of nature would probably be skipped by readers eager to know the *dénouement*.' Such gentle, deferential handling would have suggested rather the timid novice and the veteran *littérateur* than the old, experienced publisher and the raw recruit.

Some years after I had obtained a foothold in the writing world, it happened to me to receive back from a very well-known society, (too well known to be named here,) a manuscript, slashed on every page with a roystering blue pencil, which had obviously never hesitated for a moment on its murderous track. Alongside came a few bald lines, in which I was desired to send the story back when 'revised' – which, being interpreted, meant with all the spirit, all the 'vim' taken out of it – while even the very spelling and punctuation were not immune from free and fearless correction. John Blackwood would have died sooner than have sent the like.

I told him of it, and can see now his disgusted face. 'Impertinent fools! Never permit anyone to take such liberties with you, my dear young lady. And I do hope,' he added earnestly, 'you did not let them have the story? I *do hope* you didn't?'

I had not.

Let me tell, however, the experience of a fellow-sufferer who did. This was the Rev P B Power,[73] that most amusing and original of writers in his own line. Mr Power was an Irishman, and to his Irish wit was doubtless due the amazing popularity of his religious booklets, *The Oiled Feather*, etc. N.B. – My mother would order these by a hundred at a time, and scarce an evangelical family but read and distributed them.

Knowing, then, that he had his own particular world at his feet, it was delightfully interesting and entertaining to me to hear on one occasion of a 'rankle' against that very blue pencil which had raised the blue devil in me.

It appeared that my interlocutor had recently written a tale – and one could guess a racy tale – founded on a visit of a certain ultra-refined and courteous dignitary of the Church to a rough mining district where he had *un succès fou*. The miners were greatly struck by their fine friend, finally succumbed altogether to his gentle, persuasive demeanour, and thus summed up the situation:

'Us can stand up agin most things, that us can; but that bloke and his manners, he were too much for the likes o' we!'

'I named the story *That Bloke and his Manners*,' recounted Mr Power, 'and would you believe it' – here his eyes danced with mirth, – 'would you *iver* believe it,' (the Irish accent flew out), 'I got it back with a savage dash of that brute of a pencil through the words, and this on the margin – "We draw the line at 'Bloke'"!'

Not long after we had laughed together over this, I came on *The Man and his Manner* at a religious bookseller's; and while I thought of poor Mr Power with sympathy, I could not resist a certain self-gratulation in that I had not yielded as he had done, but taken my wares to another market, with orders to pay no heed to anything in blue!

⁂

While every post was bringing me in adulatory epistles, often from unknown or anonymous correspondents; while I grew almost sick of the very sight of a 'simple, noble Christian gentleman,' and was grateful if it were omitted, I was on the other hand suffering in no small degree from the attitude generally adopted by my mother's family towards *Mr Smith*.

The Colquhouns might take kindly to it: the Fuller-Maitlands did not. A few words first about the Colquhouns. My great-aunt Helen (one of those who danced a reel by moonlight on the top of Ben Lomond) being now, despite her age, above all things a woman of the world who swam with the tide, wrote, 'I hear you called a new Jane Austen on every side, and am congratulated every day on being the aunt of such a *genius*;' while my father's younger brother William, a man of leisure with clannish instincts, made it his business to hunt out press notices and collect opinions, which he freely passed on when they were laudatory – and probably they mostly were laudatory when said to his face. I had thus two adherents on that side of the house; but alas! I must own I did not greatly value the support of either. They would have supported anything done or written by one of the clan.

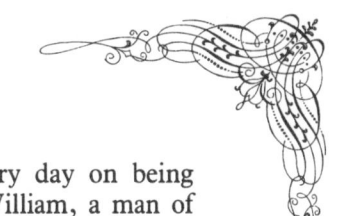

And the Colquhouns were few, and the Fuller-Maitlands many; and with all respect to my father's people, 'the English relations,' as we called them, were more intellectual than the hardy Highlanders. I looked forward to their verdict confidently. I sent copies to the heads of various houses. I pictured *Mr Smith* being read – read aloud perhaps – by uncles, aunts, and cousins; and as there were nearly forty of the latter on the other side of the Border, they formed an imposing phalanx.

Well! What the cousins said is of small consequence, since so thoroughly were we of that generation subservient to our elders, that a genuine opinion was hardly to be extracted from any of them – but the fathers and mothers were simply horrified.

They talked to each other; they wrote to each other; they shook their heads; they threw up their hands. That one of themselves should have written a novel at all was bad enough, but that it should have had for its *dramatis personae* such people as the Tolletons and the Hunts was inexplicable.

I have still a letter from one aunt to another wondering how 'the dear child' – we were always children to those relatives – 'could ever have known anything about such inferior society?' – and another deploring that she should have 'taken any notice whatever of such vulgar people,' – while a third took pen in hand to address myself on the subject. 'Your book appears to be full of nothing but silly, useless chatter, most unworthy of being recorded. I daresay *the* T's did say it, but that is no reason why I should have to read it. You might have given us *one* good woman with a heart and a character. *That* would have refreshed us and done us good; but your cold, worldly-wise, manoeuvring doll, Helen Tolleton,[74] does no one good, and her only attraction is of the shallowest kind, in her pretty face. If I had readers – which I never shall have – I would teach them to reverence womankind, and not imagine that all girls are laying horrible little traps for rich old men ... I miss in the book the warmth and colour of a wholesome, honest, noble love story, such as is lovely and a good report – I do *not* want to be reminded of ignoble flirtations.'

This was giving it me pretty 'straight'; but I had it straighter still from another quarter, and more condensed. 'I have heard it said that there may be something to be learnt even from novels. I do not know if this be true – but at any rate there is nothing whatever to be learnt from *yours*.'

The pain inflicted by this severity – for though I can smile now, I did not smile then – was increased by my electing to keep such missives to myself. I could not bear that my husband, who would have been stung to the core by them, should share my bitterness of spirit – indeed, he would have done more than share it, for he ever felt more for me than I did for myself. Accordingly I hid the mortifying budget, and of course knew by heart what it contained.

Obviously my relations had missed the whole point of *Mr Smith*: scarce a comment was passed on the man himself; no one seemed to deem him worth even a passing observation, while one and all fell tooth and nail on his surroundings.

And it was not till one very dear simple-minded creature, whom I had been trained to regard as an authority on conventions, propounded the following theory, that I drew a breath to wonder, Could she really be as ignorant of life as it evinced, and had I and all the other nephews and nieces been under a hallucination regarding her all along?

This was what raised the question. In a letter to my mother, she wrote, 'What is the poor dear child thinking of to *dream* of making her Lord Sauffrenden "hanker after the Tolletons?" The idea is perfectly *preposterous*. A man like Lord Sauffrenden would never have known that such girls as the Tolletons *existed*.' Another epistle of a like nature followed, but the kind heart of the writer sought to modify her strictures in it; 'Farrer defends the book, and says it is immensely clever – though he does agree with me that it is an extraordinary one for *your* child to have written.'

Instructed by her menfolk, my mother was able not only to receive this with equanimity, but even to appreciate the surpassing adroitness of the reply – that wonderful adroitness which, united to his great ability, eventually landed the said 'Farrer' on the Woolsack. Lord Herschell, while eminently sincere and truthful, contrived never to make an enemy. He had a marvellous way of getting round a difficulty without giving offence. And, moreover, he would disarm an opponent – and once told me that in the whole course of his life only two men had even been personally rude to him. He gave the names of the two; but my readers must be left the conjecture what these were, for of course I keep them to myself.

And while I am writing of this dear and lifelong friend in connection with my first novel, can there be any harm in admitting that he was a sworn admirer of its heroine? Years and years afterwards when some beauties of the day were being vaunted, he turned to me with his own quiet smile, saying, 'But you know, I never think I see any girls now as perfectly lovely as were your "Tolletons."'

Naturally he kept this sentiment to himself, when to have avowed it would have done me no good, and only have vexed an excellent and devoted stepmother; but when we met – and he often spent week-ends, (the thing, though not the name, was invented then,) with my husband and me when on the Northern Circuit, we had great talks over every book I wrote.

On one occasion he arrived to stay with us in Scotland – at the time of the Great

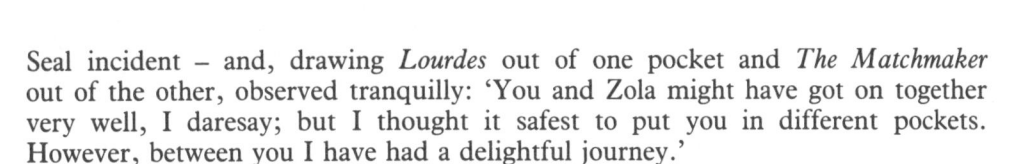

Seal incident – and, drawing *Lourdes* out of one pocket and *The Matchmaker* out of the other, observed tranquilly: 'You and Zola might have got on together very well, I daresay; but I thought it safest to put you in different pockets. However, between you I have had a delightful journey.'

While detailing family disparagement, however, I love to recall that this disparagement was not shared by my new family. The Walfords were, in the best sense of the word, people of the world. They took wider views of life than we did, were infinitely more tolerant, and, I must add, infinitely more humble-minded. It did us all imaginable good to consort with them; and for myself I can only add that no young bride was ever introduced into a family of more delightful 'In-laws.'

Having no daughters of their own, the two dear parents took every son's wife to their hearts, and their proximity to our own first wedded home was one of my chief sources of happiness.

Both of them were renowned for beauty of person, my father-in-law being a perfect model of the 'fine old English gentleman,' while she was a dainty creature of whom everyone said on an instant, 'What a little Dresden Shepherdess!'

In connection with them, and because I know now where else to insert it, I must insert here a very slight incident which amused us at the time. Many years later my husband and I were making a call on an aged lady, Mrs Whitaker Maitland, of Loughton Hall, Essex, and she thus addressed us: 'It is so strangely interesting to me, your coming to reside in this neighbourhood, for I knew long ago *all four of your grandmothers.*' Then to me, 'I knew Lady Colquhoun and Mrs Fuller-Maitland,' and to him, 'I knew Mrs Walford and Mrs Hanson' – Mrs Hanson was only a great-aunt, but we let that pass.

As it was, the old lady's acquaintance with our forebears was surprising enough, as she continued: 'What a horsewoman *old* Mrs Maitland was – Ebenezer's mother, I mean! She rode to the day of her death, and she died at ninety. They tried to stop her, and she did stop for a little; but one day she saw a butcher's pony at her door, and took a fancy to have her saddle put on it, and her habit put on her, and away she went round the paddock. She bought that pony; and there is a picture of her somewhere, on its back, and her big, stolid coachman, on a big horse close behind!'

'Yes, I knew your grandmothers too,' continued our aged friend, scanning my husband with the musing eyes of old age, then suddenly rousing up: 'The Walfords *were* a handsome race!'

We went away laughing; my people were out of it on that occasion.

A Walford, my husband's grandfather, was High Sheriff of Essex in 1815, the 'Waterloo year;' and we now possess the dining-table of dark mahogany at which this High Sheriff entertained the Waterloo heroes on their return to their native land. I must be forgiven for this digression.

One letter much prized by me anent *Mr Smith* came in a roundabout way which doubled its value. 'It is the book of the year,' wrote Mr Mudie,[75] the then head of the well-known firm; 'none other can touch it at present for popularity. As to whether it is by a man or a woman is much discussed, but general opinion is in favour of the former.'

This was also attested by others, and some went so far as to affirm in the most positive manner that not only was 'L.B. Walford' a pseudonym, but that they 'knew the fellow who took it' – that he was, in fact, a brother-officer.

'They are saying in your eldest brother's regiment that he is the author of *Mr Smith*,' wrote Mr Blackwood. 'There is no harm in its being supposed to be so, provided you and he don't mind. People don't think a woman can know as much as you do about sport.'

Of course we did not 'mind' – in fact we both enjoyed the joke; but when it came to one newspaper critic alleging that the young author 'knew more of woodcock-shooting than of religion' my mother looked grave. She who had instructed us all so carefully, so anxiously, on this highest of all subjects, to have it, as it were, 'cast up' at her that she had brought me up in ignorance! It was not till I had explained that the jeer simply referred to a Biblical passage which I had failed to verify before quoting, that she recovered her equanimity, while I took the hint to heart and never after fancied I knew a text, or texts, of Scripture too well to need looking them up before writing them afresh.

From across the Atlantic there soon sounded a welcome note. I had heard of piracies and infringements of copyrights, but these terms conveyed nothing to my ignorant mind; indeed, I should willingly have made a present of *Mr Smith* to the whole American continent if he would have been accepted as a colonist, so that a letter from one of the leading New York publishers astonished as much as it pleased me. It ran thus:

> 'Dear Madam, – I hope that you will not be unpleasantly surprised at receiving by mail an American edition of *Mr Smith* and the enclosed draft for £20 – which the profits of the book enable my house to forward with compliments. Although it is made payable to the order of "L B Walford" – a name that we take for granted to be fictitious – you are justified in signing it for the purpose of collecting the draft. Your book has done exceptionally well here for one by a new author, and should you enable us to publish as good ones in future, we can show our practical appreciation more liberally. Personally, I beg leave to express more admiration for your work than it is often my pleasure to experience, and
> I beg to remain, –
> Respectfully yours, etc.'

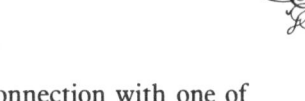

This was the beginning of a long and lucrative business connection with one of the most charming Americans I have ever met.

It was not till twenty years later that we did meet, and during that period he had not only published American editions of nearly everything I wrote, but introduced me to other useful fellow-countrymen who ran my serial novels contemporaneously with their appearance in this country.

I was also indebted to him for making known to me many agreeable acquaintances, who first sought me out in my English home, armed with letters of introduction, and subsequently entertained me with their well-known royal hospitality on the other side of the Atlantic.

⁂

Let me now ascend to an exalted sphere. *Mr Smith* had been out about six months, and though the post still continued to bring me many exciting epistles of one sort or another on the all-important subject, the first flood had abated when I received one whose envelope bore the stamp of 'Windsor Castle.'

Windsor Castle? I started, as well I might. For though we had relations holding offices about the Court, my parents seldom went there, and were absolutely indifferent to any advantages that might have been obtained by cultivating their goodwill. As for seeking them out? – however, here was somebody apparently seeking me out, which was quite another thing.

And I am not ashamed to own that I did feel proud and pleased as I read the letter, which was from the then Duchess of Roxburghe,[76] who was First Lady-in-Waiting to the Queen at the time.

The Duke of Roxburghe and my father were third cousins – not a near relationship certainly, but it still counts for something north of the Tweed, especially when friendship is added to it. His wife now wrote to me; and little did I think how many, many more letters I was to receive from her, bearing on the same subject with variations; but as this was the first, I may be forgiven for transcribing it verbatim.

> 'My dear Mrs Walford, – I have just come in from driving with the Queen, who said she wanted to read *Mr Smith*, and I undertook to say you would be proud to send it. Will you do so *directly* – (not waiting for binding) – addressed to the Countess of Erroll,[77] as I leave early tomorrow? I am sure you will like what I have promised in your name? Lady Erroll is to read it aloud to Her Majesty. – Catching the post, yours most truly, S Roxburghe.'

Here indeed was a pleasant note for a young author to receive.

And scarcely had *Mr Smith* been despatched, and the Queen's gracious message

Queen Victoria, a Royal fan / The Kylin Archive

of thanks received *via* Lady Erroll, (which to me and mine meant the close of the affair), when their came another letter from this new friend.

I need not quote it: its *raison d'être* was one from Lady Erroll to herself, which her kind heart impelled her to forward on the instant. The latter ran as follows:

> 'My dear Duchess, ... I have been reading *Mr Smith* to the Queen ever since it arrived, and I *can* say with what interest the Queen listens to the readings. How interesting it is, and how delightfully it is written! I wish we had more literature of this kind. Novels written with so good and righteous an end in view. I have written to thank Mrs Walford from the Queen. – Believe me, my dear Duchess, ever yours sincerely, E A Erroll.'

I have not quite done with this subject, which indeed wove a thread into all my future literary career; but as this chapter deals only with my first novel, I will just mention a trivial incident which took place in connection with it at my presentation at Court a year or two later.

At that precise moment the Duchess of Roxburghe, who was to present me, was taking the place of the then Mistress of the Robes, absent from indisposition, and, sending for me beforehand to see her privately at Buckingham Palace, she told me that she would in consequence be close to the Queen's ear on the occasion, and had been desired to whisper 'Mr Smith' on my approach. 'I believe Her Majesty intends to speak to you,' added she.

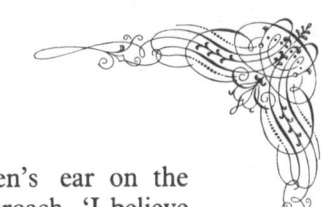

'If so, what am I to say?' inquired I, somewhat fluttered.

'Nothing. Only bow, unless you are asked a question. *Then* you will know better than I what reply to make. And do be early,' continued my kind sponsor, who forgot nothing, 'for the Queen will not stay till the end of the Drawing-Room, and may retire very soon.'

Acting on this hint, our small party, consisting of my eldest brother, (lately married), his bride, and myself, secured seats in the front row of the room, and I was the eighth lady to pass into the Royal Presence.

But nothing happened! The Queen afterwards scolded the duchess, who, she averred, had omitted to do as she was bid; the duchess could not reply to her august mistress, but assured me that she had whispered so loudly that she thought I must myself have heard; be it as it may, 'Mr Smith' passed on with the rest; and whether I were glad or sorry, I declare I don't know.

The Queen might, of course, have sent for me afterwards; but she did not – I believe she was not well at the time, – and as I lived far from London, and was fast tied and bound in my own home, I was well pleased that future intercourse with the Court should be epistolatory.

Now comes a curious touch of human nature.

My good uncles and aunts in the south, who had been so *down* on my first essay into the realms of literature, were quite unmoved by popular feeling striking a different note – indeed, this only served to exasperate them. They were overheard saying to each other, 'The worst of it is *she'll go on doing it!*' – and groaning.

My mother, who had become converted to another view of the case after a second perusal of 'the horrid book' – (for I am bound to own she too had at first mourned in secret over what was to her a bitter disappointment) – in vain strove to induce her people to follow her example. No, they would not; among themselves they agreed that it was perhaps natural, and certainly it was 'Fanny all over' to stand up for her own children, but that if *Mr Smith* had not been written by one of them, she would have been more severe upon it than anyone.

Well, as luck would have it, this disarmed critic was staying with me in my own new home when there arrived the letters from Windsor Castle already quoted – and she soon had them all round the family.

What a sensation they made! To be able to appreciate it, one must have lived from start to finish, if the expression may be used, in the Victorian era. My mother's people were no *snobs*; the sudden revulsion which took place in my favour was not due to snobbery; it had its origin in the profound and ingrained reverence for Queen Victoria which was with them and others of their kind a species of religion.

Had she not seen with her own eyes that the dreadful book of which they were all so ashamed was being read aloud to her adored Sovereign, my aunt, Mrs Herschell, who affirmed that the very existence of such girls as the Tolletons would be unknown to Lord Sauffrenden, would have pronounced as unhesitatingly that the very existence of such a book as *Mr Smith* would be unknown to the Queen. And that the three select ladies who were Her Majesty's chosen friends and companions, and who were equally as herself above reproach, should be vying with each other in their encomiums, and writing them moreover to the poor, misguided child? It was incredible – impossible.

The shock must have been terrific; for it was followed by a silence which told its own tale. And though it was not till after this new experience was as old as the hills, and *Pauline, Cousins, Troublesome Daughters*, and *The Baby's Grandmother* were affording opportunities for a change of front, it certainly did in some instances come about with singular rapidity upon the heels of royal favour.

Queen Victoria may or may not have been a good judge of a book; but the verdict of the finest critic in the world would not have carried the same weight as did that of Her Majesty with those nineteenth-century relations of mine.

But I must now speak of some other antagonists of *Mr Smith*, not so soon nor so surely silenced.

It was alleged in my own neighbourhood – the neighbourhood in which the book was written – that every single character in it was drawn from life. This common accusation against character-novelists derived intensity from the fact that there was unfortunately an admixture of truth in it, – yet the strange thing was that those persons who really did serve as prototypes, who heard it so said on every side, and would doubtless have found it out for themselves if it had not been said at all, were not by any means the ones to feel resentment.

That was reserved for insignificant, obscure individuals, some of whom I had never even heard of, but who chose to imagine themselves and their belongings held up to ridicule. Thus one poor man could not hear me spoken of without anger, and would not permit himself to be introduced to my acquaintance for years and years, because of a casual remark in which his name had been introduced. In vain he was assured by those who knew me best – and by myself through them – that I had merely heard by chance a name which suited me, and had no knowledge that a person bearing it lived in our locality, to be wounded by its being coupled with the epithet 'Fool.' He stoutly held to his own opinion; and when at last, quite a dozen years afterwards, he consented to relinquish it, his doing so was a fresh instance of human inconsistency. He and I met by accident at a country house, and, horror of horrors! he was told to take me in to dinner. Naturally, *Mr Smith* was never mentioned; but, as often happens, my neighbour, out of sheer nervousness, introduced the very topic he may be credited with wishing to avoid

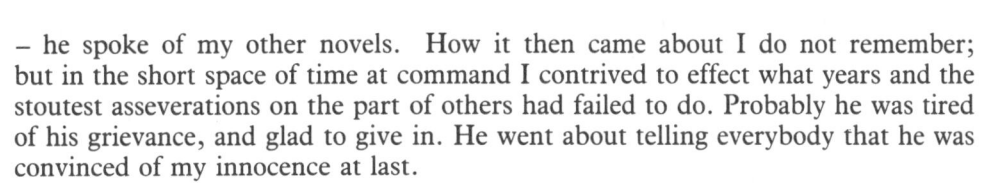

– he spoke of my other novels. How it then came about I do not remember; but in the short space of time at command I contrived to effect what years and the stoutest asseverations on the part of others had failed to do. Probably he was tired of his grievance, and glad to give in. He went about telling everybody that he was convinced of my innocence at last.

The mistake I made, and it was a very serious one, was in using too many characters from one neighbourhood for the same book. It is true that many more were assigned to me than I did use; but I confess to some – and also to having drawn them more closely from life than occasion warranted.

But I was very young, and like a lion or bear-cub, unaware of my power. I never supposed – *never* – that caps would be fitted as they were.

Moreover, I did not feel ill-natured, and it did not occur to me that I was doing an ill-natured thing. The uproar that was created petrified me.

And it is no exaggeration to use the word 'uproar.' Even a respectable Liverpool paper allowed itself to print a column of abuse, under the heading of a 'Second Notice,' since *Mr Smith* had already been reviewed in its pages; and our country doctor – a fine specimen of the old Scotch doctor, who was always my fast friend and staunch ally – reported to me one day that he had found an elderly patient one day too much engrossed by the new novel to think of his ailments. 'For,' quoth he, 'I'm told that I shall find everyone I know in it, and I have already found a lot.'

'Said I, "Bless me, sir, am I the doctor?" chuckled my good friend, Doctor Main, very happily aware that he was not – and I may add that no one was. The 'Dr Hunt' of *Mr Smith* evolved himself out of no real person.

I have written too much on this theme – naturally more interesting to myself than to others; but when one begins to think over old days, how vividly one thing after another rises to view! – and I cannot resist adding two curious little incidents connected with my first novel which may at least entertain my fellow-writers.

The first of these was the discovery in a Highland parish that it possessed in its midst an authoress hitherto content to be anonymous, but resolved to be so no longer.

She was a servant girl at the Free Church manse; and she proclaimed *Mr Smith* to be the child of her brain, winning credence for the assertion at the hands of all her associates. Her master alone was sceptical.

Maggie, or Jenny, or whatever her name was, nevertheless persisted; she had thoroughly mastered her part, and 'got up' the book – which probably the worthy minister had not, – and all he had to go upon was his conviction that one so illiterate could not possibly have written *any* book, *Mr Smith* or not; and as things became increasingly disagreeable, (strangers coming to the manse, and demanding to see 'the inspired lassie'), he took what no doubt was to him a strong measure – he wrote a statement of the case to the Blackwoods.

From them I heard of it – for the letter was sent on to me, – and of course we both laughed together over the imposture; but will it be believed that our emphatic denials were met in a manner so ingenious that they failed of their end?

'Ah,' said the girl, 'that's what they say, is it? Shame upon them! The writin' itsel' is no mine, that's true; but I find a' the rest. I mak up the tale, tho' a' the money and the credit gaes to anither.' (*Sic vos non vobis*, she might have added, but that would have been beyond her.)

Nevertheless, so stoutly did she hold to this amended assertion, and so satisfactory was it considered by her followers, that shortly afterwards she made a marriage far above her station on the faith of it – though whether the deluded husband finally learned the truth or not, history does not say.

—⁂—

The second nefarious proceeding to which my first novel gave rise emanated from the other side of the Atlantic.

This time *Mr Smith* had not merely a new author, but a new name. A story entitled *A Sudden Change* appeared in an American journal, described as 'A magazine of pure literature,' which caught the eye of a Scotch editor, who, thinking it would suit his readers, made arrangements to reproduce it for their benefit.

This he did in all innocence; but, unluckily for him, the new tale caught the eye of one to whom its outlines seemed strangely familiar. This gentleman showed it round in his circle, where his opinion was not only confirmed, but a voice was raised unhesitatingly to proclaim, 'Why, this is *Mr Smith*!'

The Blackwoods were again applied to, and an amusing correspondence ensured.

Naturally, the American fought every inch of the ground. The MS. had been sent him as authentic; he had no reason for supposing it was not so, with more of the kind, (all of which I have before me as I write); but eventually, being compelled by threats of exposure to give up the alleged 'authentic MS.,' it proved to be simply *Mr Smith in print* – with the named altered, and paragraphs here and there struck out.

The whole was considerably abridged; every page was mutilated; 'Mr Smith' himself was 'Mr Adams,' 'Miss Tolleton' was 'Miss Podmore,' and other names throughout were likewise changed – well, indeed, might the whole be called *A Sudden Change*! – but no further concealment of the fraud was possible.

We inflicted a fine of ten pounds – the man was down upon his knees, so we had to let him off cheap – and I handed the cheque over to the Royal Literary Fund.

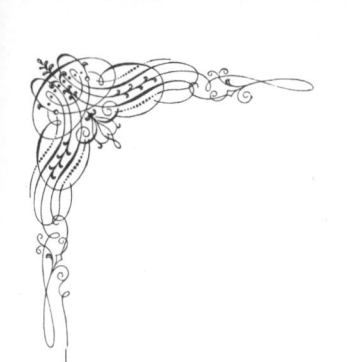

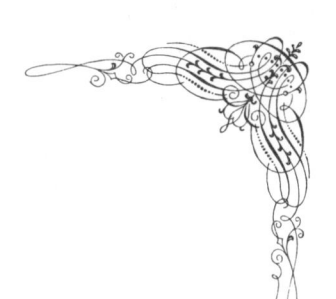

Last days at Arrochar

Arrochar, which had been my dear parents' first Highland home, was to be their last. A sad and tragic event had occured to make their future residence in the county of Dumbarton a matter of expediency, and though there are many still living to whom details of this will not be new, I may perhaps be forgiven for recalling them.

All who have ever sailed among the thickly-wooded islets of Loch Lomond will remember, amongst the group at the lower end, one of the largest, names Inch Lonaig, covered by a fine natural forest of old yew trees. It lies on the right as the steamer bears away to the north after leaving Luss pier, and on a calm day its reflections in the lake are singularly beautiful.

Nearly all the islands belong to the Colquhoun family, and Inch Lonaig has been used as a deer-park by them for generations. A couple of foresters reside there; otherwise it is uninhabited.

It was the custom of my uncle, Sir James, to make a deer-stalking expedition to this spot just before Christmas every year, in order to provide venison for an annual distribution to the poor people on his lands, and, albeit an old man in 1873, he set forth one December day early in the forenoon, accompanied by my younger uncle, who lived with him at Rossdhu, and who, like himself, was a first-rate shot.

With them they took four keepers and a boy, and remained for some hours on Inch Lonaig, having excellent sport; after which they proceeded to load the larger of the two boats in which they had come, with the dead bodies of the deer, and Sir James took his seat at the helm.

As the sky looked dark and threatening, and squalls from the hills were flying about, he urged his brother to accompany him, and leave the skiff to be fetched home at another time. My uncle William replied, however, (as he told us afterwards), that he did not think there was any danger, and would prefer to warm himself, for he was chilly, by rowing home alone in the skiff.

The two boats left Inch Lonaig at the same time, the larger, with its four stalwart oarsmen, taking the lead. But presently as the dusk fell, the squalls grew stronger, and the solitary occupant of the skiff decided to avail himself of the shelter of Inch Conachan, another well-wooded islet, which lay on his right hand. He last saw the big boat as he entered what are known as 'The Straits' at this point. Whether it was caught in a gust then and there, or attempted to round Inch Conachan on the other side, cannot never be known, for it was never seen again.

Not without difficulty either did the skiff make the shore, and then only did the sole survivor of the fatal expedition realise that he was not followed.

Search was made instantly, but to no purpose; the first traces of the missing boat did not appear till two days afterwards, when the hat worn by Sir James – a high white felt hat – how well we knew it! he always wore a bunch of bracken in front to hide it from the deer – was cast ashore on the other side of the loch.

The boat itself followed; floating in bottom upwards, – and next, the dead bodies of two deer. But of the other dead, the human dead, two still lie hid in the dark depths where they sank, for all efforts for their recovery proved unavailing. The bottom of Loch Lomond is by weed and wood entangled, and it is thought these must have caught and held fast their prey.

And my father never spoke of that terrible time when day after day, the woeful search went on – between thirty and forty boats taking part in it – until at last the dear familiar features, peaceful and unaltered, were drawn to light.

He was silent, too silent, about the whole scene. He altered. For the first time we saw grey in his hair. And although after a while the first shock wore off, and the grief and the loss became less keen, we noticed there were things he never did, and places he never went to, after that dread period, that agonising ordeal in the home of his childhood.

Perhaps it will not be intruding on his inner feelings now that so many years are passed and that the two so fondly affectioned on earth have been so long re-united above, if I append part of a letter he wrote to his second daughter at this time, which to us who knew him so well was very touching:

> 'We had need of your comforting letter, dearest child, for your poor uncle's body was found last evening, by the Duke's[78] boat of trawlers. Finlayson asked us to see him, as he was so little changed. William and I therefore went in to where he lay, and there were no marks of suffering or struggle – but he looked calm and peaceful as if only asleep. I gave my adieu to his poor body till I meet him on the resurrection day. I could not help kissing his forehead. We have never had one rough word between us, and he has always been to me the kindest and most loving of brothers. The funeral takes place to-morrow, and we have to-day summoned by telegraph all your brothers for it. I need not say how much William and I were gratified by the Queen's sympathy, – Ever your truly affectionate old FATHER'.

Arrochar not being on Loch Lomond, nor sufficiently near Rossdhu to be fraught with harrowing associations, my parents were content to go there when it was desirable that they should reside for a time on the Colquhoun territory.

By his brother's death my father had again become heir-presumptive to the baronetcy and estates of Luss; and as these were left in trust and he was also one of the trustees, he was obliged to give time and attention to business matters connected with the management.

His nephew, the new Sir James, had been delicate all his life, and was wintering in Egypt for his health, when news of the accident reached him. His immediate return was not to be thought of – and, indeed, at no time then or thereafter was he able to live permanently in the humid climate of the west of Scotland.

This, his father had foreseen; and on this account alone he had made a will which was fully as great a surprise to his nearest kith and kin as to the world at large. I mention this because of some misapprehension on the subject. No slight was intended, no offence was taken; and my cousin was on the most cordial and intimate terms with us all to the day of his death only a few years ago.[79]

To return to Arrochar. Things being as they were, we could not but lead a very quiet life there throughout our first summer sojourn. Our mourning was shared by all around us; there was not a house within reach which had not lost a kind landlord and a good friend; there was not a poor working man or woman who had not something to say, some tale to tell, of one who had truly dwelt among his own people, and whose sterling worth was perhaps known to them alone.

No doubt this was a good thing; I fancy it soothed and cheered my dear father, whose devotion to his brother dated from boyhood; but it constituted a period of monotony which yields nothing to memory, and I shall therefore take the opportunity of reverting to something else which has not perhaps been hitherto made clear.

It may have seemed that in the old Scottish home which overflowed with such joyous life wherever it was implanted, time was mainly spent in sports and pastimes, interwoven by pursuits of a higher order, but still ministering only to our own pleasure or happiness.

This was not so; and I should be doing injustice to all, but especially to those dear ones who are gone, if I left standing so false an impression. Wherever my parents went, wherever they pitched their tent for the time being, they made it first their business to know and visit the poor around them. To relieve their wants and brighten their lives was a matter-of-course with both my father and mother, and though naturally the latter was to be found most frequently at cottage doors, they often went together, he carrying her basket, in which were medicines and delicacies.

My mother was a great doctor. She had a passion for doctoring. She could not move without an army of bottles and pill-boxes to which an entire cupboard was assigned – and the cupboard often resolved itself into a small room. She would have shelves put up all round the room, and only when these were stacked from end to end was she satisfied.

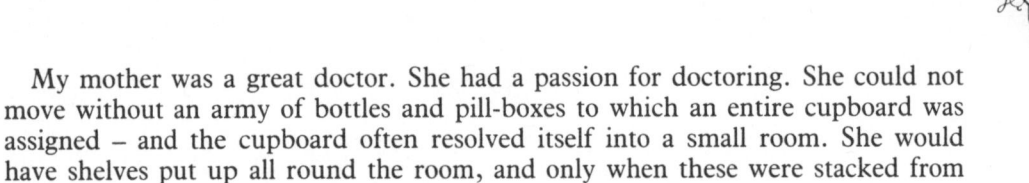

Of course on this being spread abroad whenever we went to a new place, patients were now slow to appear. Whether they liked their physic or not, they liked what was pretty sure to follow in the shape of chicken-broth and beef-tea, with possible flannel shirts, or waistcoats.

Now and then a sick person would be taken into the house and nursed, and on one occasion this gave rise to a diverting piece of impudence. A shepherd lad threatened with consumption – indeed, it was more than a threatening – had been taken in hand by my mother, who put him under Aiky's charge, and the combined efforts of both did eventually result in a cure.

One of poor Hectors's colleagues on the hill, however, cast an envious eye on the coddling and comforting, the snug corner by the fire in Mistress Aitken's own room, and the easy jobs about the garden which took the convalescent into the open air without fatigue.

It all seemed very nice and pleasant to Donald. Why should he not have a turn at the same?

Accordingly he presented himself, coughing. And hearing that Hector had spat blood, and that it was this which had worked the charm in the first instance, he had his story pat. 'Awfu' it was, maist awfu'. To be spittin' bluid a' nicht lang! An' it cam up as cauld, as cauld' – shivering at the recollection.

'Cauld?' ejaculated Aiky, eyeing him. 'Did ye say "cauld," man Donald?'

'Jist cauld – cauld as ice,' responded the infatuated Donald, thinking the trick was done now. 'Cauld – cauld,' and he sighed delightedly.

'Then ye may tak yersel and yer cauld bluid awa' wi' ye,' was the unexpected response; 'tak it whaur ye'll get fowks to believe in it. But anither time when ye're makin' up a likely tale, I wadna mak the bluid *cauld* till ye hae dippit yer finger in't to see! Awa wi' ye!' –and the imposter was driven from the door.

My parents had also their winter work among the poor. For thirty years my father had a district in the Grassmarket – part of the Old Town of Edinburgh – and never once failed to take this up directly he arrived from the country.

Every Tuesday he held a religious meeting in a small room which he rented for the purpose; and this meeting was carefully prepared for, though none of us ever knew how it was conducted.

Simply enough, I daresay. He had his Bible by him, and was to be seen busily writing and transcribing on certain mornings of the week; but as he did not confide in anyone his method of procedure, nor whether he gave his humble audience an extempore address or one from a written paper, we forbore to pry. Either way, I am sure the substance was his own, and that it was well pondered over beforehand.

A distribution of coal and bread tickets followed each meeting, and no doubt gave it a little extra flavour – but whether or no, he had always a good attendance. His own personality would, I think, have ensured this at any time.

'Slumming', as practised by young ladies in these days, was not regarded in favourable light by our forefathers – indeed it could hardly have been carried out with safety under the conditions that then prevailed.

We visited cottagers in the country – unless the house were prohibited by our elders, as occasionally happened; but in Edinburgh personal ministrations in early youth had to cease. One of my sisters, however, who was earnestly concerned at this, and has since become known as a leader of religious and philanthropic work, prevailed on our parents to place at her disposal a Biblewoman, whom, when older grown, she sometimes accompanied on her rounds – and on returning from these, she often had odd tales as well as pathetic ones to relate.

Having a gift of humour, like our aged friend the large-hearted and lovable Miss Marsh, (author of *Memorials of Hedley Vicars*, etc.), my sister could also enjoy a laugh against herself, when her district days provided it; and on one occasion she told in her own inimitable manner a story of an old woman to whose wants, spiritual and bodily, she was endeavouring to minister. Having unpacked a basket of good things, she took no notice as a wrinkled hand went and came between them and the wrinkled lips, but talked of higher things, trusting from the silence with which she was heard that an impression was being made. On and on she talked; and on and on the old creature ate. She had found something much to her taste.

At length she heaved a sigh, and her visitor paused hopefully. A meditative eye was raised as it were in deep reflection; there was another sigh, and a pensive voice murmured, '*What a lot o' that cheese I hae eaten!*'

With respect to the same subject, I should like to add one more word. It often happened that the remote parts of Scotland in which my parents took up their temporary residence were unfortunate as regarded religious observances.

'We do seem *always* to have a poor minister, and a neglected parish,' my mother once lamented to a friend in my hearing.

'For that very reason, perhaps, you and your husband are sent there,' was the calm reply.

It sank in; from that time forth there was an increased sense of responsibility, and desire to be blessing and blessed wherever my father and mother went. In many and many a lonely spot they did veritably leave a name not soon forgotten.

The summer of 1874 being exceptionally dry and warm, we lived a more out-of-doors life during that, our first year at Arrochar, than is usually possible in a climate whose conditions are well described as being 'shooery – shooery – and rain between.' The little straggling village, delightfully situated in its picturesque basin at the head of Loch Long, would seem to have a special attraction for clouds, doubtless drawn thither by the rugged and precipitous mountain-peaks around.

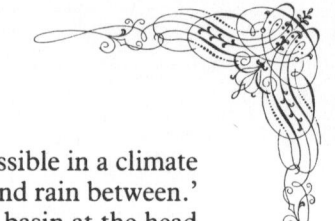

Of course, no one minds a 'Scotch mist' – no one to the manner born, that is; but one cannot sit in it, read in it, work in it, and when July and August, the two wettest months in the west, do transform themselves for once, how beautiful, how enchanting is the scene!

Although debarred from gaieties, we took advantage of the long spell of fair weather to go about a good deal in a quiet way. Nearly every afternoon we boiled our kettle on the shores of the loch, some driving, some rowing to the selected spot; and if no more distant excursion suggested itself, there was always the 'Buttermilk Burn' at the entrance to Glencoe, where the foaming waters came down from the hills in a series of falls white as milk – hence its name.

We were sitting there one day – the fire smoking, the kettle hissing, everybody waiting – when the post-bag was brought across from the house, and there was in it a letter for me, which was not exactly like any other letter I had ever had before. It accompanied my first cheque from Messrs William Blackwood & Sons.

This may seem inaccurate, as *Mr Smith* was now ten months old; but payments for that book did not begin till the year was up, and in the meantime I had written a short magazine story, and perhaps may here venture to tell a little about that story.

The success of my first novel did not at first have a stimulating effect on my energies – rather it humbled them. I felt like many another young writer, as though I had said all I had to say, and there was no more to be got out of me.

By-and-by, however, chancing to come across Miss Yonge's simple little magazine, *The Monthly Packet*, and noting that its standard was not superlatively high, I thought I might manage a few thousand words without undue mental strain, and in easy fashion set to work. No sooner had a beginning been made, however, than the pen flew like fire, and the story was written with scarce a breathing-space.

Forthwith it was despatched to Miss Yonge[80] – and forthwith it came back again. 'It is,' wrote that esteemed editress, 'a pretty tale, but not quite in the tone of *The Monthly Packet*.'

To own the truth, that stung me. I felt mortified, yet put on my mettle. I re-read the MS., and then and there without alteration of a word, despatched it the same day to Mr John Blackwood.

Of course it would come back; I told myself a dozen times a day that it would come back; and yet I hardly anticipated seeing the large envelope turn up as soon as it did, for a week had not transpired when there it was, with the Edinburgh postmark.

However – I opened the envelope. Out came the little MS. certainly, but something else came too. Proofs? Could they be proofs? 'Kindly let me have corrected proofs by return,' wrote Mr Blackwood, 'for we are just about to go to press for the August number of *Maga*, and have displaced another story for yours.'

It was to be in *Maga*, and *Maga* at the height of its fame! Wonderful! Incredible!

In the first volume of the new series of *Tales from Blackwood* there re-appeared *Nan: A Summer Scene*; it was re-produced in various forms again and again; some of my happiest memories are connected with it.[81]

And not the least of these was the reception of the cheque by the Buttermilk Burn. Thirty-five pounds! I could scarce believe my eyes. Always generous in his dealings, I cannot but think the great publisher had special pleasure in sending a sum so much overstepping its merits to the author of so slight a contribution – and if so, I would he had come up the burn-side that day.

Shall I be thought malicious if I relate what happened fifteen years later in connection with this same little tale? It chanced that I had a letter from Miss Yonge, whom to my regret I never met, but who wrote to me on some business matter, and after disposing of it, subjoined: 'I have just read with the greatest pleasure such a charming story of yours called *Nan*.'

Just read!

Well, I never enlightened her, for worlds I would not have done so; and the mystery, if mystery there were, remains one to this day.

The following January *Pauline* began to run as the serial for the year in *Maga*, to be followed before very long by *The Baby's Grandmother* and *A Stiff-necked Generation* in the famous pages. But my dearest mother, my kindest sympathiser, my most invaluable counsellor, only lived to see the first five parts of *Pauline*, for she died after a few days' illness on the 27th of May 1875.

The only incident of any note I recall during our second year at Arrochar, (where my father for the last time assembled his children and grand children round him in a Highland home) was a visit from General Ulysses Grant,[82] who, with his wife and son, and several other relations, was touring in Scotland that autumn.

As the party was desirous of seeing Loch Lomond, it behoved them to be conducted and entertained by the Colquhouns, and the head of the family being still an absentee, the duty of doing so would have devolved on my father, but for his recent bereavement.

The American general, however, was not to be denied an interview. He was very willing to accept the escort and hospitality of my eldest brother, who was now married and also resided on the estates; but after lunching with him and his charming young wife at Ben Cruach, near Tarbet, he announced that he would still like to see his father, if it would not be thought intrusive.

Several of us from Arrochar were of the party at Ben Cruach, and the general turned to us: 'There's a question,' he said, 'I want to ask him.'

We entertained General Grant, who later became President of the United States, and his family / The Kylin Archive

It was then arranged that though all the strangers could not be received at Arrochar, General and Mrs Grant were to go over next morning, taking us *en route* for Inveraray, where they were to be the guests of the Duke and Duchess of Argyll.

My father was anxious to know what the famous soldier was like? It was a somewhat rough-hewn face, we told him, ruddy and sunburnt, with a beard. 'Not unlike Lord Seafield,' said one, pointing to an engraving of a former Earl of Seafield which hung on the drawing-room wall.

But we little expected that the 'question' to be asked by the Grant from over the water, related to this very resemblance.

Out it came, almost immediately after greetings had passed. 'You are Grants, aren't you?' quoth the general, with frank disregard of ceremony. 'I know you are, for the heiress of Luss married a Seafield, and that is why you Colquhouns had to get a new creation. I know all about it; and now tell me' – he looked a little self-conscious, actually a little shy – 'people say it, but I don't know if it is humbug or not; am I like the late Lord Seafield?'

'You are his living image,' replied my father – and took him up to the picture.

He spoke the simple truth, and I think I never saw a man more pleased than this American descendant – for he was a descendant, albeit through several generations – of the ancient Scottish family.

He stayed a long while and talked of many subjects; he was in a more genial and expansive humour than at the luncheon party of the day before – doubtless social entertainments were not in his line, – but always his eyes kept wandering back to the Seafield portrait.

Presently my brother accompanied the elderly couple to the verge of the Colquhoun lands, and came back smiling. 'I believe they would have turned back if they could,' said he; 'they said they were more sorry than they could express to leave behind the beauties of Loch Long and Loch Lomond.'

'He said that?' My father knew human nature. 'Those are the sort of things people say, but' – and he laughed a little – 'the general was more taken up with being a *Grant* than with all the beauties of Loch Long and Loch Lomond.'

And probably this shrewd opinion was correct, for in a letter which I had subsequently the honour of receiving from Ulysses Grant, he did not refer to the 'beauties,' but reiterated his intentions of looking into the genealogical tree of the Seafields.

Inveraray is twenty-three miles from Arrochar. I record the distance with elation, for I walked it. It is perhaps a pardonable weakness on the part of my own sex to boast of our feats in this line; and alas! that I should say it, but too often our estimate of their extent is based on no surer foundation than the word of a Swiss innkeeper or Highland ghillie.

They of course see which way the cat jumps, and what more easy than to oblige a lady who eagerly asks for an opinion of her prowess? But a good coach road, with milestones all the way, is a witness to be depended on, and surely to traverse on foot three-and-twenty miles of this was a creditable performance on the part of a Mid-Victorian lady, brought up at a time when hockey (for women) was not, and golf was not, and hunting and skating were looked upon askance. NB – Hunting, the most daring and dangerous of forbidden sports, was oddly enough the first to be admitted to favour when a reaction set in; but I never had an opportunity of trying it, much as I should have liked to do so.

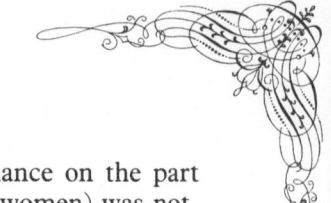

However, that walk – how beautiful, how glorious it was! I had a delightful companion in my brother-in-law, Dr Norman Macleod,[83] and we set off one brisk September morning while yet the dew was glistening and the cobwebs flying. The long ascent of Glencoe had first to be traversed – and how clear were the wimpling tarns beneath a cloudless sky! – then on over moor and fell to lonely Cairndow, where we halted for food and rest, and where began, if I remember right, the descent.

But how many little worlds we seemed to find, how many snug little villages, each nestling in its own sea-creek, we seemed to pass through, before, on rounding the bend of Loch Fyne, we sighted our goal! Welcome to me was that sight, I own – and as the coach had brought thither others of our party, we had a merry evening, and all returned together at Arrochar the following day. Personally, however, I did not see much of Inveraray!

⁂

Nor did anyone stay late that autumn at Arrochar. The sojourn there on the whole was a failure, and was never repeated.

And although my father survived his widowhood for ten years, he took no more moorland homes after finding that they could never again be to him what they once had been.

There is always something of sadness in approaching the last phase of a long and honoured life, and I need not dwell on this one, save to say that while my dear father felt his sorrows keenly – and others were to follow in the loss of his dearly-loved eldest and youngest sons within six months of each other – his health was not affected thereby, and he retained to a very remarkable degree the vigour of his younger days.

His fine physique enabled him to repel the advances of old age, and surmount various attacks of illness. To the last his eye was as keen and his tread as firm as ever, and at eighty-one he eluded precautions and despised luxuries. To this was due perhaps the fact that he did not live even longer than he did.

One chilly day in spring, seeing that the sun was shining, he took no heed that the wind was in the east, slipped out by himself without his greatcoat, and caught a cold. A bronchial attack set in; and eventually on the 27th of May 1884 he followed his beloved wife to the grave on the same day of the same month that took her from him.

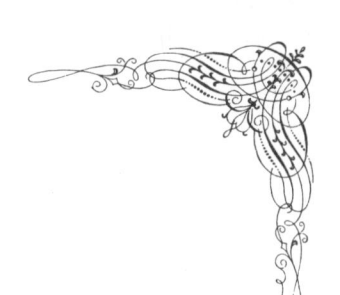

Literary Memories

And now I have come to the last chapter. Not that I have no more to say, for I have much, only too much; but it cannot be said. The story of my full, busy, happy married life is far too near and dear to my heart – too many of those who have taken part in it are still doing so, too much that has happened is still in a sense happening.

Into it, therefore, with all its joys and sorrows, its extended sphere, its accumulated experiences, I will not enter, but confine myself to what may just possibly interest a few of my readers, or fellow-writers – namely, such features of my literary career as can be supplied by memory, supplemented by a box of old letters.

Perhaps the only person who ever asked me for a copy of one of my books was Queen Victoria. This very great compliment was paid *Pauline* at the close of its career in *Blackwood's Magazine*, when I received the following notes (the first being from the Duchess of Roxburghe, already referred to in these pages; and the other, enclosed by her from Miss Drummond,[84] one of the Queen's Maids of Honour). That from the duchess, who was then in the Riviera, was as follows:

> 'My Dear Mrs Walford, – This moment have I received the enclosed from Miss Drummond, forwarded from Floors. Pray sent *Pauline directly* to Osborne. I am sure you will, – and will also kindly at once relieve *my* anxiety as to this note's reaching you, as I have been so stupid as to have mislaid your last letter, and am therefore not *certain* of your address. – Believe me (catching the post), very sincerely yours
> S Roxburghe.'

N.B. – She was always 'catching the post,' this dear, kind, energetic lady – but she never failed to catch it; and the better I got to know her the more I appreciated that warmth of heart and fervour of sympathy which made her so truly beloved as well as admired by all who knew her.

The letter which had been received only 'a moment' before being despatched to me, was worth the haste bestowed on it – at least in my eyes. It was dated from Osborne where the Court was then assembled, and ran thus:

> 'My dear Duchess, – I have just had a message from the Queen to say that the authoress of *Mr Smith* who was to have sent the Queen her last book called *Pauline*, has not done so yet, and I was to let you know this, as H. M. wishes to have the book...'

The rest of the sheet had reference to private affairs.

And what was *Pauline* about that she had not already flown to the feet of her royal mistress? *Pauline* was putting on her Court dress, *i.e.* the book was at the binders'; and, never imagining that there was any hurry, since my special Lady-in-Waiting was not at hand to present it, I had not set them a time-limit.

Here was a dilemma. Should I send the book in its ordinary attire of neat, plain, dark-green cloth, or wire the binders to 'rush' the Queen's copy in its navy-blue calf? 'You *can't* send it in its common binding,' pronounced my father, who was staying with my husband and me at the time. 'Certainly not, I had *The Moor and the Loch* beautifully bound. It's only proper respect.'

But was it not more respectful to be obedient? We really were perplexed – we two, my husband and I, who were always one in everything – and what would have happened I know not, if by a stroke of luck the glorified *Pauline* had not arrived by parcel-post the same day, when it was sped forth on its southern way then and there.

Forthwith I received a letter in the fine, delicate writing of the then Lady-in-Waiting, the Marchioness of Ely,[85] to the effect that the Queen was much pleased, 'and desires me to say that she likes *Mr Smith* so much that she is most anxious to read *Pauline*, as H.M. hears it is so highly spoken of.'

After this I never again failed to have the Queen's copy of every new novel bound in time, and up to the date of her death Her Majesty always had them read aloud to her, and took care that her appreciation reached me through one or other of her ladies.

The Queen, however, could criticise on occasion: I am not sure that she ever greatly cared for *The Baby's Grandmother*. 'Lady Matilda' was, I take it, a little too sprightly for Queen Victoria's very Victorian ideas; though she pronounced the story 'absorbingly interesting,' and could never make up her mind whether Challoner ought to have married the girl he was engaged to or not.

Of *Leddy Marget: A Girl of Eighty* – the last book of mine to be sent Her Majesty

– she was also at first a little shy. Probably in the last years of her life the aged Queen did not feel sufficiently in sympathy with the gay-spirited old heroine, who played pranks whenever she was out of sight of her faithful dragon, Gibbie; – and it is only human nature not to care for others to do what we cannot do ourselves as the years pass. Be that as it may, I gathered from those then about Her Majesty that she listened coldly to *Leddy Marget*, which, to confess the truth, I had rather expected would be a favourite with my Royal reader.

Then came a second letter. Quite unexpectedly, Lady Erroll had been asked to read the book aloud a second time, and had looked up to behold the tears running down the face of her Royal Mistress! 'Afterwards I saw Her Majesty re-reading it quietly to herself,' subjoined my kind correspondent; 'and as for *my* opinion, if it is worth having, I do think I never read a more beautiful book – the last chapters are quite perfect.'

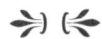

⁂

At the time of the death of the Duke of Clarence,[86] I had a short but interesting correspondence with the Queen (through those about her) on the subject of Her Majesty's letter to the nation.

This most touching and admirably expressed letter was permitted to be published by Raphael Tuck, and was of course widely bought for such loyal subjects as could afford a shilling for the purchase.

But it seemed to me that there were many thousands of very loyal subjects who would willingly have adorned their cottage walls with this memento of their Sovereign, but to whom a shilling was a shilling, and not to be parted with unnecessarily.

I therefore made bold to propound to the Duchess of Roxburghe the suggestion that a copy of the letter should be sold for a penny, and the idea caught her fancy at once.

'I enter into all you say *most* warmly,' wrote she, replying, as usual, on the instant, 'and have sent on your letter of this morning by this post to Sir Henry Ponsonby,[87] begging his advice, and if favourable to your suggestion, asking him to take the Queen's pleasure on it.'

Sir Henry's reply, however, was not favourable. 'This is a difficult question to answer, my dear duchess,' wrote he, 'If Raphael Tuck had given a facsimile of the letter at once, for a penny, he would have made a fortune. But he waited for the expensive surroundings which no one cared for, and so made but little. Still, the Queen promised to stand by him, and she cannot now give leave for any other reproduction.'

To the latter statement, however, the duchess demurred. 'It seems to me that, once published and sold, *anybody* can copy *anything*,' cried she. 'I enclose Sir Henry's letter, and you will see what I mean. I do not understand the subject, *do you*? But at any rate, cannot the same publisher now issue a cheaper edition?

Shall I ask Sir Henry if this idea could be proposed to the Queen?

As, however, I find no further mention of the subject among my letters, many of which have got lost, I must conclude that the one finally dismissing it is among these, and that the project fell to the ground – a pity, for nothing so good of its kind had ever before been given by Queen Victoria to her people, and now it has probably sunk into oblivion, to be heard of no more.

Pauline had not reached its last instalment in *Blackwood* ere I was at work upon *Cousins*, which was published the following year.

This novel I wrote with greater ease and pleasure than anything I had ever written before, for the following reason. It depicted the kind of life to which I was born. *Mr Smith* was the work of an alien; I did not look at my characters ill-naturedly – indeed, I regarded them with the liveliest sympathetic interest; but I had often to stop and think what they would say and do under certain circumstances: whereas my 'cousins' Simon and Hetty, likewise Jem, Bertie, Agatha – all of these talked, and acted, of themselves. I knew just how angry Agatha would be when Simon put his arm round Hetty in the boat, and felt every wince of the poor little crushed Hetty when 'all the starch was taken out of her' thereafter.

The fateful blunder of Simon's proposal to the wrong sister had been criticised as improbable – nay, as impossible; but two cases of the kind in real life were communicated to me, not indeed to be expected, but by men who knew the facts and vouched for their truth. This was not, however, till after the book was published; so all that can be said is that if the case were an abnormal one, I did not give it proper attention, being only bent on finding some peg, however slight, on which to hang the thread of the tale. Simon had got to be parted from his true love, and the parting had got to be of a painful and, as I thought, probable character.

Mr Blackwood's first opinion of the new novel was a shock to me. I had grown accustomed to his favourable verdicts and to depending upon them.

When therefore he wrote, though kindly and courteously as ever, that he was not quite sure that *Cousins* was 'equal to its predecessors' and 'would like to see me about it,' I could hardly believe my eyes. Honestly, I thought the book as good as *Mr Smith*, and better than *Pauline*. But as I never showed a manuscript to anybody before submitting it to the arbiter of fate himself, I could only take it for granted that my opinion was wrong, and with a sinking heart present myself at the old house in George Street.

Ah! that old house! It seemed to wear a forbidding aspect now, and I had grown to love it so!

It was not quite the time for which my interview was appointed when I reached

Blackwood's literary salon / The Kylin Archive

the outer steps, and down and down went my courage till it was clean out of sight before the chime of St Andrew's clock rang out the dreaded hour.

However, the thing had to be done, and a brother who accompanied me, having no idea of anything amiss, had the cruelty to open the door and beckon me to lead the way, on the instant. We went into the historic Blackwood room where the portraits of Scott,[88] Hogg,[89] Christopher North,[90] George Eliot,[91] and others known to fame adorn the walls, – and there we waited, while fancy conjured up a frowning publisher and a rejected MS. Of course, he would do it nicely – of course, he would do his best to soften my disappointment; but I must be prepared, and would be prepared, to take with a good grace whatever was in store.

John Blackwood came forward to receive us. He certainly was not frowning; his face wore its most genial expression, and he did not delay a moment in putting me out of my misery.

'Now I have got good news for you'; (perhaps he saw how little the 'good news' was expected, for he took me again by the hand and shook it heartily), – 'I am going to climb down about your book. It's a capital book; I have read it all through again; I sat up till the small hours over it last night, and cannot imagine what I was about to take such a grumpy view of it the other day. The only thing I can think of' – and he laughed slyly – 'is that I had had fearful drubbing at golf on St Andrews Links that afternoon; and when I got back to Strathtyrum, (where I was stopping for a match, and had taken *Cousins* with me to read), I was feeling not fit to live! My dear young lady, you can have no idea of what we golfers suffer when we have had a real bad day – when luck's been against us, and we have played abominably into the bargain. We ... '; but here he pulled himself up with a laugh. 'It's not *that* you want to hear about, and I am just like all other golf men, start me on the one great subject, and it's all up with any other. However, *Cousins* is all right, and we shall have the greatest pleasure in publishing it.

With my head swimming and ears ringing, I feebly stammered out my willingness to make any alterations, to – to – add anything, or – or omit anything.

'You will not need to alter a syllable,' said Mr Blackwood emphatically. He then proceeded, 'Well now, Mrs Walford, here we have a full-length portrait of the author of *The Moor and the Loch* at last. We have had several snapshots; we catch a glimpse of him here and there; but 'Sir John Manners' is my old friend John Colquhoun to the life.'

It was then arranged that *Cousins* should be brought out the following October, and my brother and I flew home on wings.

I think it was on this visit to Edinburgh that I dined with the Blackwoods to meet George Eliot.

To meet George Eliot? That was my one thought. Colonel Chesney (afterwards Sir George Chesney,[92] author of *The Battle of Dorking*) was also present, and there was a large dinner-party, of whom nearly all were interesting and notable people, but George Eliot alone engrossed my attention. She was at the height of her fame, having just produced *Middlemarch*. But she did not shine in society – at least, she certainly did not shine that evening; and I am inclined to think that those who met her only in public found her as destitute of personal charm as I did. Here I recall the tale of an undergraduate.

The famous authoress was being fêted at Cambridge, and a few enthusiastic and very youthful admirers were permitted to join a luncheon-party given in her honour, though accommodation could only be found for them at a side-table. They could, however, look and listen – and as there was not much to look at, they listened the more. The large, full lips seemed to be emitting words of wisdom; they craned their necks, they stretched their ears – suddenly the tension was relieved, they leaned back in their chairs, and laughed as only boys ever laugh. What had they heard? The deep voice that should have pronounced judgement on a Cicero or a Sophocles, had exclaimed with fervid protest: 'But surely, Mr So-and-so, you do not mean to say you really like that bitter Bairisch beer?'

Cousins was followed a year later by *Troublesome Daughters*, which was written from start to finish in three months. As this comprised the writing out for the press, it will surprise no one to learn that, in the teeth of all protest, I was at work from eight to ten hours every day; and as I was suffering a good deal from asthma at the time, and had to change my attitude every short while – from sitting to standing, from standing to kneeling, from kneeling to lying flat on my face on the floor (while the pencil still steadily pursued its way), – it will surprise no one either to hear that something like collapse ensued directly the strain was over, or that I never again defied health and authority in like manner.

The book was 'on time,' however, for the next opening in *Maga*, and then – then came a heavy loss and bitter disappointment.

Of the loss first. My kindest of friends and most invaluable of supporters, Mr John Blackwood, died rather suddenly, and as no formal arrangement had been made for *Troublesome Daughters* running serially in the magazine, and as the new head of the firm preferred a tale called *The Private Secretary* (which was believed to be by Sir George Chesney, but to which his name was never attached), my three months of vehement overwork was in a sense thrown away. The new novel was indeed published by the old firm, but it did not run in *Maga*.

It was much liked, but I have already been too frank over the kind receptions accorded my work and shall say no more on this head. One little reminiscence, however, may perhaps be pardoned. I was standing with a party of my own people in Chester Station when Mr Gladstone, who was travelling south from Hawarden, and naturally the centre of a good deal of attention, popped his head out of a carriage window, and called something after a retreating figure. 'Did you hear what he said?' demanded those about me, laughing.

I had not; my attention had been momentarily diverted.

'Oh, you ought,' rejoined they; 'it was, "If you want the third volume of *Troublesome Daughters*, you will find it on the little table beside my bed." And then I felt rather sorry not to have heard for myself the great statesman say it.

❧ ☙

Troublesome Daughters elicited a letter from a daughter of Robert Chambers[93] (and sister of Lady Priestley, in whose reminiscences she figures as 'Annie') which is so brimful of sprightly charm – rare in a middle-aged woman – that for its own sake I append a portion of it.

'My husband happened to be kept at home yesterday – *no vera weel* – (awful business a man in the house, and not ill enough to be in bed – only able and willing, alas! to go poking and prying about, discovering mares'-nests in every sort of unexpected and unthought-of quarter) – when I set him down to *Troublesome Daughters* and peace ensued. I had no further trouble, except to get him to put out the *candle*, which one night in the middle of the second volume he would *not* do. We fought and struggled, till he jumped out of bed, flung on his dressing-gown, and bounded and banged into the spare room. No sheets there, of course, – but that was a trifle – he had *your book*, and peace to devour it. Where do you get all your wonderful knowledge of life from? You are as much at home in the whirl of London society as in the lonely castle or farmhouse. As for your handling of *Scotch*, you beat William Black hollow.'

Now I must own I am a little proud of my Scotch, so this from such a thorough Scot was delightful. On the same subject wrote Dr Donald Macleod, editor of *Good Words*. 'Your Scotch sometimes beats me, and I flatter myself I am not easily beat. What is 'a drink of the Dodgill Reepan?' I repeat, it marvels me where you have picked up such idiomatic and vigorous Scotch.'

For the benefit of those equally ignorant of the 'Dodgill Reepan' and its qualities, I may explain that it is a herb which grows among the red mosses of Galloway, and if brewed by a despairing lover, and presented by him to the lady of his affections, is supposed to be all-potent in causing them to turn in his favour.

Throughout my writing career, now extending over thirty-seven years, I have had the full share of reprobation, animadversion, and instruction, which inevitably falls to the lot of a novelist endeavouring to depict the manners and customs of her day. I was told by one indignant correspondent, among other items, that I must be completely ignorant of how men really talk when I could make them use such an expression as 'By jove!' He railed through three sheets at this unfortunate expletive, assuring me it never had been and never would be in use 'among gentlemen,' and wound up by the complacent announcement that he might be supposed to know, as he had been among boys all his life, and was now in a responsible position attached to the Y.M.C.A.!

From among a host of other humorous epistles I select one which pleased us much. It also adopted an aggrieved and contemptuous tone. Did I suppose that the aristocracy (*sic*) ever had dessert on the table for luncheon? I ought not to have made a mistake like that. Biscuits and cake – *never* fruit – were alone 'served' in the middle of the day. Again, I offended against the susceptibility of one whom I judged to hold a position in a great household similar to that obviously held by the above writer. 'You seem to know a good deal,' she was good enough to allow, 'but permit me to set you right on one point. The aristocracy, (again the aristocracy), *do not use davenports*. Davenports[94] are never to be seen in their houses.' And, to enhance the value of this instruction, this writer, like the other, added for my information a synopsis of her own status: 'You may believe me, *as I am writing in the room with a Countess.*'

On the other hand, a heated pen accused me roundly of prejudice and ignorance in depicting the family of Tufnells in *The Baby's Grandmother*, and I was told that I knew nothing whatever about such people; that they might not have handles to their names, and might only live in a simple, provincial town, but they could be every whit 'as refined and cultivated and well-bred,' as my Lady Matilda and her brothers for all that. To poke fun at them was 'not like a lady,' whatever I might think. Here again was a letter a yard long.

But the climax of these was perhaps reached in one before me now, though not written directly to myself.

Perhaps it would be best to suppress the name of the editress to whom it was addressed, and who, with a fine sense of humour, passed it on.

> 'Madam, – Allow me as an old subscriber to your magazine, to say that if you admit many more such stories as *A Carrier of Parcels*, by L B Walford, you will lower the tone of it by many degrees. The vulgar slang which runs through the whole of it would do no discredit to the *Referee*, or the *Pink 'Un*, – papers which I hope you have never seen. – Yours faithfully '*A Saddened Reader*'

I was also frequently proffered advice. One writer could not any longer endure to find me year after year deliberately choosing for my novels such heroines as Kate Newbattle, Lady Matilda Wilmot, and Rosamund Liscard. Was it possible that I did not know any other kind of girls? They abounded in my native land. In the writer's own neighbourhood she (I felt sure it was a 'she,' though only initials were appended in this instance) could enter at least half-a-dozen houses, where were to be found dear, sweet, *good* girls, living useful and beautiful lives, devoted to their home duties, to the poor, to books, music, and pleasant, wholesome recreations, etc., etc.

Obviously it never dawned upon the mind of this other 'saddened reader' that the lives of such 'dear, sweet, *good* girls' were not laid absolutely bare before her approving eye, and that if they did not, as she proceeded to allege, 'give men a thought,' there would hardly have been in them material for a novelist.

Another well-wisher began by being complimentary. So far she liked my books, but thought I had now exhausted the subjects of country-house life, and ought to turn to something new – something altogether different. 'Why not try our hop-pickers, for instance?' continued she. 'They come down every year from the East End, when the hops are ready, and are really a most interesting set of people,' etc.

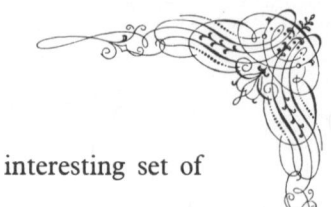

Hop-pickers and me! To compare a small thing to a great, I could not but think of the suggestion made to Miss Austen, by the Librarian to King George IV, that she should 'delineate in some future work the habits of life, character, and enthusiasm of a clergyman who should pass his time between the metropolis and the country, who should be something like Beattie's Minstrel, fond of and entirely engaged in literature.'

⇒) (⇐

Nor was this attempt to turn the current of my thoughts into another channel by any means a solitary one, and I will only add that if I ever did try to conform to some well-meant counsels, the result never justified them.

How to introduce a comical little piece of miss-fire which happened on one occasion, I do not know. It connects with nothing, and yet we have laughed so often over it that I must risk dragging it in by the heels.

A novelette of mine, yclept *The Havoc of a Smile*, had for its hero a figure in my own eyes lovable and pathetic. Young Gregory Pomfret is nobody in his father's pompous mansion, and leads a lonely, neglected life there, because, owing to the circumstances of his lot, he is unable to keep the hours and enter into the amusements and occupations of the rest. The story has eventually a happy ending for Gregory, which makes ample amends to him for all he has had to go through beforehand.

But I was not prepared for the feelings the book aroused in a country squire who overtook me one day when out walking, and holloed from horseback his heartiest applause, waxing more and more eloquent, till, with fiery red face and blazing eyes, he finally burst forth, 'I feel I could *just kick that Gregory*!' What was in his mind to bring about such a state of savagery, we were never destined to know, then or thereafter.

In 1889 I had a difference of opinion with Messrs Blackwood as to issuing cheap editions of my novels; my husband's view of the case – and he had an excellent insight into such matters – being that these would bound to come sooner or later (which prediction has been amply fulfilled, we all know), while the fine old conservative firm held out stoutly against the idea of any such innovation.

We parted company, with the greatest reluctance on my part, – though I have had no reason to regret my course of action from any other point of view than that of friendship and gratitude.

In Messrs Longman, to whom after a short time my novels and books of all sorts were ultimately transferred, I found all the steady, sound, reliable support and generous treatment which had so smoothed my literary path in its early stages, and which is still so invaluable to me as a veteran.

After ceasing to write serials for *Maga* (the last of them being *A Stiffnecked Generation*, in 1888) I started with *The Mischief of Monica* in *Longman's Magazine* in 1890.

I was then at my busiest. I was pouring out at one and the same time novels, magazine stories, essays, poems, anything and everything. Referring to my literary record, which has been faithfully kept ever since the first faded entry of *Mr Smith* in 1874, I find that I have produced forty-five full-sized books, and may add that there are two smaller ones in the press at the present moment.

This number does not, it is true, rival that of my friend Mrs Maxwell (Miss Brandon[95]), but who could rival that fertile and wonderful pen? Moreover, *Lady Audley's Secret* came out when I was in my teens, – and though there are, no doubt, many writers of to-day who can claim to have been, and to be, as industrious as I during any given time, there are few, alas! for whom the writing-time has been so prolonged.

In addition to other work, I was for four years, namely from 1889 to 1893, London Correspondent of the New York *Critic*, for which I wrote a fortnightly budget of literary news; and when it is added that my predecessor was Mr W E Henley, it will be seen that I had to put my best foot forward.

Moreover, the articles had to be sent in punctually, and it will always be a source of triumph to me that such a born free-lance as myself should have faithfully fulfilled this binding engagement, and only once, and that on an almost excusable occasion, forgotten the day. Had I said beforehand I should do this, no one would have believed me. But I did it, and had pleasure in doing it; it was, I repeat, a triumph, and, to confess the truth, a triumph little likely to be ever wiped out by repetition. To do anything *regularly* is, and always has been, foreign to my inclinations.

I also wrote fugitive pieces for the *World*, then edited by Edmund Yates, and one of these was composed under rather unusual circumstances.

It was a perfect summer day, and Henley Regatta was in full swing, when, under cover of my parasol, indeed using it as a species of desk, I added line upon line, and verse upon verse, to a poem a column long entitled *A Henley Ghost*.

The whole was written from first to last in the midst of the Regatta – now in a boat, now in a tent, now on the seething brink of the river.

As the evening shadows fell, my husband, who had to go back to town, carried off the pencilled scrawl in his pocket, handed it in at the *World* offices, and next day it appeared!

Mr Yates's brief notes in the tiniest of handwritings – such a contrast to his big, burly self – were curiosities. One ran: 'Dear Mrs Walford, Do go on. Yours, E Yates.' Another, still more brief and equally to the point was: 'Dear Mrs

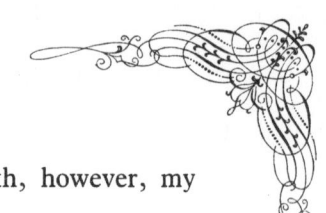

Walford, – Hooray! – Yours, E Yates.' With Mr Yates's death, however, my connection with the *World* ceased.

❧ ☙

Some who read these pages may remember, and will never forget the advent of a singularly endearing young American amongst us, about eighteen years ago. Wolcott Balestier[96] came over to this country with a few introductions, and in an incredibly short space of time he had turned the subjects of these introductions into friends – some of them close and intimate friends. There was scarcely a literary man or woman in England whom he had not approached on behalf of the large publishing firm in New York which he had been sent hither to represent, and very, very few whom he had not drawn into his net.

He had a unique personality. He took the most cold and cautious hearts by storm. His wit, his enthusiasm, his absolute and unqualified self-reliance, untinged as it was by any personal vanity or egotism, inspired us with the same faith.

On the one hand lay old associations, reluctance to trust a stranger, (and that stranger a 'smart' Transatlantic cousin), together with the lurking inbred conservatism which makes change of any sort detestable in the eyes of a true-born Briton; on the other was a slight, fragile form whose persuasive tongue neither man nor woman could resist.

Our first meeting took place at Cranbrooke Hall, in Essex, which my husband and I had taken for a term of years. Mr Balestier asked leave to run down shortly after his arrival in England, and only the day before he did so, we heard of him simultaneously from one or two quarters. From such celerity and vivacity what was to be expected but a forward, irrepressible, impossible young man?

Never were prognostications more agreeably disappointed. When he had opened his mission and found me disinclined to negotiate, the subject was quietly dropped. By-and-by, however, and that in the most natural manner possible, it was again on the *tapis*. I began to listen, to hesitate, to deliberate.

'We are prepared,' said the young American, 'to be reasonably reckless.' It was an odd phrase – one of Wolcott Balestier's many odd phrases; but it forcibly conveyed his meaning, as I subsequently found – for though the matter stood over for a time, it ended as anyone can guess.

But there came a sad day all too soon, when a little band of mourners, with more than ordinary grief in their hearts, stood on the platform of Liverpool Street Station to see a train go out, bearing some of their number to a foreign land where, after a few days' illness, death had cut short that bright young life, so full of promise – and I know that none of those who stood there will ever forget Wolcott Balestier. Shortly afterwards his sweet young sister married Mr Rudyard Kipling, and the same little circle reassembled; but influenza, which was raging at the time, struck me down upon the wedding-day, and I lost the pleasure of being the bride's only feminine friend present. Readers of a stirring tale, *The Naulaka*, may recall that it was written conjointly by Rudyard Kipling and Wolcott Balestier.

Although I have never written stories for children, I have written about them, and a small book (not worthy of being included in the forty-five referred to above) contains four, which appeared first in *Atlanta*, to which magazine at one time I was a regular contributor. The most popular of these little tales is *Such a Little Thing*, and though it was not founded on fact, it was founded on what might have been fact. A child's disappointment, a child's suffering under a sense of its offerings being slighted, and the great things of its life shown to be of small account in the eyes of others – that is what I never can bear to see, and on one occasion, unwittingly, I and others all but inflicted it.

We were skating on the pond at Cranbrooke, and it was a glorious winter afternoon, and the fun was at its height. Two little faces watched us from the nursery window, and on a sudden we remembered – just in time.

They, the little ones, had prepared for us – for *us*, not we for *them* – a Christmas tree. It had cost them weeks of preparation beneath the care of an affectionate and intelligent nurse, and we were within an ace of forgetting it!

But all went well; at the cost of no little self-sacrifice, sisters and brother cheerfully tramped across the snowy gardens up to the house, leaving behind the merry scene, the frosty air, the rising moon, to take part in a poor little, loving festivity; and as I, the mother, looked round the tables which told so much, I thought of all that might have been, had the bidden guests refused to come. Thereupon I wrote *Such a Little Thing*.

The small, square volume, named *For Grown-up Children*, is now issued by Messrs Ward Lock & Co.

It may interest some readers – or, at any rate, some writers – to know that *The Matchmaker* was the last three-volume novel accepted by Mudie's Library.[97] Perhaps I was one of the writers of fiction hit hardest by the sweeping away of that ancient landmark.

Still, I have had my day; I have never until within a year or two ago had a single unpublished MS. in my possession; and what I have now are – shall I confess it? – the abortive efforts of a novelist who would fain be a playwright!

Nature has denied me this gift, and so I must e'en do without it.

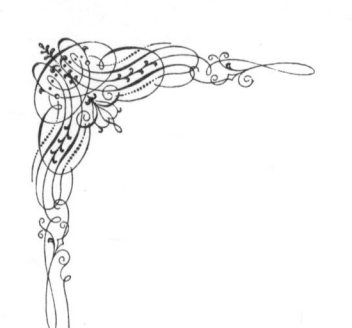

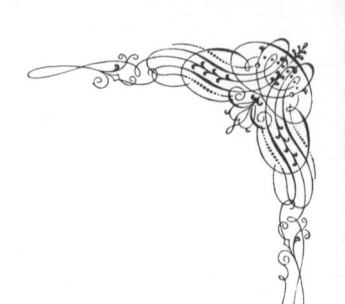

Chapter Notes

1. Powdered

2. In fact, the first edition came out in 1840, five years before Lucy was born. The book she saw her parents working on was probably one of the later editions, or *'Rocks and Rivers'*, which was published in 1849. *'Salmon Casts and Stray Shots'* came out in 1858 and *'Sporting Days'* in 1866.

3. Bethia Fuller-Maitland's *'Hymns for Private Devotion'* was published in 1827, and republished 1863. Fanny and her eldest sister Esther both contributed two hymns.

4. *'Rhymes and Chimes'* was published by Macmillan in 1876, the year after its author's death.

5. 'Powan' is described by the author as a kind of trout, only found in Loch Lomond.

6. Samuel Rogers (1763–1855) was a poet, sufficiently celebrated to be offered the laureateship in 1850, which he refused. His breakfast gatherings are remembered in *'Recollections of the Table Talk of Samuel Rogers'* ed. Dyce (1856) and in his memoirs.

7. *'Ministering Children'* was published in 1854 by Maria Louisa Charlesworth (1819–80). The children devote every leisure moment to ministering to the needs of the poor. It had sold 100,000 copies by the time the sequel appeared in 1867.

8. *'The Little Duke'* and *'Heartsease'* both appeared in 1854. Miss Charlotte M. Yonge (1823–1901) was influenced by John Keble to express her religious views in fiction. She produced 160 books at the rate of about three per year from 1850 and edited *'The Monthly Packet'* from 1851–98. In many ways she was the last of the 'old school' of writers for children, stressing above all the duty of obedience to parents.

9. Struwelpeter or shock-headed Peter and the chubby Augustus are characters in a colourful book of rhymes published in 1845 by Dr Heinrich Hoffman (1809–94). Augustus refuses to eat his soup, becomes thin, and dies.

10. *'Holiday House'* is a book of Children's takes by Catherine Sinclair (1800–64). It was published in 1839 and went through many editions, to 1919. Miss Sinclair wrote over 35 books, most of which went through several editions.

She portrays real children in her books, often wilful, mischievous or dirty, and probably wrote initially with the idea of amusing her nephew, Lucy Colquhoun's cousin, George Boyle, the son of her sister Julia who married the Earl of Glasgow.

11. Sir John Sinclair (1754–1835), the first baronet, was a politician and agriculturalist. He trained as a lawyer and was an MP from 1780–1811. In 1784 he wrote a *'History of the Revenue of the British Empire'* and helped to establish the Board of Agriculture in 1793. His *'Statistical Account of Scotland'* 1791–99 was a description of every parish in Scotland, compiled with the help of the local ministers. His letters were published in 1831 and a biography was issued in 1837.

12. In Lady Colquhouns's entry in the DNB, her biographer is more complimentary about her 'feeble religious booklets,' saying that she might lack artistic skill but her books are like the conversation of their compiler, genuine and inartificial, spontaneous and heartfelt and he insists on their graceful ease and natural truthfulness. Lady C. died in 1846, when Lucy was one.

13. *'Modern Accomplishments or the March of Intellect'* (1836) *'Modern Flirtations or a Month at Harrogate'* (1841) and *'Beatrice'* (1852). All these books went through at least three editions. Miss Sinclair also wrote an account of the Queen's visit in 1842 and a series of *'Common Sense Tracts'*.

14. Lord Benholme (1795–1874), known at the Bar as Hercules Robertson, passed as an Advocate in 1817, was raised to the Bench in 1853 and took his place in the Second Division in 1859. For many years he was the oldest man to act as Judge in any Supreme Court in Great Britain. In 1842 he had also been appointed Sheriff of Renfrewshire.

15. Charles, Lord Neaves (1800–76) was one of the greatest case lawyers of his day, and also contributed prose and verse to Blackwood's Magazine for over 40 years. A collection of his brilliant satires was published in 1868. He was a great attender of literary banquets including the 1827 one at which Scott admitted authorship of the Waverley novels and the 1841 Dickens banquet, and that given in 1857 for Thackeray.

16. Sir James Simpson (1811–70), was the Edinburgh Professor of Midwifery from 1840. He originated the use of ether as an anaesthetic in childbirth (1847) and discovered the anaesthetic properties of chloroform by experimenting on himself – a discovery which became accepted after his attendance at the birth of Prince Leopold in 1853. He was the Queen's physician for Scotland from 1847 and was created a baronet in 1866.

17. Giulia Grisi (1811–69) was especially famous for her Bellini roles – 'I Puritani' having been written especially for her. Her husband, Giuseppe Mario (Don Giovanni de Candia) (1810–83) had a long series of operatic triumphs in Europe and America but lost his fortune after his retirement, through speculation (see Pearce & Hird *'Romance of a Great Singer'* 1910).

18   This was not the Queen's first visit to Balmoral (1848) but she only bought the estate in 1852, with the proceeds of a legacy from a Scottish eccentric. The new house was built by September 1855, the original building being demolished the following year, so Lucy may be referring to her first visit to her new house.

19   'Uglies' were common from 1790 onwards, to shield the wearer from the sun, but by 1850 they were becoming a little old-fashioned, as bonnets got larger.

20   Mr Ebenezer Fuller-Maitland (1780–1858) was MP for Lestwithiel, Wallingford and Chippenham. He was also a JP and Deputy Lieutenant for Berkshire and High Sheriff for Berkshire in 1825 and for Brecon 1830. The Maitland family can be traced back to 1238 (G H Rogers-Harrison *'Genealogical & Historical Account of the Maitland Family'* – (1869) but Ebenezer's was not the senior branch.

21   Spencer Percival (1762–1812) became Lord Chancellor in 1807 and succeeded the Duke of Portland as Prime Minister, when he had the problem of trying to limit the powers of the Regent during the incapacity of George III. (He did not succeed in this). He was shot by a madman.

22   Her grandmother, Bethia, (1781–1865) was the only child of the banker Joshua Ellis and she also inherited a considerable fortune through her mother, the daughter of Thomas Fuller of Fuller's Bank in Lombard Street. She married Ebenezer (who added the name Fuller to his surname) on 9th January 1800.

23   Park Place was substantially rebuilt in the French Renaissance style in 1870 and is now a school. An obelisk erected by Ebenezer to commemorate Queen Victoria's accession is, in fact, the top spire of St Bride's Church in the City, and the grotto, said to incorporate stones from Reading Abbey, still exists. The Druidic Temple is a stone circle found in Jersey in 1785 and given to the then owner of Park Place. Horace Walpole called it 'very high priestly' (Pevsner).

24   Princess Helena married Prince Christian of Schleswig-Holstein on July 5th 1866. (Percy Noble in *'Park Place'* 1905) says that Jane was embarrassed when she recognised the Queen since she had been remarking freely on the royal portraits, for instance that Queen Charlotte was not as ugly as people said.

25   The first ever University Boat Race took place at Henley in 1829 and the memory of it encouraged the foundation of the July regatta from 1839 onwards.

26   Bishop Wilberforce (1803–75) was the son of the reformer William Wilberforce. He became one of Prince Albert's chaplains in 1841 and was Bishop of Oxford from 1845 to 1869, when he was transferred to Winchester. He was a model of reforming zeal in his diocese and founded one of the first theological colleges in 1854, but is now chiefly remembered for his debate with

T.H. Huxley in 1860 about Darwin's theory of evolution and 'man's descent from the apes'.

27 Thomas Day (1748–89) was a barrister who devoted himself to reform work. Sandford and Merton are the two main characters in a children's story which came out between 1783–9. The book relies on the ideas of Rousseau, and, in rather a heavy fashion, teaches that virtue pays. It was written at Aybridge, only half a dozen miles from Mrs Walford's home at Cranbrooke Hall, Essex.

28 Lucy is a little unfair here about a lack of desire to give back any contribution. The DNB has a most appreciative article of her Uncle William (1813–76) who was an art connoisseur and helped to popularise painters then neglected, such as Botticelli. He contributed largely to the success of the Royal Academy – Old Masters Exhibitions and nine of his paintings are now in the National Gallery.

29 John Alexander Fuller-Maitland (1856–1936) was music critic of *'The Times'* from 1889–1911 and edited the second edition of *Groves Dictionary of Music*. He was also distinguished for his work on early music, especially the Fitzwilliam Virginal Book.

30 Blackwood's published Mrs Ella Fuller-Maitland's volume of verse *'Parva'* in 1886.

31 *'Uncle Tom'* had come out in 1852, but *'Dred'* had just been published at the time of this trip. It furthered the anti-slavery cause by showing the demoralising influence of slavery on the whites. On this visit Mrs Beecher-Stowe (1811–96) was honoured by Queen Victoria, but many people turned against her in 1870 when *'Lady Byron Vindicated';* which alleged Byron's incest with his sister, was published.

32 From *'The Lord of the Isles'*, a poem which Sir Walter Scott (1771–1832) wrote in 1815, about the return of Robert the Bruce to Scotland in 1307, culminating in the Battle of Bannockburn. Sir Walter, of course, really 'rehabilitated' the highlands and made his version of Scottish history and culture popular, with the series of 'Waverley' novels.

33 The Indian Mutiny broke out in July 1857 after a period of discontent over such problems as the issue of Enfield cartridges said to contain cow and pig fats. One of the most horrifying atrocities was at Cawnpore where a garrison of 1000 Europeans, half of them women and children, surrendered after a 19 day siege under a safe conduct. The men were massacred as they left the fort and the women and children locked up under horrifying conditions. When a rescue mission was expected they were butchered and their bodies thrown down a dry well.

34 Susan Edmonstone-Ferrier (1782–1854) was a friend of Sir Walter Scott and wrote three good novels of Scottish life, marked by a sense of humour and high comedy. *'The Inheritance'*, the middle work, came out in 1824.

35 The 'Royal Charter' was wrecked near Anglesey on the 26th October 1859.

36 Mrs Mary Martha Sherwood (1775–1851) was the author of numerous children's books, including *'The History of the Fairchild Family'* which came out from 1818–47 and was frequently reprinted.

37 The Misses Macdonnell of Glengarry, were sisters of the last great chief of the name. Alexander Ranaldson Macdonnell, supposedly the model for 'Fergus MacIvor' in *'Waverley'*, famous for his feudal, lawless way of life, his generosity and warm-heartedness and for his uncontrollable temper, which led to his trial for murder. He was drowned in the wreck of the steamer 'Stirling Castle' in 1828, leaving seven daughters and a son, Aenaes, who sold the mortgaged family lands and emigrated to Australia.

38 Gladstone & Carlyle were severally installed Rectors,
Gladstone on the 16th April 1860. His address was on the function of universities.

39 Professor Blackie (1808–95) was Professor of Greek at Edinburgh to 1882. He helped to reform the university and as a keen nationalist, helped found a Celtic chair.

40 His address embodied his moral experiences in the form of advice to the younger members of his audience. He was greatly shaken by the death of his wife three weeks later, and the discovery of how his irritability and lack of consideration had caused her unhappiness and ill health.

41 Dr John Caird (1820–98), principal of the University of Glasgow, was one of the greatest Scottish preachers, attempting to demonstrate that the organic development of Christianity was not inconsistent with its divine origin. His *'Religion in Common Life'* preached before the Queen at Crathie in 1855 was said by Dean Stanley to be the greatest single sermon of the century.

42 Norman Macleod, who died on the 11th December 1911, became Principal Clerk of the General Assembly of the Church of Scotland. He married Lucy's sister Helen Augusta.

43 Mr Joseph Farquharson (1846–1935) lived at No 5 Eton Terrace. First exhibited his work at the age of 13 and exhibited annually at the London Royal Academy exhibitions from 1873–1904, chiefly landscapes. He was an A.R.A. in 1900 and an R.A. in 1915.

44 Dinners at Highland inns were often unreliable. In her journal for 8th October 1861, Queen Victoria recorded of the inn at Dalwhinnie that 'Unfortunately there was hardly anything to eat, and there was only tea, and two miserable starved Highland chickens, without any potatoes! No pudding, and no *fun* … it was not a nice supper. The servants had to make do with the remnants of the chickens.'

45 John Millais (1829–96) was already an established painter by this time. He had first exhibited in 1846, joining the

Pre-Raphaelites in 1848. He painted 'Isabella' in 1849, and the notorious 'Christ in the House of His Parents' (which for many people was shockingly realistic, or just ugly) in 1850 and 'Ophelia' and 'The Order of Release' in 1853. 'Autumn Leaves' and 'The Blind Girl', which marked a new depth of feeling in his art, were painted in 1856. He also produced outstanding woodcuts for 'Cornhill' and other magazines.

46 The late Lord Herschel (1837–1899) was the stepson of her maternal aunt and he was one of her closest friends when she lived near London in the period after her marriage. He became Lord Chancellor in 1866 (The Great Seal was his badge of office).

47 Caroline Agnes, third daughter of Lord Decies, married James Graham 4th Duke & 7th Marquis of Montrose (1799–1874). Among other appointments, he was Hon. Colonel of the Stirling, Dunbarton, Clackmannan & Kinross militia.

48 The latest guidebook to Rossdhu tells us that Dr Johnson had got himself drenched in a boating expedition on Loch Lomond and came into the drawing-room with water splashing out of his boots and this was how he incurred Lady Helen's comment.

49 'Proudly our pibroch has thrill'd in Glenfruin,
And Bannachra's groans to our slogan replied;
Glen Luss and Rossdhu they are smoking in ruin,
And the best of Loch Lomond lie dead on her side'.

50 'Nascitur non fit' – born not made.

51 This collection is now housed in its own room at Rossdhu, 'The Moor and Loch Room', and there are notes on the collection in the official guidebook at Rossdhu.

52 HMS Warrior was a very new ship at this time. She was the first British ironclad, being finished in October 1861 at a cost of £376,000. She marked the beginning of a long and hard-fought transition from the 'wooden walls' of the fully rigged sailing ships of Nelson's era and the early powered ships. Her general shape was that of a wooden ship, but she incorporated new ideas, such as that of watertight compartments. She was armoured with 4 ½" iron plates and was 380 feet in length. She was sold in 1923 and in the 1960s rediscovered at Pembroke as C77, an oil fuel pier.

53 Margaret Gatty (1809–73), a children's writer, was the daughter of Nelson's chaplain in the 'Victory', the Rev A Scott, whose life she wrote. Married the vicar of Ecclesfield in Yorkshire, where there is a memorial window to her. Her most popular book was *'Aunt Judy's Tales'* (1858). She also wrote a series of 'Parables from Nature' illustrated by herself. In 1866 she started *'Aunt Judy's Magazine'*, with which her celebrated daughter Juliana Horatio Ewing helped. Her writing is conspicuous for its identification with the point of view of the young, humour, cheerfulness and truth.

54 Mr James Ferrier lived at 12 Queen Street, Edinburgh. He exhibited at the London R.A. in 1873.

55 The Walkers of Dalry were an old landed family (now subsumed in the Robertson-Luxfords – see Burke's Landed Gentry 1914). Lady Hall was the wife of the baronet.

56 Mr Ferguson of Kilkerran – presumably the son of the baronet.

57 Mary Elizabeth, baroness Ruthven (1784–1864).

58 Sir William Fraser (1816–98), was deputy keeper of the records of Scotland 1880–92. He was knighted in 1887. In addition to his antiquarian studies he endowed the Chair of Scottish History at Edinburgh financed the *'Scottish Peerage'* and founded the Fraser homes.

59 Sir Joseph Noel Paton and his charming wife (1821–1902) lived at 33, George Square after 1856. Bryan's *Dictionary of Painters & Engravers* (1920) says of him 'a most courteous, kind-hearted and sympathetic man distinguished by a considerable amount of religious fervour'. ... 'His paintings were elaborate and full of detail, but distinguished by a hardness of texture and an over-strained pathos and sentiment in their subject' ... 'in Presbyterian circles their vogue was immense'.

60 On the 22nd November 1860 the King of the Belgians wrote to Queen Victoria, 'Eugénie's expedition is most astonishing. She also coughs much and I never heard Scotland remembered for Winter excursions. I believe that the death of her sister affected her a good deal ... (because) she had been dancing in Africa when that poor sister was dying. Next to this, there seems a difference of opinion (with her husband on his anti-papal religious policy).'

61 The Reel of Tulloch or 'Hullachan' usually follows the Strathspey as an alternative to the Highland Reel. For a description of how it is danced see *'Highland Dancing'* (Thos. Nelson 1955). The Triumph is an old English Dance where the couple pass up and down between the lines of men and women who form arches. It was one of the first dances always to be danced to its own tune. J.T. Surenne *'The Dance Music of Scotland'* (1852) says '50 years ago the fashionable dances in Edinburgh and other large towns were minuets, cotillions, reels and strathspeys and country dances. Now, with the exception of the reels and strathspeys, all these dances have disappeared.'

62 Waterspout is a pillar of cloud extending downwards from low masses of cloud, rotating with great velocity, rather like a tornado and fed with moisture from the waves over which it passes (which accounts for 'rain' of frogs, small fishes etc.) It moves forward slowly at about 15–20 mph (Chambers Encyclopaedia adapted).

63 George Boyle, (1825–1890) later 6th Earl of Glasgow was the son of the 5th Earl of Glasgow and his second wife Julia (Lucy's relation through the Sinclairs). He became Lord Clerk Register of Scotland and was famed for his piety. It will be remembered that he was the favourite of his aunt, Miss Catherine Sinclair,

and many of her stories were written to amuse him as a boy.

64 Robert Smith Surtees (1805–64), created the fox-hunting grocer, Mr Jorrocks. *'Mr Jorrocks Jaunts & Jollities'* appeared in 1838.

65 Sir John Powlett Orde of Kilmorey (1803–78), the 2nd baronet, was educated at Oxford. In 1826 he married the co-heir of Peter Campbell of Kilmorey, and the names were jointly held by their descendents.

66 Edward Gibbon (1737–94) published the *'History of the Decline & Fall of the Roman Empire'* from 1776–88.

67 Charles Rollin, French historian (1661–1741), a Jansenist who wrote rather uncritical ancient history. His 'Histoire Ancienne' appeared from 1730–8, a useful *'Traité des Études'* in 1726–8 and he had completed 8 volumes of the *'Histoire Romaine'* before his death. (Adapted from Oxford Companion to French Literature).

68 Bulwer Lytton (1803–73) – later Lord Lytton. A versatile best-selling novelist and poet who also wrote three plays. *'My novel'* appeared in 1853 and is the story of a self-taught poet brought up in a peasant family who turns out to be the son of a distinguished politician. It appeared in *'Maga'* (Blackwood's Magazine) and, in spite of being in four volumes rather than the usual three, sold well, although Mudie at first took only half the number he would have ordered if the novel had been shorter.

69 William Scrope died in 1852, aged 81. He was a noted illustrator and sportsman. His books include *'Days & Nights of Salmon Fishing in the Tweed'* (1843) and *'The Art of Deer Stalking'* (1858) and *'Deer Stalking & Other Sports in the Highlands 50 Years Ago'* (1865). He also contributed to the *Westminster Review* and *Maga*.

70 John Blackwood (1818–79) was the third son of William Blackwood, the founder of the publishing house and *'Blackwood's Magazine'*. He succeeded his two elder brothers as head in 1845 and pursued a vigorous policy of expansion and action against American piracy. Among others, Mrs Oliphant and George Eliot owed their first encouragement as novelists to his discernment and generosity. *'Middlemarch'* made publishing history by being issued in 8 parts, rather than four volumes and, with most of George Eliot's other novels, was a great money spinner for the house. (See F.D.Tredney *'The House of Blackwood'* 1954 and Mrs Oliphant *'Annals of a Publishing House'* 1897).

71 Miss Jean Ingelow (1820–97), the poetess. She was a great friend of Lucy who was considered for the post of Poet Laureate but Queen Victoria decided that the responsibility was too great for a woman – presumably the post of monarch was less onerous.

72 Sir Frederick Locker (1821–96), the poet, a friend of Tennyson, Ruskin and the Pre-Raphaelites. He became a Roman Catholic in 1864. In 1889 he published a series of articles in the *'St James's Gazette'* under the heading *'Principles in Art'*. He published his *'Religio Poetae'* in 1893.

73 Rev Philip Bennett Power was vicar of Christ Church, Worthing. The *'Oiled Feather'* series was a selection from his writings which initially came out in two volumes (1866–7).

74 The rather 'fast' Helen Tolleton and her sisters are spurned by good society at the instance of Lady Sauffrenden, though the kind-hearted Lord Sauffrenden would have very much liked to befriend them, until she is tamed by the wisdom and goodness of Mr Smith, a middle-aged man who comes to reside in the neighbourhood, and whom she at first wishes to captivate for his wealth. The manner in which she bears his tragic death, which follows close upon their engagement, leads to her social reinstatement.

75 Mr Charles Edward Mudie (1818–90) was originally a stationer. From 1842 he developed the idea of the circulating library, the subscription being one guinea per ticket. (At this time a new novel cost a guinea and a half for 3 volumes). The firm grew to occupy vast premises and books could be sent all over Britain and to the 'colonies'. He alone selected novels, on grounds of the strictest propriety, and the need to please his tastes had an effect on the fiction market since he bought up to half the copies of a book, and advertised the novels widely. It is often said that the three-volume form of novels survived so long because it was in his interest to keep novels expensive, and, in theory, three subscribers could be reading the same book at once.

76 Susanna Stephenia Dalbiac married the 6th Duke of Roxburghe in 1836. She was a lady of the Bedchamber and Queen Victoria's friend and companion for many years and accompanied her on many of her Highland tours. She died in 1895.

77 Dean Davidson described Leila, the Countess of Errol, as a 'hot Evangelical' and while in attendance on the Queen she divided her time between handing out Temperance tracts and campaigning against Windsor theatricals, which she regarded as 'works of the devil'. (Tom Cullen, p230).

78 The Duke of Montrose.

79 He was succeeded by Mrs Walford's second brother, who as Sir Alan Colquhoun, died in March 1910. He was succeeded by his son, Sir Iain, a lieutenant in the Scots Guards.

80 Miss Charlotte Yonge – see reference 8.

81 So general a favourite was this little tale, that, as it was out of print, Mrs Walford obtained the kind permission of Messrs Longman to reproduce it as an appendix at the end of the first edition of *'Recollections of a Scottish Novelist'*.

82 General Ulysees Grant (1822–85), the distinguished Civil War commander, became the 18th President of the USA in 1868 & 72. In 1884, as 'sleeping partner' in a bank, he lost his money and began to write his autobiography to help support his family. Unfortunately, at this time he was diagnosed as suffering from cancer, and public

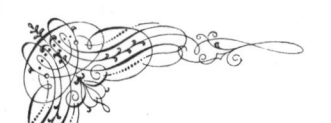

opinion ensured that he was restored to his rank of general, which he had had to relinquish on taking the presidency.

83 Dr Norman Macleod – see reference 42.

84 Miss Drumond was the Queen's maid of honour.

85 Jane Hope-Vere married John 3rd Marquess of Ely in 1844. She was Lady of the Bedchamber for a long period and died in 1890.

86 The Duke of Clarence was the eldest son of the Prince of Wales and died of cholera a few days before the date set for his wedding to Princess Mary of Teck, who later married his younger brother and became Queen Mary.

87 Sir Henry Ponsonby, was the Queen's Private Secretary from 1879. His letters from Court to his wife give a lively and informative picture of Court life in this period.

88 Scott – see reference 32.

89 James Hogg was a poet discovered by Scott. (1770–1835). He was known as 'The Ettrick Shepherd', which gives a clue to his pastoral verse. He contributed to *Maga* (Blackwood's Magazine).

90 Christopher North was the nom de plume of John Wilson (1785–1854) who became professor of moral philosophy at Edinburgh, and who joined the magazine's editorial staff in 1817. He was one of the first critics to do justice to the poetry of Wordsworth.

91 George Eliot (1819–1880) had been launched as a novelist by John Blackwood, whose dealings with her were marked by patience, critical discernment and generosity. (Gerald Bullett p117). '*Middlemarch*' was published 1871-2. She was self-conscious about her rather unprepossessing appearance. She also had difficulty with social small talk, as Gerald Bullett says 'her notion of talk ... was the interchange of real thought between intimate friends. In personal intercourse of the less intimate kind she had no lightness of touch'. Mrs Walford never learned to appreciate her as a person. She may have been prejudiced by the circumstances of G E's 'marriage' to George Lewes.

92 Sir George Chesney (1833–95) was a distinguished Indian Army General. Published the '*Battle of Dorking*' in '*Maga*' May 1871 – it caused a sensation, being an imaginary account of the invasion of England, designed to show the lack of military preparedness. In 1876 he published '*The Dilemma*' – a powerful story of the Indian mutiny.

93 Robert Chambers (1802–1871) was an Edinburgh bookseller and publisher and author of '*Vestiges of Creation*'. He left three sons and six daughters.

94 Davenports is used in the English sense as a kind of small writing table popular in Victorian homes, and not in the American sense of a sofa.

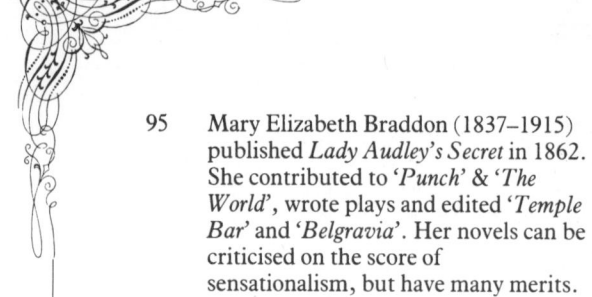

95   Mary Elizabeth Braddon (1837–1915) published *Lady Audley's Secret* in 1862. She contributed to *'Punch'* & *'The World'*, wrote plays and edited *'Temple Bar'* and *'Belgravia'*. Her novels can be criticised on the score of sensationalism, but have many merits.

96   Charles Wolcott Balestier (1861–91) wrote several novels and short stories, but is now best known for his collaboration with Kipling on *'The Naulakha'* (1892), in which he did the American chapters in this novel about a Californian speculator in India.

97   Last three volume novel accepted by Mudie's Library – See reference 75.